Delectable Collectibles

With recipes from and tested by
CAMPUS CRUSADE FOR CHRIST
staff members

NEW REVISED INDEXED EDITION

Published by HERE'S LIFE PUBLISHERS, INC.
San Bernardino, CA 92402

© Campus Crusade for Christ, Inc. 1971, 1981

Published by Here's Life Publishers, Inc.
P. O. Box 1576
San Bernardino, CA 92402

Library of Congress Catalogue Card 81-66594
ISBN 0-86605-006-X
HLP Product No. 70-062-5

Printed in the United States of America.

1971 edition compiled by
Midge Piedot and Dorothy Gregory

INTRODUCTION

Although Campus Crusade's emphasis is on <u>winning</u> <u>men</u>, <u>building men</u> and <u>sending men</u>, the needs of the body have not been forgotten. We realize that to be spiritually strong, physically fit and mentally alert, our bodies, the temple of the Holy Spirit, must have proper care and nourishment. With a time-pressured schedule--that many times demands superhuman strength--and a limited budget, much thought has had to be given to nutritious and inexpensive foods that can be quickly and easily prepared.

Early in this ministry, as staff women came together at training time, there was much sharing of recipes, time-saving hints and short-cuts to housekeeping which would help us to be as effective as possible in running our households, while, at the same time, maintaining an active outreach ministry. As the ministry has grown, significant contributions have been added from time to time. So many people outside of the ministry have requested an opportunity to benefit from it, that we have been inspired to put this first printed copy together.

All of us as staff women have desired that our cooking be "as unto the Lord," whether it be a quick snack to tide us over, or an elegant dinner, practicing hospitality. We feel that Jesus was very much interested in the details of food and social events, since He performed His first miracle at a wedding party.

Henry Ward Beecher once said, "If you want your neighbor to see what Christ's Spirit will do for him, let him see what it has done for you." One of the most effective ways for a person to see the Holy Spirit in your life is to observe you "at home." The motto for my kitchen is, "Let my celestial knowledge affect my domestic action."

Through the years, hundreds of staff women have worked together in sharing, testing, typing, editing and collecting recipes--all of them making their contributions "as unto the Lord." The present edition of this book has, in its various forms, been a vital part of my kitchen library through the years. May I wish for all of you who try these recipes, the pleasure of cooking "as unto the Lord," plus the opportunity to share your faith through your hospitality.

Vonette Bright

LOVE

"Love forgets mistakes; nagging about them parts the best of friends" (Proverbs 17:9 TLB).

"A new commandment I give to you, that you love one another as I have loved you, that you also love one another" (John 13:34 NASB).

"Love is very patient and kind, never jealous or envious, never boastful or proud, never haughty or selfish or rude. Love does not demand its own way. It is not irritable or touchy. It does not hold grudges and will hardly notice when others do it wrong. It is never glad about injustice, but rejoices when truth wins out. If you love someone, you will be loyal to him no matter what the cost. You will always believe in him, always expect the best of him, and always stand your ground in defending him" (1 Corinthians 13:4-7 TLB).

HOME

"She is a woman of strength and dignity, and has no fear of old age. When she speaks, her words are wise, and kindness is the rule for everything she says. She watches carefully all that goes on throughout her household, and is never lazy. Her children stand and bless her; so does her husband. He praises her with these words: 'There are many fine women in the world, but you are the best of them all!'" (Proverbs 31:25-29 TLB).

"A wise woman builds her house, while a foolish woman tears hers down by her own efforts" (Proverbs 14:1 TLB).

"...But as for me and my house, we will serve the Lord" (Joshua 24:15b KJV).

"A worthy wife is her husband's joy and crown; the other kind corrodes his strength and tears down everything he does" (Proverbs 12:4 TLB).

WOMEN

"Who can find a virtuous woman? For her price is far above rubies" (Proverbs 31:10 KJV).

"Don't be concerned about the outward beauty that depends on jewelry or beautiful clothes, or hair arrangement. Be beautiful inside, in your hearts, with the lasting charm of a gentle and quiet spirit which is so precious to God" (1 Peter 3:3, 4 TLB).

"Charm can be deceptive and beauty doesn't last, but a woman who fears and reverences God shall be greatly praised" (Proverbs 31:30 TLB).

HOSPITALITY

"Honor goes to kind and gracious women" (Proverbs 11:16 TLB).

"Kind words are like honey--enjoyable and healthful" (Proverbs 17:24 TLB).

"A friendly discussion is as stimulating as the sparks that fly when iron strikes iron" (Proverbs 27:17 TLB).

"Withhold not good from them to whom it is due, when it is in the power of thine hand to do it" (Proverbs 3:27 KJV).

"...Let all be harmonious, sympathetic, brotherly, kindhearted and humble in spirit; not returning evil for evil, or insult for insult, but giving a blessing instead" (1 Peter 3:8, 9 NASB).

"When God's children are in need, you be the one to help them out. And get into the habit of inviting guests home for dinner or, if they need lodging, for the night" (Romans 12:13 TLB).

"She sews for the poor, and generously gives to the needy" (Proverbs 31:19, 20 TLB).

DEDICATED TO ALL

THOSE COOKS WHOSE KITCHENS

ARE DEDICATED TO GOD

MICROWAVE CONVERSION

1. Selecting the proper time is the most difficult conversion. A basic rule would be
   to cut the suggested cooking time to 1/4.
   It can be helpful to find a similar microwave recipe and adapt that power time and
   setting.

2. Do not salt meats or poultry before cooking. Salt causes meat to toughen and dry
   out. Other seasonings and herbs may be
   added before cooking.

3. Baked goods rise higher and lose more
   moisture when cooked in microwave ovens.
   Reduce leavening agents by 1/4 and increase liquids by 1/4. Baked goods will
   not brown.

4. Ingredients for casseroles, stews, etc.,
   should be cut into a uniform size and
   shape to insure more even cooking.

5. When using cheese to top a casserole, add
   it during the final 1 or 2 minutes of cooking time. Cheese will cook faster and
   harden if cooked the full time.

6. If in doubt about what size dish to use,
   always use the large size especially if
   the recipe calls for milk.

CROCKPOT CONVERSIONS FOR MAIN DISHES

1. Brown meats and poultry in a little oil first for the best flavor and appearance.

2. Decrease liquids in the recipe by 1/3 to 1/2.

3. Place vegetables on the bottom with meat on top. Meat tends to cook faster than vegetables in crockpot.

4. Stir in milk, yogurt and sour cream at the end of cooking to prevent scorching and curdling.

5. Add frozen vegetables when partially thawed in order to maintain the temperature of the hot mixture.

6. Use whole spices or leafy herb spices instead of ground spices. Ground spices tend to lose their flavor after long periods of cooking.

7. Add fragile vegetables, such as mushrooms, zucchini and Chinese vegetables, an hour or two before serving in order to preserve the flavor and appearance.

8. Add fish or seafood, instant rice or pasta only one or two hours before serving in order not to overcook them.

9. If a crisp topping such as bread crumbs or corn flakes is desired, sprinkle it on 30 minutes before serving and finish cooking without the cover.

NUTRITIONAL CONVERSIONS

7/8 c. whole wheat flour	1 c. white flour
1 1/2 c. barley flour	1 c. white flour
1 c. corn flour	1 c. white flour
1 1/3 c. oat flour	1 c. white flour
3/4 c. potato flour	1 c. white flour
3/4 c. ride flour	1 c. white flour
1 1/3 c. rye flour	1 c. white flour
1 1/3 c. soy flour	1 c. white flour
1 c. tapioca flour	1 c. white flour
1/2-3/4 c. honey	1 c. white sugar
1/4 c. molasses	1 c. white sugar
3/4-1 c. brown sugar	1 c. white sugar
7/8 c. cold press oil	1 c. shortening
1 T. arrowroot	2 T. flour
1 T. arrowroot	1 T. cornstarch
1 egg	1/2 tsp. baking powder
1 tsp. salt	1 tsp. sea salt
3 T. carob and 1 T. butter	1 square chocolate

Many of these conversions depend on individual tastes. Remember that using honey or molasses instead of sugar may change the texture.

Fructose can also replace your white sugar. Read your individual packages for conversion amounts.

MAKE-YOUR-OWN CASSEROLE GUIDE

1. Use fresh ingredients or combine left-overs for a new dish.
2. In a skillet, saute meat and seasoning vegetables.
3. Select one food from each of remaining groups, in quantity given, and combine in a casserole.
4. Bake uncovered at 350° for 25 minutes or until heated through.
5. Makes 4-5 servings.
6. A variation would be to have vegetable casseroles and omit the meat.

I
1 lb., cooked

Beef   Poultry
Pork   Fish
Lamb

II
1 c. seasoning vegetable

Mushrooms   Celery
Onions   Bell peppers

III
1 c. cooked or canned vegetables, drained

Peas   Asparagus
Beans   Broccoli
Carrots   Mixed vegetables
Spinach, etc.

IV
1 c. cooked starch

Noodles   Rice
Macaroni   Hominy
Spaghetti   Grits

V
Sauce

Tomato
Canned soup
Sweet and sour

VI
1/2 tsp. seasonings

Salt   Marjoram
Pepper   Parsley
Thyme   Curry
Oregano   Tarragon
Basil, etc.

VII
topping

Grated cheese   Corn chips
Bread crumbs   Potato chips
Cracker crumbs   Wheat germ
Croutons, etc.

COMPANY BREAKFASTS AND BRUNCHES

Orange Juice
Light-As-A-Cloud Pancakes, 60
Sausage Patties   Applesauce

+ + + + +

Sliced Pears
Savory Eggs, 63
Sour Cream Coffee Cake, 54   Hot Chocolate, 29

+ + + + +

Pineapple/Grapefruit Drink
Poached Eggs in Toast Cups, 49
Bacon Slices

+ + + + +

Gingerbread Hot Cakes, 61
Melon Balls   Baked Ham Slices

+ + + + +

Eggs with Celery, 63
Orange Cinnamon Rolls, 57
Mincemeat-Stuffed Peach Halves, Broiled

+ + + + +

Ham 'n Eggs, 62
Baked Apples and Bananas, 377
Tomato Juice   Toast

+ + + + +

Grapefruit Halves
Apple Pancakes, 62
Swedish Egg Coffee, 31

LUNCHEONS

Paradise Chicken Salad on Pineapple Boats, 243
Carrot and Cheese Casserole, 264
Pickles   Olives
Pink Cloud Dessert, 136

+ + + + +

Tuna Rolls, 169   Celery and Carrot Sticks
5-Cup Salad, 234
Delicious Cheesecake Tarts, 130

+ + + + +

Pineapple Lace Fruit Plate, 235
Banana Bread, 50   Danish Creme, 135

+ + + + +

Chicken Monte Carlo, 160
Ranch Biscuits, 45   Pine-Cot Salad, 228
Cream Puffs and Filling, 134

+ + + + +

Salmon-Shrimp Casserole, 170
Spinach Salad, 242   Six Week Muffins, 44
Chocolate Frozen Dessert, 121

+ + + + +

Spinach Salad, 242
Cauliflower and Carrots, 264   Fun Tasties, 57
Frosty Ambrosia, 121

+ + + + +

Souffle'd Cheese Sandwich, 254
Vegetable Salad, 238
Cherries in the Snow, 122

+ + + + +

Hot Onion Soup
Quiche Lorraine, 209
Fruit Cup   Angel Biscuits, 45
Peach Melba, 116

FAMILY DINNERS

Spaghetti and Meatballs, 195, 212
Garlic Bread   Overnight Cole Slaw, 241
Cherry Crisp, 117

+ + + + +

Meat Loaf, 186
Baked Potatoes   Green Beans
Sunrise Salad, 231   Oatmeal Muffins, 43
Hot Fudgey Pudding, 127

+ + + + +

Hamburger-Bean Casserole, 196
Spinach Salad, 242   Zucchini or Summer Squash, 273
Apple Crisp, 114

+ + + + +

Spanish Rice Pronto, 180
Asparagus Amandine, 258
Cheese Bread, 42   Three-Bean Salad, 238
Lemon Sponge Custard Cups, 112

+ + + + +

Sweet and Sour Chicken, 161
Chinese Broccoli, 259
Quick Onion Rolls, 41   Gingerale Salad, 229
Lemon Fluff Pie, 226

+ + + + +

Salisbury Steak for Six, 194
Lithuanian Kugelis, 267   Angel Biscuits, 45
Nobby Apple Cake, 74

+ + + + +

6-Hour Stew, 176

Spinach-Apple Toss, 242
Grace's Sour-Dough Bread, 46

Harvest Table Apple Pie, 221

ELEGANT COMPANY DINNERS

Cheese Rounds, 34
Hot Fruit Punch, 28
Crabmeat Hors D'Oeuvres, 36
Javanese Dinner, 165
Frosted Fruit Cocktail, 121
Hot Spiced Tea, 30

+ + + + +

Mexican Chili Con Queso, 38   Mexican Pizza, 35
Authentic Curry Dinner, 166
Orange Bavarian Salad, 232
Cranberry Fruit Bread, 52
Lemon Angel Pie, 225

+ + + + +

MENUS FOR LARGE GROUPS

Sloppy Joes, 197 Or Hot Dogs
Potato Chips   Hawaiian Beans, 262
Apples   Punch
Cookies   Jello Salad   Cake

Lee Etta Lappen

+ + + + +

Meat and Potato Casserole, 199
Hot Vegetable or Green Salad
Hot Rolls   Punch and Coffee
Chocolate Sheet Cake, 65

Sharyn Regier

Veal-Pineapple Surprise, 206
Lemon-Chive Potatoes, 267
Creamed Asparagus, 258

Lorraine's Layered Jello, 230

Poppy Seed Bread, 48

Lemon Snow, 113

+ + + + +

Cheese Pennies
Dilly Bread, 48   Herb Spread, 36
Oriental Dinner, 202
Iced Tea   Cranberry Shrub, 32
Orange Charlotte, 132

+ + + + +

Tuna Casserole, 168
Fruit Salad   Biscuits and Jelly
Lemonade   Cookies
Miscellaneous Serving Needs:
paper plates, cups, napkins, forks,
butter, sugar and ice

Sharyn Regier

+ + + + +

Tamale Pie, 189
Jello with Bananas   Rolls
Cupcakes

Alyne Gustafson

+ + + + +

Cheese Balls, 36

Broccoli Chinese-Style, 259

Sweet-Sour Pork, 203
Louisiana Crab-Stuffed Potatoes, 269

Refrigerator Rolls, 42

Cinnamon Apple Slices, 234
Tropicana Pie, 219

KITCHEN KWICKIES

"A virtuous woman is a crown to her husband"
(Proverbs 12:4).

Grate the rind of whole oranges or lemons and store in
refrigerator in small jar for future use - frostings,
etc. (Linda Skulte)

If you use a lot of grated cheese, you may find it
very handy to grate 2 lbs. at a time and store in
a large Baggie in the refrigerator. Then it is handy
for use on scrambled eggs, casseroles, salads, etc.
You need only clean grater once and it saves quite
a bit of time and muss. (Paula Carter)

About 7 drops of lemon juice added to a pint of
whipping cream makes it beat up firm in about half
the time. (Dorothy Gregory)

Prepare a list of all the items you need to buy at
the grocery store. Arrange it in the same order in
which the items appear in the store. This way the
shopping cart can move right down the aisles without
back-tracking or even stopping except to pick out
tomatoes, potatoes, etc. Craig calls this his
"Shopping Strategy." (Craig Claybrook)

Make your own 2% milk by dividing one carton of whole
milk into two cartons. Mix up powdered skim milk and
fill up cartons. When chilled for several hours, it
tastes just the same and is much more economical.
(Nan Green)

Don't throw away any left-over bacon. Instead, return
it to the pan and fry until very crisp. When crumbled,
it may be added to scrambled eggs, to soups, or even
to the peanut butter that you spread on the children's
sandwiches. (Dorothy Gregory)

KITCHEN PRAYER
Bless my little kitchen, Lord
And the food Thou dost afford;
May joy and happiness abound,
As in Thy service we are found.

"Every wise woman buildeth her house"
(Proverbs 14:1).

Eliminate last-minute work by making and freezing
sandwiches ahead. Peanut butter and fruit fillings
freeze especially well. (Candace Steele)

Know how to score a cucumber? First pare it, then
run the sharp tines of a kitchen fork down the length
of the cucumber. After the cucumber is thinly sliced,
the slices will have a pretty scallop-type edge.
(Dorothy Gregory)

To prevent gummy noodles, rice, macaroni and spaghetti and to help keep them from boiling over, add
2 teaspoons of cooking oil to the water before cooking. This makes the noodles glisten and stand apart.
(Midge Piedot)

When lemons become dry, put them in a warm oven for
a few seconds and see them become plump and juicy
again. (Dorothy Gregory)

Add lemon juice to fresh peeled fruit to keep from
discoloring - such as peaches, apples, bananas, etc.

Add salt to water when boiling eggs; it will keep
them from cracking and makes them easier to peel.

Cover left over egg yolks with water while storing in
refrigerator to keep from drying out.

Grease jello mold with mayonnaise before pouring in
gelatin.

Add a sprig of fresh mint to water when cooking green
peas and carrots.

Add a pinch of nutmeg to spinach, carrots and squash
while cooking.

Cocoa will never lump if you mix the cocoa and sugar
before adding the hot milk.

Put candles in refrigerator a few hours before using.
This will prevent tallow from dripping.

To increase the amount of juice from citrus fruit -
dip fruit in hot water before squeezing. (E. Bromberg)

12

"A happy marriage = the union of two good forgivers."

If Hollandaise Sauce separates, remove from heat immediately and add an ice cube and beat.

Peel an onion under running water to keep back the tears. (Evelyn Bromberg)

An economical syrup to use is the Mapleine flavoring by Crescent. A little bottle makes 24 pints of syrup - all you do is add hot water and sugar. This goes a long way and is much cheaper than buying ready-made syrup. (Karen Kuhne)

A note to sugar-watchers: Best Foods Mayonnaise and Hellman's Mayonnaise do not have any sugar. This may be a help to those of you who cannot use sugar in your diets. (Marilyn Heavilin)

A few drops of peanut butter placed in the bottom of each muffin pan before batter is added gives muffins a fine nutty flavor.

Orange or lemon juice does not produce a distinct flavor in baked goods -- but grated rind of either does.

To make pure celery salt, put the leaves from celery into a pie plate and place in warming oven to dry. When dry, roll on a piece of paper until very fine. Put into a salt shaker and use instead of celery salt. It is fine served in soups.

To give baked apple a delightful flavor and to color and sweeten, add a few cinnamon drop candies. Remove core from bud end but do not cut clear through; this keeps the candies in the apple.

To one pound of butter, gradually cream in one tall can of evaporated milk and a little salt. Chill and you have two pounds of delicious spread.
(Dorothy Gregory)

Imaginative use of herbs and spices and some tomato sauce can turn the lowly leftover into an interesting dish. (Candace Steele)

"Every house where love abides and friendship is a guest, is surely home, sweet home; for there the heart can rest." (Henry Van Dyke)

Buttermilk is very low in calories and very good for you. You can add a glass of 2% milk to the carton for several times when you pour out a glass of buttermilk; shake once and it will make more buttermilk. (Nan Green)

A grated raw potato added to each pound of hamburger makes for jucier hamburgers. (Midge Piedot)

Use powdered skim milk in cooking and in soups. Economical and less calories. (Nan Green)

An eye-pleasing dish always seems to taste better too! Garnish your platter with parsley sprigs, lemon wedges or radish roses. (Candace Steele)

When cutting marshmallows or chopping dates, if you dip your scissors into water and cut when wet, they won't be as sticky. (Midge Piedot)

You can overcome the problem of keeping bread fresh by wrapping it carefully and storing in the refrigerator. It will stay fresh much longer. (Dorothy Gregory)

Dried fruits keep best in tightly closed containers at room temperature. Refrigerate only in warm, humid weather.

Apples keep better than most fruits and may be stored for a reasonable length of time in a cool place. (Candace Steele)

Frozen vegetables will taste fresher if defrosted before they are cooked.

Generally, vegetables that grow above the ground should be cooked uncovered, those that grow underground should be cooked covered.

To measure half an egg, beat the whole egg lightly, then measure 2 tablespoons.

Use minced parsley stems in dishes for flavor and save the leaves for garnishing. (Dorothy Gregory)

KITCHEN KWICKIES

"Be not forgetful to entertain strangers; for there-
by some have entertained angels unawares"
(Hebrews 13:2).

To whip or beat small amounts of cream, egg white,
etc., use a small mixing bowl. If the bowl is too
large, the amount will be considerably smaller than
usual.

Melt chocolate in a double boiler, for frosting or
coating, over simmering - not boiling - water. When
the water boils, the escaping steam moistens the
chocolate and the frosting won't dry properly.

To reheat leftover baked potatoes, dip the potato
in warm water, and bake in 250° oven until heated
throughout.

Stir a teaspoon of flour into sour cream before adding it to a sauce that must boil. The flour will
prevent the sour cream from curdling.

When substituting dried herbs for fresh, be sure
to use only 1/3 to 1/2 as much.

Saute' minced onion before adding to meat loaf for
a more delicate flavor.

Raw meats are easier to slice if slightly frozen.

Allow at least 15 minutes for a roast to cool before
carving. This allows the juices to settle back in
the meat and you don't lose any.

Combine equal parts dry mustard with mild, prepared
mustard to flavor sauces, salad dressings, etc.

A quartered potato added to gravy or soups that are
too salty will remove some of the salt taste.

Steep pieces of lemon with tea leaves for a stronger
lemon flavor.

For delicious and crisp celery, let stand in cold
water to which 1 teaspoon sugar per quart has been
added.

To separate lettuce leaves easily, cut out core and
place lettuce head under running water so that it
runs into cavity. Drain and dry leaves before using.

SUGGESTIONS FOR THE GENERAL PLAN OF A DAY'S MEALS

BREAKFAST:

Fruit - fresh, dried, canned or fresh stewed
MILK - or cocoa for children; milk, tea or coffee
        for adults
Cereal - preferably whole cereal for all the family.
Egg, meat or cheese
Bread and butter - toast or muffins
If a heartier meal is needed, it may be desirable
to add doughnuts, cookies, jam, jelly, marmalade
or pancakes and syrup. These, however, should be
considered desserts, even at breakfast, to be eaten
after more wholesome foods have been taken.

LUNCH or SUPPER:

Meat, egg, cheese or milk dish
Vegetable or fruit
Bread and butter
Light dessert
Milk - for children
The meal may be made more elaborate if desired, but
should partake of simplicity.

DINNER:

Meat or other flesh or an egg or cheese dish - dried
        beans may be used if milk or eggs are provided
        in the meal.
Potatoes - or dried beans, macaroni or rice
Vegetables
Salad - fruit or vegetable
Bread and butter
Dessert - such as fruit, puddings, gelatins, souffles
        and whips; or something heavier such as pie,
        cake, cobbler, shortcake, plum pudding or
        cookies.
If a more elaborate dinner is desired, the meal may
begin with a soup or an appetizer such as fruit cock-
tail, grapefruit, oysters in some form or a canape'.

SHORT CUTS TO MEAL MANAGEMENT

Make menus for one week at a time.

Plan simple meals - one dish casseroles, etc.

Buy according to menu. If you don't use everything
that week, plan a menu to use what was left over.

Plan foods according to budget, color, and food value.

If food looks good, it is good.

Serve fruit and vegetables raw because it saves time
and vitamins and uses fewer dishes and cooking utensils.

When preparing meals, have sink or pan of soapy water
to wash dishes as you go.

Plan and fix ahead so you don't have to rush and worry
when meal time comes. Do as much in advance as possible
such as mixing dry ingredients for baking; bake cakes,
cookies, etc. ahead; prepare sauces, etc. ahead. If
you use a double-boiler, it's easy to re-heat. Wash
greens, chill, but don't slice or cut until you're
ready to use them - preserves vitamins. Grease pans,
make casseroles, etc. ahead.

Use ready prepared foods or mixes (Bisquick, Jiffy,
etc.)

Most men like simple foods, so cook to please them.
Simple food is less expensive.

Lana Jones and Jane Prall

Just remember that most of this world's useful work is
done by people who are pressed for time--or are tired--
or don't feel well.

Live now as you shall have wished you lived when you
stand at the judgment seat of Christ. (Wm. Culbertson)

THINGS TO DO IN THE STORE AND AT HOME TO CUT DOWN THE
HIGH COST OF EATING:

1. Check the mid-week grocery ads and take advantage
of "specials."

2. Plan your meals before you shop instead of in the
store.

3. Make a list (and remember to take it with you).
Then stick to it. Impulse buying can put you in the
poorhouse.

4. When making up your list, check recipes for the
amounts you need. Overbuying can cost you extra money,
especially if it is wasted.

5. Make your list a little flexible. This way, if
you find a lower priced food of equal nutritional
value, you can substitute and be money ahead.

6. Clip and use coupons that fit in with your menus.
Keep them together, and go over them when you make up
your list. Take just the ones you'll be using this
week to avoid fumbling (and maybe deciding to forget
about it) at the checkout counter.

7. Be a label reader. Labels contain a lot of useful
information, such as weight in ounces, number of servings, government grading and ways to serve. You can
often save by buying the large size of a product you
use frequently. But before you buy it, be sure to
compare price per ounce to see which size is the best
buy for you.

8. When deciding whether you should buy something
fresh, frozen or canned, take into account the likes
and needs of your family, the space you have in your
freezer, as well as price and what is in season.
Accent restores the natural flavor in food; use generously in the preparation of meats, poultry, fish, gra-
vies, soups, vegetables and salads.

HINTS FOR COOKING FOR 2:

1. Plan ahead. Don't throw out leftovers. Make them "planned" leftovers.

2. Invest in a few small skillets and pots to make small-scale cooking easier.

3. Avoid waste of canned, packaged or frozen foods by purchasing the size suited to your needs. Many items are made to order for one, two, four, six or eight.

4. Buy chicken by the part even though it may cost a little more per pound. You can just get the parts you prefer and save money by having less waste.

5. Freeze your meat with two servings in each package. Cook a roast occasionally on weekends. What's left will make great sandwiches, plus an interesting meal or two the next week.

6. When using convenience foods such as cake mixes, serve half now and freeze the remainder for serving later.

7. Make a large casserole, then freeze it in quantities just right for two. You'll be time and money ahead.

8. Keep instant non-fat dry milk and evaporated milk on hand, thus avoiding fresh milk spoilage.

9. Keep your bread in the freezer section. Frozen bread stays oven fresh, spreads more easily for sandwiches, and can go directly into the toaster. For table use, just take out the number of slices you need. These will thaw in a jiffy.

HOW MUCH TO BUY TO SECURE WHAT YOU NEED AND THUS
PREVENT WASTE

DAIRY PRODUCTS

American Cheddar cheese, ½ lb. = 2 cups grated
Butter, 1 lb. = 2 cups
Butter, 1 stick = ½ cup
Cottage cheese, ½ lb. - 1 cup
Cream cheese, 3-oz. pkg. = 6 tbls.
Cream, whipping, ½ pt. (1 cup) = 2 cups whipped
Cream, coffee, ½ pt. = 8 servings (2 tbls. each)
Egg yolks, 12-14 fresh = 1 cup
Egg whites, 8-11 fresh = 1 cup

FRUIT, FRESH AND DRIED

Apples, 1 lb. (3 med.) = 3 cups pared
Bananas, 1 lb. = 3 medium
Dates, 7¼-oz. pkg., pitted = 1¼ cups cut up
Raisins, seedless, 15-oz. pkg. = 3 cups
Lemon, 1 med. = 3 tbls. juice
Orange, 1 med. = 1/3 cup juice
Peaches or pears, 1 lb. = 4 medium

POULTRY

Broiler, up to 2½ lbs. = 2-4 servings
Chicken, 4 lbs. = 3½ to 4 cups diced, cooked
Duck 4 lbs. = 3-4 servings
Fryer 2½ - 3½ lbs. = 3-4 lbs.
Roaster, 4 lbs. = 6-8 servings

MEATS

Bacon, ½ lb., sliced = 9-10 slices
Frankfurters, 1 lb. = 9 frankfurters
Fresh pork sausages, 1 lb. = 15 small links

NUTS

Almonds, 1 lb. in shell = 1 to 1 3/4 cups meats
Pecans, 1 lb. in shell = 2¼ cups meats
Walnuts, 1 lb. in shell = 1 2/3 cups chopped

VEGETABLES

Peas, 1 lb. in pod = 1 cup shelled
Peas, 1 pkg., frozen = 2 cups cooked
Onion, 1 med. = 3/4 cup
Sweet potatoes, 1 lb. = 3 med.
Tomatoes, 1 lb. = 4 small
White potatoes, 1 lb. (3 med.) = 2 1/3 cups diced

TABLE OF EQUIVALENTS

3 tsp. = 1 tbl.
16 tbls. = 1 cup
4 tbls. = ¼ cup
2 cups = 1 pint
4 cups = 1 quart
2 eggs = ¼ cup
Coffee, 1 lb. dry ground = 5 cups
Cornmeal, 1 lb. = 2 2/3 cups
8 eggs = 1 cup
Flour - White, 1 lb. = 4 cups
       Rye, 1 lb. = 3 7/8 cups
       Graham, 1 lb. = 3½ - 3 3/4 cups
       Rice, 1 lb. = 2 cups
Lemon, juice of 1 = 3 - 4 tbls.
Nuts in shell, 1 lb. = about ½ lb. shelled
Sugar - Granulated, 1 lb. = 2 cups
       Brown, 1 lb. = 2 3/4 cups
       Powdered, 1 lb. = 2½ cups
Grated chocolate, 1 oz. = 3 level tbls.

TABLE OF PROPORTIONS

For bread use - 1 cup liquid to 3 cups flour
For muffins use - 1 cup liquid to 2 cups flour
For batter use - 1 cup liquid to 1 cup flour
Use 1 tsp. baking soda to 1 pint sour milk
Use 1 tsp. baking soda to 1 cup molasses
Use 1 tbl. unflavored gelatin to thicken 2 cups liquid
Using salt:
In soups and sauces - use 1 tsp. salt to 1 quart sauce
In dough - use 1 tsp. salt to 4 cups flour
In cereals - use 1 tsp. salt to 2 cups liquid
In meats - use 1 tsp. salt to 1 lb. meat
In vegetables - use ½ tsp. salt to 1 quart water.

COMMON CONTAINER SIZES FOR CANS

# 1 = 1 3/4 cups	# 5 = 7 1/3 cups
# 1 tall = 2 cups	# 10 = 13 cups
# 2 = 2½ cups	# 300 = 1 3/4 cups
#2½ = 3½ cups	# 303 = 2 cups
# 3 = 4 cups	

SUBSTITUTIONS

IF YOU DON'T HAVE...	YOU CAN SUBSTITUTE...
1 tbl. cornstarch (for thickening)	1 3/4 to 2 tbls. flour (or 4 tsps. tapioca)
1 whole egg	2 egg yolks plus 1 tbl. water (in cookies, etc.)
1 whole egg	2 egg yolks (in custards and such mixtures)
1 cup fresh whole milk	½ cup evaporated milk plus ½ cup water
1 cup fresh whole milk	1 cup reconstituted nonfat dry milk plus 2 tbls. butter
1 cup fresh whole milk	1 cup sour milk or butter-milk plus ½ tsp. soda (decrease baking powder 2 tsps.)
1 cup sour milk or buttermilk	1 tbl. lemon juice or vinegar plus enough fresh whole milk to make 1 cup
1 sq. unsweetened chocolate (1 oz.)	3 tbls. cocoa plus 1 tbl. butter
1 cup honey	1¼ cups sugar plus ¼ cup liquid
1 cup molasses	1 cup honey
1 tsp. baking powder	½ tsp. soda plus ½ tsp. cream of tartar
1 cup sifted cake flour	1 cup minus 2 tbls. sifted all-purpose flour
1 cup butter	4/5 cup clarified bacon fat 2/3 cup clarified chicken fat 7/8 cup vegetable oil 7/8 cup lard 1/2 cup suet 1 cup shortening plus ½ tsp. salt
3/4 cup salad oil	1 cup solid shortening
1 cup sour cream	2/3 cup sweet milk plus 1/3 cup butter

+ + + + +

22

SUBSTITUTIONS

IF YOU DON'T HAVE...	YOU CAN SUBSTITUTE...
1 cup canned tomatoes	1 1/3 cups cut-up fresh tomatoes, simmered 10 minutes
1 cup tomato juice	½ cup tomato sauce plus ½ cup water
1 cup catsup or chili sauce	1 cup tomato sauce plus ½ cup sugar and 2 tbls. vinegar (for use in cooked mixtures)
1 cup tomato sauce	1 can tomato paste plus 1½ cups water --measure according to what is needed; store remainder in refrigerator
3/4 cup cracker crumbs	1 cup bread crumbs
1 tbl. fresh chopped herbs	1 tsp. dried herbs
1 sm. fresh onion (approx. ¼ cup)	1 tbl. instant, minced, dehydrated onion
1 tsp. dry mustard	1 tbl. prepared mustard
1 clove garlic	1/8 tsp. garlic powder
1 tsp. garlic salt (This proportion can be used on other seasoned salt combinations such as celery or onion.)	¼ tsp. garlic powder plus 1/2 to 3/4 tsp. salt

+ + + + +

ABBREVIATIONS USED IN THIS BOOK:

tsp. = teaspoon
tbl. = tablespoon
MSG = Monosodium Glutamate
oz. = ounce
lb. = pound
" = inches
o = degrees

sm. = small
med. = medium
lg. = large
pt. = pint
qt. = quart
opt. = optional

Use the extra space on the pages to write in your own favorite recipes.

BASIC HERBS

"Better is a dinner of herbs where love is, than a
stalled ox and hatred therewith" Proverbs 15:17

BASIL - Mild flavor of anise and spice, slight mint
aftertaste. Basil and tomatoes are natural
partners. Use in all egg dishes; in tomato
sauce; in poultry stuffings and poultry.

BAY - Strong aromatic, pungent flavor. Use sparing-
ly in hot tomato juice or bouillon. Add to
corned beef, ham, when cooking meats for cold
plates and with vegetables around roast.

DILL - Sharp, aromatic, caraway-like flavor. Good
in sour cream over cucumbers; finely cut leaves
or seeds in potato salad or tossed green salad.

MARJORAM - Sweet, spicy flavor, mint aftertaste. Good
with cottage cheese or cream cheese. Use only
in sauces to go with eggs, such as sharp
cheddar cheese sauce.

MINT - Refreshing, fruity, aromatic flavor. Use in
hot or cold fruit beverages, fruit cocktails.
Suitable garnish for any fish, lamb, veal.
Good in fruit salads.

OREGANO - Strong clove flavor, slightly bitter.
Sprinkle over pizza or in mushroom dishes.
Sprinkle lightly on soft cooked eggs. Use
in Spanish sauces and with all game birds.

PARSLEY - Sweet, spicy, rather peppery flavor. Combines with all herbs and all egg dishes.
Use as both seasoning and garnish.

ROSEMARY - The meat herb; pungent, piny and resinous
in flavor; quite aromatic. Use in jams and
jellies.

SAGE - Fragrant, aromatic, slightly bitter flavor.
Ideal for cheese spreads; on cheese-topped
canapes. Good with sausage, pork, veal and
lamb.

SAVORY - The bean herb; warm, aromatic, resinous in
flavor. Good in bean salads, tomato juice,
all egg dishes, cheese souffles - a mild herb.

TARRAGON - Aromatic, licorice-anise flavor, slightly
bitter. Good in all egg dishes if used lightly.
Its greatest use is in vinegar.

THYME - Strong, warm, clove-like flavor. Blends with
strong cheeses; all fish and shellfish. Good
with all meats, if used with restraint.

SPICE AND HERB USES

Do you want to "spice" up your cooking? Try some of the following.

SALADS AND VEGETABLES:

BEETS - Sprinkle in tarragon while they cook. For tart flavor, use tarragon vinegar.
CABBAGE - Cook with caraway or mustard seed.
CARROTS - Season glazed carrots with ginger.
CAULIFLOWER - Flavor with rosemary.
COLE SLAW - Sprinkle with caraway or dill seed.
CORN - Flavor canned corn with chili powder; garnish with green pepper rings.
EGG PLANT - Add just enough basil or thyme to enhance flavor.
FRUIT SALAD - Add allspice or mace to whipped-cream dressing.
GREEN BEANS - Add mustard to cream sauce.
ONIONS, CREAMED - Add mustard
PEAS - Drop in mint flakes or pinch of savory while they are simmering.
POTATOES, MASHED - Sprinkle in dill seed as you mash, or season with rosemary as they cook
TOSSED SALAD - Cautiously add curry powder to an oil-vinegar dressing.

EGGS - CHEESE:

Any cheese dish will respond to a dash of sage or marjoram.
CHEESE RABBIT - Include basil and marjoram in the cheese sauce.
CHEESE SAUCE - Add ½ tsp. mustard for zest.
CREAM CHEESE - Blend in basil or parsley flakes. Spread on thin rye or use as a dip.
COTTAGE CHEESE - Add onion salt, dill or caraway seed.
CHEESE SPREAD - Season snappy soft cheese with thyme and celery salt.
DEVILED EGGS - Add savory and mustard.
FRENCH OMELET - Put a dash of basil in the eggs.
SCRAMBLED EGGS - Sprinkle lightly with savory.
SOUFFLE - Add from ¼ to ½ tsp. marjoram to 4 eggs - serve with hot tomato sauce.
TOMATO OMELET - Just a bit of oregano.

MEATS, FISH, POULTRY:

BEEF STEW - Add flavor with basil. Or cook with mixed
     vegetable flakes or dash of mixed herbs.
CHICKEN STUFFING - Use poultry seasoning; or sage,
     thyme, onion salt.
FISH FILLETS - Sprinkle with marjoram, tarragon or
     curry powder before cooking.
FRIED CHICKEN - Use paprika, or sprinkle pieces with
     thyme and marjoram. Roll in flour; fry.
HAMBURGER PATTIES - Add basil or curry powder.
HAM LOAF - Mix in a bit of rosemary for complementary
     flavor.
HASH - Add a pinch of marjoram or savory.
MEAT BALLS - Season with savory, mustard or garlic salt.
PORK CHOPS - Sprinkle with sage or thyme. Or add a
     shake of cinnamon.
PORK ROAST - Blend marjoram, savory - add to basting
     sauce.

BREADS:

BISCUITS - Add mustard and thyme to dry ingredients.
     Bake and serve with any meat dish.
BLUEBERRY MUFFINS - Add dash of nutmeg to dry ingre-
     dients.
CINNAMON TOAST - French type - dip in egg, milk; fry.
     Sprinkle with cinnamon and sugar.
COFFEE CAKE - Mix anise in the batter just enough to
     taste.
CORN BREAD - Mix rosemary in batter.
CROUTONS - Toss toasted bread cubes with melted butter
     seasoned with onion salt, basil, and marjoram.
     Serve with soup.
DATE MUFFINS - Add a dash of pumpkin pie spice to
     batter.
DOUGHNUTS - Add mace to dry ingredients; after frying,
     roll in cinnamon sugar.
DUMPLINGS - Mix parsley flakes in the batter.
GARLIC BREAD - Slice French bread partly through.
     Spread slices with butter seasoned with garlic
     salt. Wrap; heat.
ROLLS - Add caraway seed to batter or put dill seed
     on top.
WAFFLES - Add poultry seasoning, serve with creamed
     chicken. Or add a dash of allspice and cinnamon.

SPICES AND HERB USES

DESSERTS:

APPLE PIE - Add cinnamon to crust.
BAKED APPLES - Core and fill center with brown sugar
     or stick cinnamon.
CHERRY PIE - Add a dash of mace or nutmeg.
CHOCOLATE CAKE - To one package chocolate-cake mix,
     add 1 tsp. cinnamon, ½ tsp. nutmeg, ¼ tsp. cloves.
CHOCOLATE PUDDING - Add a dash of cinnamon or mace.
GRAPEFRUIT - Sprinkle halves with ginger and coconut;
     chill to serve.
MOLASSES COOKIES - Add pumpkin-pie spice to dry
     ingredients.
PEACH PIE - A shake of cinnamon picks up the flavor.
PEARS - Dot fresh or canned pears with butter; sprinkle
     with sugar, cinnamon; broil.
PINEAPPLE - Top slices with cream cheese, add shake
     of cinnamon; broil.
RICE PUDDING - Season with apple pie spice, serve with
     stirred custard sauce.
SPICE CAKE - To one package spice cake mix, add 2
     tbls. instant coffee.
SUGAR COOKIES - Stir anise seed into dry ingredients.
YELLOW CAKE - To one package yellow cake mix, add
     ½ tsp. nutmeg and ¼ tsp. allspice.

SOUPS - APPETIZERS:

BEEF SOUP - Add mixed vegetable flakes while it
     simmers.
CHICKEN SOUP - Add a pinch of rosemary or dash of
     paprika or marjoram.
CONSOMME' - Season with allspice or a dash of savory.
CRANBERRY JUICE - If served hot, spice with whole
     cloves; if served chilled, add cinnamon or ground
     cloves.
FISH CHOWDER - Cook with lots of vegetables, then add
     thyme.
OYSTER STEW - Add light touches of mace or cayenne.
POTATO SOUP - Try a dash of mustard or basil.
SPLIT-PEA SOUP - Sprinkle in savory.
STUFFED CELERY - Mix caraway seed with cream cheese
     for stuffing; sprinkle with paprika.
TOMATO-JUICE COCKTAIL - Try a pinch of dill seeds or
     a bit of oregano.
TOMATO SOUP - Shake in sage and garlic salt.
VEGETABLE SOUP - Add thyme or a dash of chili powder.

TAKE TIME FOR TEN THINGS

Take time to work --
    It is the price of success.
Take time to think --
    It is the source of power.
Take time to play --
    It is the secret of youth.
Take time to read --
    It is the foundation of knowledge.
Take time to worship --
    It is the highway of reverence and washes the
    dust of the earth from our eyes.
Take time to help and enjoy friends --
    It is the source of happiness.
Take time to love --
    It is the one sacrament of life.
Take time to dream --
    It hitches the soul to the stars.
Take time to laugh --
    It is the singing that helps with life's load.
Take time to plan --
    It is the secret of being able to have time to
    take for the first nine things!

                  Submitted by Libby Trest

WARM CHILDREN AND LOVE

Take 5 or 6 children - sprinkle over a wide field.
Add some water - a cool babbling brook. Stir in some
excitement. Add a generous portion of love and a
pinch of laughter. Cover with a clear blue sky and
allow to bake for several hours in the warm summer
sun. When done and a golden brown, wash and tuck
them into a soft bed.

                  Submitted by Libby Trest

"There is nothing better for a man than that he should
eat and drink"   (Ecclesiastes 2:24).

CRANBERRY TEA

4 cups or 1 lb. fresh cranberries
2½ quarts water
2 cups sugar (scant)
1 cup orange juice
30 whole cloves

Cook cranberries in 2 qts. water until they all pop;
strain. Save juice and discard cranberries. Dissolve
sugar in 2 cups water. Add to cranberry juice. Add
orange juice and cloves. Serve hot. (If too thick
or strong, several cups of plain tea may be added.)
Serves 12.

Marilyn Heavilin

+ + + + +

HOT FRUIT PUNCH

3 cardamon seeds
1 cinnamon stick
6 whole cloves

Simmer spices ½ hour in 1 cup water.   Strain.   Add:

4 cups unsweetened pineapple juice
1 cup apricot juice
2 cups apple juice
1 cup orange juice
3/4 cup sugar

Serve hot.   Donna Chapman

+ + + + +

RUSSIAN TEA MIX

2 cups Tang   1 tsp. cinnamon
1 cup instant tea   1 pkg. sweetened lemonade (opt.)
½ tsp. ground cloves   1 cup sugar (if desired sweet)

Mix all ingredients together and store in a covered
container. Use desired amount of tea mixture to water
to suit your taste (1 to 3 tsps. per cup).

Dixie Sylvester

REAL FRENCH CHOCOLATE

½ cup semi-sweet chocolate pieces
½ cup white corn syrup
¼ cup water
1 tsp. vanilla
1 pt. (2 cups) whipping cream
2 qts. milk

Blend chocolate and syrup and water over low heat
until melted. Pour into cup and refrigerate until
cool. Add vanilla. In large bowl beat cream at medium
speed and add chocolate syrup gradually. Continue
beating until mixture mounds. Spoon into serving bowl
(such as punch bowl) and chill. Scald milk. Pour into
heated coffee pot. Spoon chocolate cream into cups
and pour hot milk over the chocolate (about 2 tbls.
chocolate mixture). Stir. Serves 16.

Lee Etta Lappen

+ + + + +

INSTANT HOT CHOCOLATE

1 8-qt. box Instant Carnation milk
1-1b. box Hershey Instant Chocolate
1 6-oz. jar dry cream
½ cup sifted powdered sugar

Mix all ingredients together. Combine 1/3 to 1/2 cup
of dry milk mixture to each cup of water. Heat but do
not boil.

Carol Barger

+ + + + +

SWEDISH EGG COFFEE

Boil 10-12 cups water. Add 1 cup regular grind coffee
to 1 egg and mix all together. Add a little hot water
to coffee and egg mixture. Put coffee mixture in hot
water, stir, put back on stove until it boils over.
Remove from heat and add one cup of ice cold water.
Let set for 10 minutes (egg and grounds settle to
bottom and coffee is a lovely, dark honey color).

Barbara Ball

HEALTH DRINK

Mix in blender:		To make in quantity:
3 tbls.	Carob-Tigers milk powder	3 cups
1 tbl.	powdered milk	1 cup
1 tbl.	protein powder	1 cup
1 tsp.	yeast powder	1/3 cup
1 tsp.	powdered liver	1/3 cup
½ cup	water	
1 or 2	eggs	
1 tsp.	wheat germ or energoil (liquid)	
(or more)		

Sweeten with Sweet 'n Lo or other artificial sweetener.
For flavoring use: 1 teaspoon of extract, maple,
lemon, vanilla or others. Add several variations:
1 tablespoon honey (instead of sweetener), 1 tablespoon peanut butter, 1 banana or any fresh fruit.
When mixing quantity, add 1/3 cup or 6 tablespoons
powder to liquid. Contains 197 calories with only
one egg and without variations added. Add several
crushed ice cubes while blending.

Vonette Bright

+ + + + +

HOT SPICED TEA [OR PUNCH]

[Especially nice during the holiday season to serve
drop-in guests.]

1 tsp. whole cloves
1 stick cinnamon
½ tsp. allspice
1 gal. water
2½ tbls. tea leaves (or 3 tea bags)
1 can (or more) frozen orange juice
1 can frozen lemonade
1½ cups sugar

Tie spices loosely in a bag and bring to boil in
water. Add tea tied loosely in a bag and steep 5
minutes. Remove bags, add juices and sugar; bring to
a boil and serve. (For a stronger spicy taste, return bag of spices to steep.) May be made ahead and
stored in refrigerator. Reheat when ready to serve.

Dorothy Brooks

BANANA ALE

[This is a terrific, refreshing, summer fruit drink
or can be an appetizer on hand in the freezer for
ready use. Great for morning breakfast cup.]

This recipe makes a large batch to be stored in a
plastic container in freezer.

Boil together for 3 minutes:
    6 cups water
    4 cups sugar
Cool.
Mix in blender:
5 oranges, juiced with pulp
5 bananas, mashed
4 lemons, juiced with pulp
1 (46-oz.) can pineapple juice
Mix sugar-water and fruit mixture together. Set in
freezer for at least 3 hours before serving. To
serve: spoon mixture into individual glasses - ½
full. Fill up the rest of glass with 7-Up or ginger
ale.

                                        Sue Cowan

                    + + + + +

HONEY CUBES

Honey ice cubes are cool and refreshing when added to
iced tea or fruit beverages. Keep a supply on hand
in the freezer. Blend ½ cup honey with 2 cups very
hot water and 2 tablespoons lemon juice. Pour into
ice cube trays and freeze at once. Crush and serve
in iced tea or float in punch.

                                    Dorothy Gregory

                    + + + + +

SHERBET PUNCH

2 quarts ginger ale
1 quart sherbet (pineapple or orange is best)

Chill ginger alle and mix together with chunks of
sherbet.

CRANBERRY SHRUB

½ pint cranberry juice
1½ cups tangerine juice (frozen or may substitute
      orange juice)
1 pint orange sherbet

Place ingredients in blender. Beat on high speed for
5 seconds. Pour into small glasses and serve.

Carol Williams

+ + + + +

CRANBERRY PUNCH

[A two-way punch]

2/3 cup sugar
6" of stick cinnamon (broken)
2 tbls. whole allspice
1-2 tsps. whole cloves
¼ tsp. salt
1 qt. cranberry juice cocktail
1 #2 can unsweetened pineapple juice
1 large bottle ginger ale

Combine sugar, spices, salt, cranberry juice and
pineapple juice. Cover and simmer 10 minutes. Strain
and chill. Float orange slices on top. Add ginger ale.
HOT: Omit ginger ale and add 2 cups water. Serve
hot. This punch can be served hot in the winter or
cold in the summer.

Helen Lovell

+ + + + +

SURPRISE TOMATO COCKTAIL

Tomato juice
Lemon/lime carbonated drink
Lemon slices

Mix equal quantities of tomato juice and lemon/lime
drink just before serving. Pour into stem glasses
and garnish with a lemon slice.

Ethelwynne Reeves

PUNCH BASE

2 small frozen cans of orange juice
6 small frozen cans of limeade
4 small frozen cans of lemonade
½ gal. cranberry juice
2 cans pineapple juice
4 qts. water
1 large pkg. jello - raspberry or strawberry

To serve punch use:
2 quarts of punch base and
2 quarts of ginger ale
May add more water if needed and sugar to taste.
May make green color by eliminating cranberry juice
and using lime or apple jello and apple juice.

+ + + + +

BRIDE'S PUNCH

[Add Kool Aid for economy to the punch below]

6 (6-oz.) cans frozen orange juice
6 (6-oz.) cans frozen lemonade
5 quarts cold water
2 quarts (or large bottles) chilled ginger ale
2 pkgs. frozen strawberries or other fruit

Mix juices and water. Chill. Add ginger ale and
berries just before serving. May float a frozen
fruit ring in bowl if desired. Serves 100.

Lois Mackey

+ + + + +

BUBBLING JADE PUNCH

1 sm. pkg. lime gelatin
1 cup hot water
2 cups cold water
1 (6-oz.) can frozen lemonade
1 cup pineapple juice
1 bottle ginger ale
1 (10-oz.) pkg. strawberries

Dissolve gelatin in hot water. Add cold water,
lemonade and pineapple juice; blend well. Just before serving, add ginger ale, ice cubes and strawberries. For a bubbling and smoking effect, put a small
piece of dry ice in punch bowl. Let it rest on a piece
of foil in your bowl. Serves 25

Lois Mackey

DEVILED HAM CORNUCOPIAS

[Use as appetizer at Thanksgiving -- yummy!]

Cornucopias: Cut 20 slices of thin sliced white bread with round cookie cutter. Flatten with rolling pin, spread mayonnaise on both sides. Roll up to form cornucopia, fasten with toothpick. Bake on ungreased cookie sheet at 350° for 12-15 minutes, until lightly brown. Remove toothpick. Fill with:

3 tbls. mayonnaise
1 (4½-oz.) can deviled ham
2 hard cooked eggs, finely chopped
1 tbl. prepared mustard

Combine ingredients. Chill. Fill cornucopias with one generous teaspoon.

Peggy Jones

+ + + + +

CHEESE ROUNDS

½ lb. sharp cheese, grated
1 cup margarine
2 cups sifted flour
2 cups Rice Krispies
Dash of cayenne pepper

Mix ingredients well, shape into small balls, flatten with fork. Bake on Teflon baking sheet at 350° for 15 minutes. Cool slightly before removing. Excellent for parties. Freezes well.

Jane Prall

+ + + + +

OLIVE-CHEESE SNACKS

1 5-oz. jar bacon-cheese snacks
4 tbls. butter or margarine
Dash of hot pepper sauce
Dash of Worcestershire sauce
3/4 cup sifted flour
1 sm. jar medium-sized stuffed olives (may prefer
    ripe olives)

Blend cheese and margarine together until light and fluffy. Add hot pepper sauce and Worcestershire; mix well. Stir in flour; mix to form a dough. Shape around olives using about one teaspoon of dough for each. Place on ungreased baking sheet. Bake at 400° for 12-15 minutes or until golden brown. Makes about 30.

Jerri Younkman

+ + + + +

CHEESE PENNIES

¼ cup butter
1 cup Cheddar cheese, grated
½ pkg. dry onion soup mix
1 cup flour
¼ tsp. salt

Cream butter and grated cheese. Add soup mix, salt
and flour. Blend well. Shape into a roll 1" in
diameter and chill. Cut into thick slices and bake
at 375° for 10 minutes or until brown.

Carol Carter

+ + + + +

MEXICAN PIZZA

They are so good you may decide to skip the rest
of the dinner!

Cover corn tortillas with thin slices of Cheddar
cheese and put in hot oven for 7 minutes until cheese
is melted. Chopped onions can also be included. Cut
as pizza and serve.

Ginger Gabriel

+ + + + +

HOT SHRIMP CANAPES

24 white bread slices
24 shrimp (or cold meat)
½ cup mayonnaise
1 cup finely shredded American cheese

Cut bread into small shapes with cookie cutters.
Top with shrimp. Combine mayonnaise and cheese.
Spread completely over appetizer. Broil 4" from
heat until bubbly and brown. Serves 8.

Peggy Jones

36

HERB SPREAD

1 cup butter
1 tbl. dehydrated onion
1 tbl. dehydrated parsley
1 tsp. sweet basil
2 tbls. Parmesan cheese

Soften butter and combine with rest of the ingredients. Spread on Party Rye or Melba toast. Broil
and serve.

Charlotte Day

+ + + + +

CRABMEAT HORS D'OEUVRES

2/3 sm. pkg. of Velveeta cheese
¼ cup margarine
1 can (7½-oz.) crab meat
1 tsp. Worcestershire sauce

Melt cheese and margarine in double boiler. Add crabmeat and Worcestershire sauce. Spread on Party Rye
or Melba toast. Broil for a minute or two.

Charlotte Day

+ + + + +

CHEESE BALLS

1 cup finely grated sharp cheese
½ cup flour
¼ cup soft butter
½ tsp. salt
2 tsps. seeds (caraway, sesame, or poppy)

Mix all ingredients. Shape into balls. Chill. Bake
at 375º for 10-12 minutes immediately before serving.
Serve warm.

Jerri Younkman

+ + + + +

NEW YORK CHEESE BALL

[Great for a party or as an appetizer. May also be
made in small balls and given away as gifts.]

1½ lbs. Velveeta cheese
2 3-oz. pkgs. cream cheese
2 tbls. Durkee's salad dressing
½ cup chopped pecans
1½ garlic buds, finely crushed

Mix ingredients with blender. Shape into balls or
logs with dampened hands and roll in sifted chili
powder. Place in center of platter and surround
with warmed Ritz crackers.

Carol Williams

NEW ORLEANS HOT BROCCOLI DIP

1 pkg. chopped frozen broccoli
½ tsp. salt
¼ cup water
1 sm. onion, chopped
2 tbls. butter
1 can cream of mushroom soup
1 6-oz. roll garlic cheese
1 tsp. Accent

½ tsp. salt	1 tsp. Worcestershire sauce
1/8 tsp. pepper	1 4-oz. can mushrooms
1/8 tsp. Tabasco	3/4 cup slivered almonds

Cook broccoli with ½ tsp. salt and ¼ cup water. Drain.
Set aside. Saute' onion in butter. Add soup, cheese
and seasonings. Cook on medium heat until cheese
melts. Add broccoli and cook 1 minute longer. Stir.
Add mushrooms and almonds. Serve hot with corn chips,
crackers, or tacos. Makes 4 cups. (May be made into
an exciting vegetable dish as well by adding 1 more
package of broccoli, 1 more onion and more butter to
taste.)

Libby Trest

+ + + + +

SHRIMP ROLL

Beat together:
1 cup (½ lb.) soft margarine
1 (6-oz.) can shrimp
2 cloves garlic, pressed

Chill. Roll in chopped onions or almonds; refrigerate. Serve with crackers and slice it as butter and
spread.

Andre' Rabe

+ + + + +

ROQUEFORT TOMATO VEGETABLE DIP

½ cup salad oil
½ cup Roquefort cheese
1 clove garlic (or 2 tsps. garlic powder)
½ tsp. salt
¼ cup Heinz chili sauce
½ tsp. paprika
1 tbl. lemon juice
1 (8-oz.) can tomato sauce

Blend all ingredients together in blender. Use as a
dip for radishes, raw cauliflowerettes, celery sticks,
carrot strips, even raw turnips.

Carol Williams

CHILI CON QUESO

[A dip to use with tortilla chips]

1 large onion
1 #2 can tomatoes
2 sm. cans green chili, chopped (mild)
2 tbls. flour
½ cup canned milk
½ lb. Velveeta cheese

Brown onion in oil. Add tomatoes and chili; simmer
5 minutes. Mix flour and milk and add to tomato mixture. Add cheese. Serve in chafing dish or fondue
pot.

Roselyn Shaver

+ + + + +

MEXICAN CHILI CON QUESO

1 med. onion, chopped
1 sm. green pepper, chopped
1 tbl. cooking oil
5 fresh med. tomatoes, chopped (or canned)
3 whole canned chilies, seeded and chopped
1 lb. sharp cheese, grated
Salt and pepper to taste

Brown onion and green pepper in oil in electric
fry pan at 300°. Turn control to simmer and mix
in tomatoes, chilies, cheese, seasoning and simmer
until well blended. Serve warm with an assortment
of chips.

Leslie Lewis

+ + + + +

HOT CRAB DIP

1 cup sharp cheddar cheese, grated
3/4 cup green onions, chopped
3/4 cup mayonnaise
1 tsp. lemon juice
1 large can crab, shredded

Mix mayonnaise, lemon juice and crab. Add to cheese
and onions. Heat over hot water and serve in chafing
dish.

Tested by Doris Rood

BREAD HINTS

"Those who have faith in Him as the bread of life will never die " (John 6:48-51).

Add grated Cheddar cheese to biscuit mix and use tomato juice instead of other liquid when making biscuits. Delicious served with a cooked vegetable salad for lunch. (Dorothy Gregory)

Save leftover biscuits. Split, spread with butter or margarine. Sprinkle with cinnamon-sugar or brown sugar. Warm under broiler for breakfast or snack. (Candace Steele)

Yeast grows best at a temperature between 80° and 85°. Too hot a temperature kills yeast; too low a temperature slows the growth. To hurry rising time, double the amount of yeast.

Potato water keeps bread moist longer; milk makes a brown crust and adds food value. Water makes cheap bread but adds no nutrient.

Batter or no-knead doughs cannot be overbeaten. Learn to knead bread dough thoroughly; it is a fine exercise and good for any neuroses you may be harboring.

To avoid soggy crust, remove bread from pans immediately after baking. For a tender crust, brush with butter immediately after baking. For a crisp crust, do not butter. (Midge Piedot)

"A dry crust eaten in peace is better than steak every day along with argument and strife" (Proverbs 17:1).

"If your enemy is hungry, give him bread to eat;
and if he is thirsty, give him water to drink"
(Proverbs 25:21).

+ + + + +

GOLDEN CAKE BREAD

1 pkg. dry yeast
¼ cup warm water
1 cup hot scalded milk
½ cup sugar
½ cup butter
2 eggs
1 tsp. salt

Combine milk, sugar and butter in large mixing bowl.
Cool to lukewarm. Stir in eggs, slightly beaten
(reserve 1 tbl. egg), 1 tsp. salt and yeast dissolved
in warm water. Gradually add 4-4½ cups sifted flour
to form stiff batter, beating well after each addition. Cover. Let rise in warm place until light
and doubled (about 1 hour). Beat down and let rise
again until doubled. Turn into 2 well-greased loaf
pans. Let rise in warm place until light (about
3/4 hour); brush with reserved egg. Bake at 350°
for 25-30 minutes until golden brown.

Nancy Schurle

+ + + + +

DAISY'S ROLLS

4 cups flour
2 eggs
1½ tsps. salt
2 tbls. sugar
2 tbls. shortening
1½ cups milk
½ cup warm water
1½ pkgs. yeast
About 1 cup flour to use when kneading

Dissolve yeast in warm water. Set aside. Mix all
other ingredients together, add yeast. Cover, let
rise in warm place until mixture doubles in bulk
(about 2 hours). Knead, using remaining flour.
Roll out and cut in circles, fold over, cover and
let rise until double again. Bake at 400° for about
12 minutes. Brush with melted butter just before
done. Makes about 3 dozen rolls.

+ + + + +

CASSEROLE ONION BREAD

1 cup milk, scalded
3 tbls. sugar
1 tbl. salt
1½ tbls. butter or margarine
2 pkgs. yeast
3/4 cup warm water
½ cup minced fresh onion
4 cups sifted flour

Stir sugar, salt and butter into scalded milk. Mix
until sugar is completely dissolved. Cool to lukewarm. Dissolve yeast in warm water. Stir until yeast
is dissolved. Add onion and flour; stir until well
blended; about 2 minutes. Stir batter down. Beat
well about ½ minute. Turn into greased casserole
dish. Bake at 375° about 1 hour.

Kerry Fix

+ + + + +   .

QUICK ONION ROLLS

[Light as a feather!]

2 pkgs. dry yeast
1 tsp. sugar
½ cup warm water
½ cup sugar
3 eggs
1 tsp. salt

1 cup scalded milk
½ cup margarine
4-4½ cups flour
1 pkg. dry onion soup mix

Dissolve yeast in warm water with 1 tsp. sugar.
Scald milk and add margarine. Mix eggs, sugar and
salt in large bowl. Add cooled milk and margarine;
mix in yeast. Blend in flour with onion soup and
mix thoroughly. (This is a soft dough.) Cover and
let rise in warm place until double (about 2 hours).
Roll out onto a heavily floured board to about ½"
thickness. Cut with round cutter and place rolls
on greased cookie sheet. Cover (with towel) and let
rise again. Bake at 350° for about 10-12 minutes.
Rub margarine across tops of buns while still hot.
Serve warm. Very good to use for sloppy joes, hamburgers, or just dinner rolls. (Also good without
the onion soup mix added.)

Midge Piedot

42

CHEESE BREAD

2 pkgs. yeast
½ cup warm water
1 (11-oz.) can cheddar cheese soup
1 pkg. (.7-oz.) dry garlic salad dressing
3½ cups flour

Soften yeast in warm water in large mixing bowl.
Add undiluted soup and dry salad dressing mix.
Gradually add flour to form a stiff dough, beating
well after each addition. Knead on floured surface
until smooth and elastic, about 5 minutes. Place
in greased bowl, cover, let rise in warm place until
the dough doubles in size (about 30 minutes). Shape
dough into 4 10" long loaves, place on greased
cookie sheets. Cover and let rise again until it
doubles in size (about 30 minutes). Bake at 400°
for 30-40 minutes. Remove from cookie sheets immediately. Cool on wire racks. Makes 4 loaves.

Diane Yancy

+ + + + +

OVERNIGHT REFRIGERATOR ROLLS

2 pkgs. yeast
2½ cups warm water
3/4 cup melted shortening
3/4 cup sugar
2 eggs, well beaten
8-8½ cups flour
2½ tsps. salt

Soften yeast in warm water. Add shortening,
sugar, eggs, 4 cups flour and salt. Stir and
beat until smooth, about 1 minute. Stir in remaining flour. Cover tightly and store in refrigerator
overnight or until needed. When ready to use, punch
down dough and pinch off amount needed for rolls.
Shape into rolls and place in a greased baking pan
or cup cake pan. Cover and let rise in warm place
1 hour. Bake at 400° for 15-20 minutes. (If using
wheat flour, use 5 cups white flour and 3 cups wheat
flour.)

Midge Piedot

"He took the bread and blessed, and broke it, and gave
it to them. And their eyes were opened and.....He was
known to them in the breaking of the bread"
(Luke 24:30,35)

+ + + + +

SPICY APPLE WHEAT GERM MUFFINS

1½ cups unsifted flour (unbleached)
½ cup wheat germ
3 tsps. baking powder
½ tsp. salt
½ tsp. cinnamon
½ tsp. nutmeg
½ cup raw sugar or honey
¼ cup margarine
2 eggs
1 cup finely chopped apple
½ cup milk
1/3 cup raisins (opt.)

Measure flour, wheat germ, baking powder, salt and
spices. Stir well to blend. Cream sugar, butter
and eggs thoroughly. Stir in apple and raisins.
Add blended dry ingredients to creamed mixture alternately with milk. Stir until dry ingredients are
moistened. Fill oiled muffin tins. Bake at 400°
for 20 minutes. Makes 15 muffins.

Arlene Dennison

+ + + + +

OATMEAL MUFFINS

1 cup rolled oats
1 cup sour milk
1/3 cup soft butter
½ cup brown sugar
1 egg
1 cup flour
1 tsp. baking powder
½ tsp. soda
1 tsp. salt

Soak oats in sour milk (1 tbl. vinegar in milk to
make it sour). Mix butter, sugar and egg. Sift dry
ingredients and add to oat mixture gradually. Mix
well. Fill muffin tins 2/3 full. Bake at 400° for
20-25 minutes.

Marilyn Klein

44

SIX-WEEK MUFFINS

[This makes a good breakfast or dinner accompaniment
for unexpected guests.]

3 cups All-Bran cereal
1 cup boiling water
½ cup margarine
½ quart buttermilk
1½ cups sugar
2 eggs
2½ cups flour
2½ tsps. soda
1 tsp. salt

Bring water to boiling point, add shortening and
All-Bran. Set aside to cool or cool with buttermilk. Add buttermilk. Beat sugar and eggs together
and add to All-Bran mixture. Mix dry ingredients
and gradually add to liquid mixture. Bake in greased
muffin tins at 350° for 25 minutes. (May use at
once or store batter in refrigerator up to six weeks.
Old plastic containers from sherbet in one quart
or ½ gallon sizes are handy for this.)

Jan Schules

+ + + + +

ORANGE DONUT MUFFINS

Sift:
1½ cups flour
1 3/4 tsps. baking powder
½ tsp. salt
½ tsp. nutmeg
½ cup sugar
Cut in: 1/3 cup shortening
Beat together and mix with the above:
1 egg
¼ cup milk.
Gently stir in 1 cup orange pieces. Spoon into
muffin tins. Bake at 350° for 20-25 minutes. Roll
in melted butter and then in a mixture of 1/3 cup
sugar and 1 tsp. cinnamon. Makes 1 dozen.

Kerry Fix

ANGEL BISCUITS

1 pkg. yeast	3 tbls. baking powder
2 tbls. lukewarm water	4 tbls. sugar
1 cup shortening	1 tsp. salt
5 cups sifted flour	2 cups buttermilk
1 tsp. soda	

Dissolve yeast in water. Sift dry ingredients. Cut
in shortening. Blend in yeast and buttermilk.
Knead enough to hold together. Roll dough to desired
thickness. Cut with biscuit cutter and fold in half.
Bake at 400° for 20 minutes.

Barbara Ball

+ + + + +

RANCH BISCUITS

[The yeast helps these biscuits pass for dinner rolls]

2¼ cups flour	2 tbls. sugar
2 tsps. baking powder	3/4 cup buttermilk
¼ tsp. soda	1 pkg. yeast
½ tsp. salt	2/3 cup warm water
2 tbls. melted shortening	

Dissolve yeast in water. Sift dry ingredients. Cut
in shortening. Add rest of ingredients. Knead
enough to hold together. Shape into balls or roll
out and cut. Let stand 15 minutes. Place on buttered sheet or cake pan. Bake at 450° for 8-10 minutes.
Extra dough may be kept on hand in refrigerator for
up to 2 weeks.

Sharyn Regier

+ + + + +

SESAME BISCUITS

2 cups flour	2/3 cup shortening
1 tsp. salt	¼ cup orange juice
½ cup toasted sesame seeds	

Combine flour, salt and sesame seeds in large bowl.
Work in shortening until mixture resembles texture
of coarse corn meal. Gradually work in orange juice.
Roll out pastry to ¼" thickness. Cut into strips
1" x 2¼". Place on ungreased baking sheet. Bake
at 400° for 15-20 minutes -- until golden brown.

Barbara Ball

+ + + + +

GRACE'S ALASKAN SOUR-DOUGH BREAD

STARTER: Mix one package yeast, one tablespoon
sugar, two cups warm water and two cups flour.
Store in covered dish (not plastic) in warm place
for three days. Stir daily. (For new method of
mixing or dissolving yeast: use same amount of
water as called for, but mix yeast with flour --
much easier!)

BREAD:

1 cup hot water	1 pkg. yeast
3 tbls. sugar	2 tbls. warm water
2 tbls. margarine	1½ cups sour-dough starter
3 tsps. salt	5 cups flour

Pour hot water over sugar, margarine, salt and cool
to lukewarm. Dissolve yeast in 2 tablespoons warm
water and add to the other liquid with the starter
and two cups of the flour. Beat thoroughly and add
two to three more cups flour and turn on board and
knead thoroughly. Let rise in covered greased bowl
until double. Punch down, let rise thirty more
minutes. Punch down, divide and let set ten minutes.
Shape into two loaves, put on greased cookie sheet,
covered with cornmeal. Slash across top several times
with scissors; let rise until double and bake at
400° for 30 minutes. A beaten egg white with one
teaspoon water spread on top of bread before baking
will give it a pretty glaze. (The remainder of the
starter may be stored in refrigerator until ready to
use again. To make more, add to the starter the
original starter listed above. If not used for a
long while, it may be frozen.)

Rita Harvey

+ + + + +

JEWISH BREAD LOAF

Cream 1 cup sugar and ¼ cup margarine
Add the following in order:

2 eggs (one at a time)	1 tsp. soda
1 cup sour cream	1 tsp. baking powder
1 tsp. vanilla	1/8 tsp. salt
2 cups flour	

Stir until blended. Mix ¼ cup sugar and 1 tsp. cinnamon. Pour half of the batter into a loaf pan.
Sprinkle on half of the sugar-cinnamon. Add remaining
batter and sprinkle the top with remainder of sugar-
cinnamon. Bake at 350° for 45 minutes.

Suzie Brenneman

ANISE RYE BREAD

[Good for salad luncheon. Very simple and tasty!]

2 cups warm water
2 round tbls. shortening
2 cups rye flour
½ cup molasses
1½ tsps. anise
1 tsp. salt
1 pkg. yeast
½ cup sugar

Dissolve yeast in warm water in bowl. Measure and
sift flour, salt and anise. Add shortening, sugar,
molasses and flour to yeast. Add 4½ cups white
flour. Let set overnight. Divide into 2 loaves
and bake at 350° for 1 hour.

Barbara Ball

+ + + + +

RYE BREAD

1 pkg. yeast
¼ cup warm water
2 cups water or milk (or 1 of each)
1/3 cup butter
¼ cup molasses
¼ cup brown sugar
2 tbls. salt
3 cups rye flour (may substitute partially whole
       wheat flour)
1 tbl. caraway seeds
2 cups flour

Sprinkle yeast in warm water and let stand. Scald
2 cups milk or water. Add butter, molasses, brown
sugar, salt and rye flour. When cooled, add seeds
and yeast. Add all-purpose flour gradually to make
a soft dough. Cover and let rise in warm place.
When doubled, divide into two loaves. Let rise again.
Bake at 375° for 35 minutes. When it has been in the
oven for 15 minutes, brush with warm water and again
when you remove it from the oven.

Carol Barger

HERB BREAD

1 pkg. yeast
2 cups scalded milk
¼ cup sugar
1 tbl. salt
2 eggs, beaten
1 tsp. nutmeg

2 tsps. sage
4 tsps. caraway seeds
3 cups flour
¼ cup melted butter
3-3½ cups additional
    flour

Cool scalded milk to lukewarm. Add yeast and mix to dissolve. Add sugar and salt. Stir in eggs, spices and 3 cups flour. Stir until smooth. Add butter and rest of flour. Knead until smooth and elastic. Let rise until dough doubles. Divide and shape into rolls or loaves. Let rise until double again. Bake at 375° for 25-30 minutes.

Barbara Ball

+ + + + +

DILLY BREAD

[Good with beef fondue or steak]

1 pkg. dry yeast
¼ cup warm water
1 cup warm creamed cottage cheese
2 tbls. sugar
1 tbl. instant minced onions
1 tbl. butter

2 tsps. dill seed
1 tsp. salt
1 unbeaten egg
2¼-2½ cups flour

Dissolve yeast in warm water. Mix in cottage cheese. Add rest of ingredients. Beat and form into stiff dough. Cover and let rise in warm place for 1 hour. Stir down. Put into well greased 8" round casserole dish. Let rise 30-40 minutes. Bake at 350° for 40-45 minutes. Brush with melted butter and sprinkle the top with salt. Serve hot. Serves 12.

Cinny Hicks

+ + + + +

POPPY SEED BREAD

4 eggs
2 cups sugar
1½ cups salad oil
3 cups flour
1½ tsps. soda
½ tsp. salt

1 large can evaporated milk
1 oz. poppy seeds (3 tbls.)
½ cup nuts

Beat eggs, add sugar and oil. Sift dry ingredients and add to egg mixture alternately with milk. Stir in nuts. Bake in 10" tube pan 1½ hours at 350° (or in 6 small loaf pans for 45-60 minutes).

Linda Skulte

HOT FRENCH BREAD

1 long loaf French bread
½ cup butter
¼ cup mayonnaise
Dash of garlic salt
Parmesan cheese
Paprika

Split bread lengthwise and spread with mixture
of butter, mayonnaise and garlic. Sprinkle grated
cheese and paprika on top and heat (uncovered on
baking sheet) at 350° for 10 minutes.

Dorothy Gregory

+ + + + +

TOMATO BREAD

1 long loaf French bread
2-3 med. tomatoes
Oregano
Mozzarella cheese (about 1 lb.)
Oil or butter

Slice bread in half and then into small 3" long
pieces. Butter each piece with oil or butter.
Slice the tomatoes in ¼" slices or thinner. Place
the tomato slices on the pieces of bread. Sprinkle
oregano over - use according to your own taste.
Slice the mozzarella thinly. Place a slice on top
of the oregano. Place bread on cookie sheet and
bake at 400° until cheese is melted. Serve hot
with any meal.

Bonnie Merkle

+ + + + +

TOAST CUPS

Remove crust of bread slices; butter. Place buttered side down in muffin cup. Bake at 350° for about
15 minutes. Fill with whatever you like--egg, tuna
fish, whitesauce, etc.

Gail Palmquist

PUMPKIN BREAD

3½ cups flour	2 cups pumpkin
1½ tsps. salt	2 tsps. soda
1 tsp. nutmeg	4 eggs
2 tsps. cinnamon	3 cups sugar
2/3 cup water	1 cup salad oil

Sift dry ingredients into a large bowl. Combine salad oil, eggs, pumpkin and water and add to dry ingredients. Mix thoroughly. Pour into two greased and floured loaf pans. Bake at 325° for 1-1½ hours.

Judy DeBoer

VARIATION: May add 1 cup chopped nuts.

Jane Prall

+ + + + +

PUMPKIN BREAD

5 cups flour	2 tsps. cinnamon
4 cups sugar	1 tsp. cloves
4 tsps. soda	1 cup salad oil
1 tsp. salt	1 large can pumpkin

Sift dry ingredients together. Add oil and pumpkin. Stir thoroughly and pour into 3 or 4 greased loaf pans. Bake at 350° for 1 hour and 15 minutes.

Toya Rennick and Karen Kuhne
Nan Green and Billie Thurman

+ + + + +

BANANA BREAD

1 cup sugar
½ cup shortening
1 egg, well beaten
3 bananas, mashed (over-ripe are best)
3 tbls. milk
1 tsp. soda
1 tsp. baking powder
Pinch of salt
2 cups flour

Cream sugar and shortening. Add well beaten egg and bananas. Add rest of ingredients. Bake in loaf pan at 350° for 45 minutes.

Lee Etta Lappen

HOLIDAY BANANA BREAD

1 3/4 cups sifted flour
2 3/4 tsps. baking powder
½ tsp. salt
½ cup chopped nuts
1/3 cup shortening

2/3 cup sugar
2 slightly beaten eggs
1 cup mashed bananas
1 cup mixed candied fruits
¼ cup raisins

Sift together flour, baking powder and salt. Blend
in nuts. Beat shortening until creamy. Gradually
add sugar, beating until fluffy. Add eggs, beating
until thick. Add flour mixture and bananas alternately, blending thoroughly after each addition.
Fold in raisins and candied fruits. Grease bottom
only of 4 x 8 x 3" loaf pan. Pour batter into pan
and bake at 350° for 60-70 minutes.

                              Dorothy Brooks

+ + + + +

BANANA NUT BREAD

Sift:
2 cups flour
1 cup sugar
1 tsp. soda
½ tsp. salt

Mix together:
2 eggs
½ cup butter
5 tbls. sour cream

Combine dry ingredients with egg mixture and stir
well. Add 3 mashed bananas and 1 cup chopped nuts.
Bake in greased 9 x 3½" loaf pan at 350° for 1 hour
or until done.   Carol Williams and Mrs. Stoll

+ + + + +

NUTTY BANANA BREAD

1 cup sugar
2/3 cup butter
2 eggs
½ cup broken pecans or walnuts
2-3 mashed bananas

1 tsp. vanilla
2 cups flour
1 tsp. baking powder
1 tsp. soda
Pinch of salt

Cream butter and sugar; add eggs one at a time and
cream a few minutes. Add bananas. Sift flour, soda,
baking powder and salt three times. Add to batter
gradually. Add vanilla and nuts. Bake in well-
greased and floured large loaf pan or 2 small pans
at 300° for about 1 hour. Turn out onto cake rack
and let cool. [May wrap in small plastic bags to
give to friends at Christmas.]

                              Jane Prall

CRANBERRY FRUIT BREAD

2 cups flour
1 cup sugar
½ tsp. soda
1 tsp. salt
¼ cup shortening
1½ tsps. baking powder

3/4 cup orange juice
1 tbl. grated orange rind
1 egg, well beaten
1-2 cups coarsely chopped
    fresh cranberries
1 cup nuts

Sift together flour, sugar, soda, salt and baking
powder. Cut in shortening. Combine juice and rind
with egg. Pour all at once into dry ingredients.
Mix thoroughly. Fold in berries and nuts. Spoon
into greased 9 x 5 x 3" loaf pan. Spread corners
and sides slightly higher than center. Bake at
350° for 1 hour.

                        Toya Rennick and Judy DeBoer

+ + + + +

BUTTER-PECAN BREAD

2¼ cups sifted flour
2 tsps. baking powder
½ tsp. soda
½ tsp. salt
½ tsp. cinnamon
¼ tsp. nutmeg

1 egg, beaten
1 cup brown sugar
1 cup buttermilk
2 tbls. melted butter
1 cup chopped pecans

Sift together flour, baking powder, soda, salt,
spices; blend in brown sugar. Combine egg, buttermilk and butter; add to flour mixture, stirring well.
Stir in nuts. Bake in loaf pan at 350° for 40-45
minutes.

                              Suzie Brenneman

+ + + + +

LEMON BREAD

1 cup sugar
1 cup butter
3 eggs
2½ cups flour

1½ oz. lemon extract
1 cup pecans
1 cup white raisins
½ tsp. soda in ½ tbl. hot water

Cream butter, gradually add sugar, add eggs one at
a time. Add soda in water. Alternately add flour
and lemon extract. Stir in nuts and raisins. Bake
in loaf pans (1 large and 1 small) at 250° for
1 hour and 15 minutes.

                              Nancy Scott

QUICK YELLOW NUT COFFEE CAKE

1 pkg. yellow cake mix
1 pkg. instant vanilla pudding mix (3 3/4-oz.)
4 eggs
½ cup salad oil
1 cup sour cream

Blend cake mix and pudding mix in mixing bowl. Add
eggs, oil and sour cream. Beat until thick, about
5 minutes. Grease Bundt or angel food pan well.
NUT MIXTURE:
1 cup chopped nuts
½ cup sugar
1 tsp. cinnamon

Blend. Sprinkle 1 tablespoon nut mixture mixed with
1 tablespoon bread crumbs (dry or fresh) in bottom
of greased pan. Add half the batter, sprinkle rest
of nut mixture over batter. Add remaining half of
batter. Run knife through batter to marble or mix
nuts. Bake at 350° for 1 hour. Cool 5 minutes, then
remove from pan to rack. Slice and serve hot or cold.

Charlotte Day

+ + + + +

SHORT-CUT COFFEE CAKE

2 rolls of biscuits (the canned type you pop open
                    and bake)
½ cup brown sugar, packed
2 tbls. butter
¼ cup butter, melted
½ cup white sugar
2 tsps. cinnamon

Crumble 2 tablespoons soft butter with brown sugar
in the bottom of a ring mold. Dip each biscuit in
the ¼ cup melted butter and then into the sugar and
cinnamon mixed. Stand the biscuits on edge around
the mold. (You may add some nuts between the biscuits.) Sprinkle remaining butter and cinnamon-
sugar over the rolls. Bake at 400° for about 25
minutes. Turn upside down on a plate immediately
and serve.

Elaine Hannah

SOUR CREAM COFFEE CAKE

½ cup margarine
3/4 cup sugar
2 eggs
1 cup sour cream

1 tsp. vanilla
2 cups sifted flour
½ tsp. baking powder
1 tsp. baking soda

Cream margarine until light. Add sugar gradually, beat until fluffy. Add eggs and vanilla. Mix. Sift dry ingredients together. Add dry ingredients alternately with sour cream to creamed mixture. Pour half of cake batter into prepared angel cake pan or Bundt pan. Cover with half of topping and then repeat with the remaining batter and topping. Bake at 350° for 50 minutes.

TOPPING: ¼ cup white sugar
          ¼ cup brown sugar
          1 tsp. cinnamon
          ½ cup chopped nuts
          2 tbls. butter
          2 tbls. flour
          1 tbl. cocoa (opt.)

VARIATION: Sliced apples may be placed over first half of batter; sprinkle with ½ of topping. Pour remaining batter on, repeat with remaining topping.

Betty Marquez, Merry McKean
Donna Lou Gaunt, Dorothy Brooks

+ + + + +

EASY COFFEE CAKE

BATTER: 3/4 cup sugar
         ¼ cup soft shortening
         1 egg
         ½ cup milk

1½ cups sifted flour
2 tsps. baking powder
½ tsp. salt

TOPPING: ½ cup chopped nuts
          ½ cup brown sugar
          2 tbls. flour

2 tbls. melted butter
2 tsps. cinnamon

Cream sugar and shortening, add egg and milk. Sift dry ingredients together and add to creamed mixture. Spread ½ the batter in greased and floured 8" pan. Sprinkle with ½ the topping. Spread rest of batter on and sprinkle with remaining topping. Bake at 375° for 20-25 minutes. Serve warm with extra butter.

Paula Carter

DANISH CUFF

1 cup sifted flour
½ cup butter
3 tbls. water
Mix like pie crust -- flatten onto cookie sheet
    into 2 strips about 2 x 12"
½ cup butter
1 cup water
1 tsp. almond flavoring
1 cup flour
3 eggs

Boil butter and water together until butter is melted.
Remove from heat -- add flavoring and flour all at
once and beat in fast (so it won't lump). Beat in
eggs one at a time. Spread over strips on cookie
sheet. Bake at 350° for 1 hour. When cool, frost
with a thin glaze and sprinkle with nuts.

Midge Piedot

+ + + + +

OLD FASHIONED CRUMB CAKE

[An easy breakfast cake and so good!]

2 cups brown sugar
3 cups flour
½ cup margarine

Crumble above mixture with fingers to coarse meal.
Save 1 cup for topping. To the remaining add:
1 cup buttermilk (mix 1 tsp. soda in 1 tbl. of the
    buttermilk and add to mixture).

Place in two greased 8" pans or pie pans. Sprinkle
with topping. Dot with chunks of butter and generously sprinkle with cinnamon. Bake at 375° for
30-40 minutes.

Charlotte Day

+ + + + +

"Beloved, I pray that in all things thou mayest
prosper and be in health, even as thy soul prospereth"
(III John 2, R.V.).

56

WHEAT-GERM CINNAMON ROLLS
[Healthy!]

1½ cups warm water
¼ cup sugar
1 cup wheat germ
1 pkg. yeast
2 tsps. salt

2 egg yolks
1/3 cup corn oil
1 cup dry-milk solids
2 cups wholewheat flour
2 cups white flour

Pour water into large bowl. Add sugar and wheat
germ. Sprinkle yeast over this mixture and let
stand 10 minutes. Add remaining ingredients, except
flour. Mix with a fork. Gradually blend in the
flour. Cover and set in warm place for 30 minutes.
Blend again with fork or hands. Cover and let double
in bulk. Turn onto floured surface and roll to
thickness of 3/8 inch. Spread with the following,
in layers, one after the other:

½ cup butter or margarine, melted
3/4 cup brown sugar
½ cup white sugar
1 tbl. cinnamon
1 cup raisins
1 cup nuts, chopped

Roll in jelly-roll fashion. Slice at 1½ inch intervals. Place in oiled pan with edges touching (cut-
side down). Allow to rise in warm place. Bake at
350° for 20 minutes. Turn out on rack and frost
with powdered sugar icing:

1 lb. box powdered sugar
½ cup softened margarine
About 2 tbls. milk

Charlotte Melcher

+ + + + +

BJU COFFEE CAKE

1 egg, beaten
½ cup sugar
½ cup milk
2 tbls. melted shortening
1 cup flour
½ tsp. salt
2 tsps. baking powder

TOPPING:
¼ cup brown sugar
1 tbl. white sugar
¼ cup corn flakes
¼ tsp. cinnamon

Combine all dry ingredients. Mix eggs, milk and
shortening. Combine with dry ingredients and mix
thoroughly. Pour into greased 8" pan. Sprinkle with
topping. Bake at 375° for 20-25 minutes.

Lee Etta Lappen

FAN-TASTIES

1 pkg. yeast	1 cup raisins
¼ cup warm water	2/3 cup sour cream
4 cups flour	¼ cup sugar
2 tsps. salt	1 tbl. grated orange rind
½ cup butter	3 tbls. orange juice
½ cup Crisco	2 tbls. melted butter
2 eggs, beaten	

Soften yeast in water. Sift flour and salt. Cut in
butter and shortening. Combine eggs, raisins, sour
cream, sugar, orange rind, 2 tbls. orange juice and
yeast. Add to flour mixture; mix thoroughly. Cover
with foil; chill at least 2 hours. Combine remaining
orange juice and butter. Roll out half of dough on
floured surface to a 14" x 20" rectangle. Brush with
half of butter mixture, then sprinkle with half of
filling. Cut into five 14" x 2" strips. Stack strips.
Cut strips into 1½" pieces. Place stacks cut-side
down in well-greased muffin cups. Repeat with remaining dough. Cover. Let rise in warm place until
doubled in size. Bake at 375° for 15-18 minutes.
Makes 18-20 rolls.
FILLING: Combine 1/3 cup brown sugar, 1/3 cup powdered sugar, 2/3 cup chopped nuts and 1 tsp. grated
orange rind.

Midge Piedot

+ + + + +

ORANGE CINNAMON ROLLS

Orange syrup:
    ½ cup orange juice   2 tbls. butter
    2 tbls. orange peel grated ¼ cup sugar
Filling:
    ¼ cup sugar mixed with 1 tsp. cinnamon
Biscuit dough (may use the recipe on Bisquick box)

Mix biscuits and roll into an oblong 9 x 12".
Sprinkle with sugar and cinnamon mixture. Roll up
long side (as for jelly roll) and cut into 12 buns.
Meanwhile melt butter in a saucepan, add sugar, orange
juice and peel. Beat until bubbly and slightly thick.
Pour orange syrup into 12 muffin cups. Place cinnamon rolls cut side down in muffin cups. Bake at 400°
for 15-20 minutes. Turn out muffins onto wax paper.
Allow syrup to run over them. Serve warm.

Ethelwynne Reeves

SPICE PUFFS

2½ cups flour
2 tsps. baking powder
3/4 tsp. soda
3/4 tsp. cinnamon
½ tsp. mace
¼ tsp. cloves

¼ tsp. allspice
1 tbl. cocoa
2 eggs
½ cup salad oil
1½ cups sugar
1 cup sour milk

Sift flour. Add baking powder, soda, cinnamon, mace, cloves, allspice and cocoa. Beat eggs. Add oil and sugar. Mix well. Add milk. Stir again. Add dry ingredients, mixing quickly. Fill greased muffin cups one half full. Bake at 375° for 20 minutes.

Suzie Brenneman

+ + + + +

SWEDISH COFFEE BRAID

2 pkgs. yeast
8 cups sifted flour
½ tsp. salt
1 cup sugar
3/4 tsp. ground cardamon

2 eggs
1½ cups scalded milk
1 cup melted butter

Sprinkle yeast onto ½ cup warm water--stir until dissolved. In large bowl combine salt, sugar and cardamon, then stir in 2 beaten eggs, yeast and gradually add milk and butter and 7½ cups flour. Beat until smooth. Cover; let rise in warm place until double in bulk (about 1 hour). Turn onto lightly floured board (using remaining flour) and knead about five minutes. Divide dough in half--cut each half into three even pieces. Roll each piece into a "rope" about 12" long. Braid together. Place braids in bread pans (or on a greased cookie sheet). Cover and let rise until almost double. Bake at 350° for about 25 minutes. Turn out and cool on wire racks. Brush top with butter and sprinkle with sugar.

Carol Hurd

+ + + + +

HOT GINGERBREAD

Split gingerbread and fill center with applesauce. Wrap in foil and place on grill until hot.

Midge Piedot

MAGIC MARSHMALLOW CRESCENT PUFFS

[A hidden marshmallow melts like magic and leaves a
hollow puff. Excellent to serve with dinner.]

¼ cup sugar
1 tsp. cinnamon
16 large size marshmallows
¼ cup margarine, melted
2 cans (8-oz. each) refrigerator quick crescent
    dinner rolls

Combine sugar and cinnamon. Dip marshmallows in
melted margarine; roll in sugar-cinnamon mixture.
Wrap a crescent triangle around each, completely
covering marshmallow and squeezing edges of dough
tightly to seal. Dip in margarine; place in muffin
pan. (Place foil under pan.) Bake at 375° for 10
to 15 minutes until golden brown. Remove immediately.

                                  Merry McKean

+ + + + +

OLD FASHIONED DOUGHNUTS

4 cups flour
1 tsp. baking soda
¼ tsp. nutmeg
½ tsp. salt
4 tbls. shortening
1 cup sugar
2 eggs
1 tsp. vanilla
1 cup buttermilk

Sift dry ingredients. Cream shortening and sugar.
Add eggs and beat well. Add vanilla. Add dry ingredients alternately with buttermilk and stir only
until blended. Divide dough in half and roll out
each half onto floured board about ½" thick. Cut
with 2½" cutter. Let stand for at least 10 minutes.
Place about 4 doughnuts at a time in deep hot fat
(about 365°); fry until golden brown, turning once.
Drain on paper towel. Makes 2-3 dozen.

                                  Midge Piedot

WAFFLES

2 cups sifted flour
3 tsps. baking powder
1 tsp. salt
2 tbls. sugar
2 eggs
1½ cups milk
½ cup cooking oil

Sift flour, baking powder, salt and sugar together
into large bowl. Separate eggs. Beat egg whites
until stiff, but not dry. Beat egg yolks well and
add milk and cooking oil. Add mixture to flour.
Stir just enough to moisten flour. Gently fold in
egg whites. Bake on hot waffle iron. Makes 6

Barbara Herrly

COTTAGE CHEESE PANCAKES

4 eggs
1 cup cottage cheese
¼ tsp. salt
2 tbls. cooking oil
½ cup sifted flour

Mix all ingredients in blender and blend on low
speed until cheese curds disappear.   Or beat
cottage cheese in mixing bowl until cheese curd is
partially broken; then add remaining ingredients
and beat until thoroughly blended. Drop by tablespoon into hot (375°), lightly oiled fry pan. Turn
when underside is nicely browned. Cook until second
side is browned. Serve immediately with butter and
favorite topping.

Carol Carter

+ + + + +

LIGHT-AS-A-CLOUD PANCAKES

4 eggs, separated
1 cup creamed-style cottage cheese
¼ cup flour
¼ tsp. salt

Beat egg whites stiff. In a separate bowl, beat
yolks until light. Beat in cheese, flour and salt.
Fold in egg whites. Bake on well-greased griddle.
Makes eight 5" cakes.

Stella Friend

JOHNNY SAUSAGE CAKE

8 pork sausage links
½ orange, ground
½ lb. whole cranberry sauce
½ cup flour
½ cup cornmeal
1 tbl. sugar
2 tsps. baking powder
½ tsp. salt
1½ tbls. egg (1 small)
½ cup milk
1½ tbls. oil or melted fat

Brown pork links over low heat until brown and done;
pour off excess grease. Pour 1 tablespoon of this
grease into bottom of 7¼" pan. Arrange sausage
attractively. Combine ground orange and cranberry
sauce and spread over sausage. Measure dry ingredients, mix and sift into large mixing bowl. Make
well in center. Combine milk, beaten egg and oil in
small bowl; add immediately to dry ingredients. Mix,
stirring as little as possible until dry ingredients
are dampened. Pour batter over sausage and orange-
cranberry mixture. Bake at 400⁰ for 15-20 minutes.
Cool 5 minutes; turn upside down on serving platter.

Kerry Fix

+ + + + +

GINGERBREAD HOT CAKES

[If you want to knock out a real crazy Sunday
morning breakfast, this is it!]

2½ cups flour
1½ tsps. soda
1 tsp. cinnamon
1 tsp. ground ginger
½ tsp. ground cloves
½ tsp. salt
½ cup butter
1 3/4 cups med. light molasses
1 egg
3/4 cup black coffee

Sift together the dry ingredients. Beat the rest of
the ingredients until well blended. Blend dry ingredients with molasses mixture and beat until thoroughly
blended. Bake on medium griddle. (Less heat is re-
quired than for regular hot cakes.) Serve with
coconut syrup and whipped cream.

Dorothy Gregory

62

APPLE PANCAKES

2 eggs
1½ cups sweet milk
¼ cup salad oil or melted shortening
1½ cups flour
1 tbl. + 1½ tsps. sugar
1 tbl. + 1½ tsps. baking powder
3/4 tsp. salt
1 tsp. cinnamon
½ tsp. nutmeg
1½-2 cups apple pieces with skin

Beat egg yolks; add milk and oil. Sift dry ingredients. Add to liquids; beat until all flour is
moistened (batter will be lumpy). Fold in stiffly
beaten egg whites and apple pieces. Pour batter
onto hot griddle (greased if necessary). Turn pancakes as soon as they are puffed up and full of
bubbles; but before bubbles break. Brown on other
side.

Kerry Fix

+ + + + +

EASY SOURDOUGH FLAPJACKS

1 pkg. yeast   2 cups milk
¼ cup water   2 cups biscuit mix
1 egg, beaten

Soften yeast in warm water. Beat egg, add milk and
biscuit mix. Beat with rotary beater until blended.
Stir in softened yeast. Allow batter to stand at
room temperature 1-1½ hours. Do not stir. Bake on
a hot, lightly greased griddle or in a skillet.
(For uniform pancakes, pour from ½ cup measure.)
Turn when surface bubbles break. Makes 2 dozen 4"
cakes.

Lois Mackey

+ + + + +

HAM N' EGGS

Cooked, cubed ham   Sour cream
Eggs   Grated yellow cheese

Grease individual cooking cups. Cover bottom with
cooked, cubed ham. Drop in 2 eggs; spread 2 tbls.
sour cream over them. Sprinkle grated cheese generously over sour cream. Bake uncovered at 350°
for 15 minutes.

Stella Friend

BREAKFAST IN A GLASS

[Breakfast ready in one minute!]

Blend in blender:
1 sm. can frozen orange juice (undiluted)
3 eggs
¼-½ cup powdered milk (increase amount as desired)
2 cups milk

Lee Etta Lappen

+ + + + +

SAVORY EGGS

[A delicious company breakfast]

1 cup grated cheese
2 tbls. butter
½ cup cream
¼ tsp. salt
Pepper
1 tsp. prepared mustard
6 slightly beaten eggs

Spread cheese in 8" greased baking dish. Dot with
butter. Combine cream, salt, pepper and mustard.
Pour half of this mixture over cheese. Pour eggs
into baking dish. Add remaining cream mixture.
Bake at 325° for about 25 minutes. Serves 6

Midge Piedot

+ + + + +

EGGS WITH CELERY

6 hardboiled eggs
4 tbls. butter
2 tbls. minced onion
2 tbls. minced green peppers
2 tbls. minced celery

2 tsps. curry powder
2 cups milk
½ tsp. salt
½ tsp. paprika
2 cups cooked rice

Melt butter, add and brown slightly the onion,
peppers and celery. Add curry powder and milk. Cook
3 minutes, stirring frequently. Add the eggs, salt
and paprika. Pour over hot rice placed in shallow
dish. Garnish with parsley.

Stella Friend

64

"He will take your daughters to be perfumers and cooks and bakers" (I Samuel 8:13).

+ + + + +

CAKE HINTS:

When substituting all-purpose flour for cake flour, use 2 tablespoons less per cup. When adding dry ingredients and liquid alternately to a batter, start and end with the dry ingredients.

Add ¼ cup Miracle Whip to any chocolate cake mix to add moisture and flavor. Add ¼ cup cooking oil to any box of cake mix and it will be as tender as Grandma's cakes used to be.

Use ice cream scoop to fill cupcake pans or baking cups.

"And they gave Him a piece of a cake of figs and two clusters of raisins" (I Samuel 30:12)

+ + + + +

VARIATIONS TO ADD TO CAKE MIXES
Add one of the following:
    To white cake mix, add
        1 tsp. almond flavoring
        ½ tsp. peppermint flavoring
        ½ tsp. allspice
        ½ tsp. nutmeg
    To yellow cake mix, add
        ½ tsp. maple flavoring
        ½ tsp. walnut flavoring
        ½ tsp. allspice
        ½ tsp. ginger
        ½ tsp. mace
    To chocolate cake mix, add
        1 tsp. almond flavoring
        1 tsp. peppermint flavoring
        ½ tsp. ginger
        ½ tsp. nutmeg
    To fruit cake mix, add
        1 tsp. peppermint flavoring
        ½ tsp. allspice
        ½ tsp. cinnamon
        ½ tsp. mace

Diane Yancy

CHOCOLATE SHEET CAKE

[Very moist]

2 cups flour	2 eggs
2 cups sugar	1 tsp. vanilla
½ tsp. salt	1 cup water
1 tsp. soda	1 cup margarine
½ cup buttermilk	3 tbls. cocoa

Measure and mix dry ingredients (except cocoa) into
a large mixing bowl. Add buttermilk, eggs and vanilla
and mix well. Mix water, margarine and cocoa in
sauce pan; melt but do not boil. Add to batter and
blend well. Pour into 17 x 11 x 3/4" sheet cake pan.
Bake at 350° for 20 minutes. Cool and ice with:
ICING: ½ cup butter or margarine
         5 tsps. milk (or buttermilk, if desired)
         3 tbls. cocoa
Place in sauce pan-melt but do not boil. Remove from
heat and add 1 box powdered sugar and 1 tsp. vanilla.
Blend thoroughly and spread on cake. Add nuts if
desired.
                    Carol Barger, Dixie Sylvester
          Nancy Scott, Susan Phipps and Lynn Owen

+ + + + +

GRANDMA'S CHOCOLATE CAKE

1 cup sugar
2 cups flour
4 tbls. cocoa
2 tsps. soda
¼ tsp. salt
1 cup warm water
1 tsp. vanilla
1 cup mayonnaise or salad dressing
Few drops red food coloring
1 (6-oz.) pkg. chocolate bits (for frosting)

Combine sugar, flour, cocoa, soda and salt in mixer
bowl. Add the remaining ingredients (not chocolate
bits). Pour into greased and floured 9" square pan.
Bake at 350° for 35-40 minutes or until done.
EASY FROSTING: Sprinkle chocolate bits over hot cake.
Cover for about a minute; then spread evenly over
cake.
                    Marilyn Ehle

CHOCOLATE FUDGE CAKE

[Easy as 1-2-3!]

1/3 cup salad oil (or melted shortening)
2 envelopes pre-melted, unsweetened chocolate
1 egg
1 cup sugar
1¼ cups flour
½ tsp. soda
½ tsp. salt
½ tsp. vanilla
3/4 cup water

Combine all ingredients in a 9" square cake pan.
Beat with fork until smooth and creamy--about 2
minutes. Spread evenly in pan. Sprinkle with ½ cup
semi-sweet chocolate chips. Arrange 9-12 walnut
or pecan halves over top. Bake at 350° for 30
minutes. Cool. Needs no icing.

Lynn Noble

+ + + + +

TUNNEL OF FUDGE CAKE

1½ cups butter
6 eggs
1½ cups sugar
2 cups flour
1 pkg. Double Dutch Fudge Butter-Cream frosting
    mix (2 layer size)
2 cups walnuts, chopped

Cream butter in a large mixer bowl at high speed.
Add eggs, one at a time, beating well after each.
Gradually add sugar; continue creaming at high
speed until light and fluffy. By hand, stir in
flour, frosting mix and walnuts until well blended.
Pour batter into greased 10" Bundt pan. Bake at
350° for 60-65 minutes. Cool 2 hours; remove from
pan. Cool completely before serving.
NOTE: Nuts and Double Dutch Fudge Frosting mix are
essential to success of this unusual recipe. Since
cake has a soft fudgy interior, test for doneness
after 60 minutes by observing dry, shiny brownie-
type crust.

Merry McKean
(A Pillsbury bake-off recipe)

DEVIL'S FOOD CAKE

½ cup (1 stick) margarine
2 squares bitter chocolate
1 cup boiling water
2 cups sugar
2 cups unsifted flour

2 eggs, unbeaten
1 tbl. vanilla
½ cup buttermilk (or sweet
   milk with 1 tsp. vinegar)
1 tsp. soda

Melt margarine and chocolate over hot water. Slowly add half of boiling water. Stir well; add other half of hot water. Add sugar, stir well. Let cool slightly. Sift flour and add. Add eggs, vanilla, and buttermilk with soda dissolved in it. Stir. Pour into 2 round pans, greased and lined with wax paper (oil both sides of wax paper). Bake at 325° for 35 minutes. Do not open oven until done. Remove cake from pans by pulling cake out by the paper and put on flat surface. Place pans over cakes and let cool.

ICING: ½ cup (1 stick) margarine
       1 box powdered or white sugar
       1 tbl. vanilla

Jane Prall

+ + + + +

SOUR CREAM CHOCOLATE CAKE

2 cups sifted cake flour
2 tsps. baking powder
3/4 tsp. baking soda
¼ tsp. salt
1/3 cup shortening
1 cup sugar

2 eggs, well beaten
2 oz. baking chocolate,
   melted
½ cup milk
½ cup sour cream
1 tsp. vanilla

Sift flour, baking powder, soda and salt together. Cream shortening with sugar until fluffy. Add eggs and chocolate and beat thoroughly. Add sifted dry ingredients and liquids alternately in small amounts, beating well after each addition. Pour into greased tube pan and bake at 350° for 45-50 minutes. Makes 1 8" cake.

Nancy Schurle

+ + + + +

CAROB CAKE

[Tastes just like devil's food cake]

1½ cups whole wheat flour
1 cup sugar (turbinado or kleen raw)
1/3 cup carob powder
3/4 tsp. salt
1 tsp. baking soda
½ cup carrot juice with 1 tbl. lemon juice
½ cup salad oil
1 egg
1 tsp. vanilla
½ cup boiling water

Sift together dry ingredients into large mixing bowl.
Mix wet ingredients except boiling water. Pour wet
ingredients into dry ingredients; mix for 1 minute.
Pour boiling water into batter; mix 1 minute. Do not
over mix. Bake at 325° for 15 minutes, then at 350°
for 15 minutes.
FROSTING:
Butter, powdered sugar with carob powder and instant
coffee to taste. Add milk to thin.

Mary Lou Lyon

+ + + + +

PINEAPPLE CAKE

2 cups flour   1 #2 can crushed pineapple
2 cups sugar   (not drained)
2 eggs   2½ cups coconut
2 tsps. soda   1 cup nuts

Mix dry ingredients. Blend in eggs. Add pineapple,
coconut and nuts. Bake in greased and floured
9 x 15" pan at 350° for 45 minutes.
ICING:
        ¼ cup butter
        8-oz. cream cheese
        3½ cups powdered sugar
        1 tsp. vanilla
Mix and spread on cake while hot.

Roselyn Shaver

+ + + + +

HONEY CARROT CAKE

2 cups flour
1 tsp. soda
1 tsp. baking powder
1 tsp. cinnamon
½ tsp. salt
1½ cups honey
4 eggs
3 cups grated carrots
½ cup nuts
1 tsp. vanilla
1½ cups polyunsaturated oil

Mix dry ingredients; add oil and blend; add eggs one
at a time. Add carrots and nuts and blend. Pour
into greased 9 x 13" pan. Bake at 350° for 1 hour.

Arlene Dennison

CARROT CAKE

[Good for you!]

2 cups flour
2 tsps. baking powder
1½ tsps. cinnamon
2 tsps. soda
½ tsp. salt
1 cup oil
2 cups brown sugar
4 eggs
1 cup chopped nuts
3 cups grated carrots

Mix dry ingredients; add oil and blend. Add eggs
one at a time and beat after each addition. Add
carrots and nuts and blend well. Bake in 9 x 13"
pan (or 2 9" layer pans) at 350° for 45 minutes.
FROST:
    1 8-oz. pkg. cream cheese
    ½ cup margarine
    1 lb. box powdered sugar
    2 tsps. vanilla
Mix together until smooth and spread on cake.

Charlotte Melcher, Nan Green and Jane Prall

CRUSTY POUND CAKE

½ cup shortening
2 sticks whipped margarine
3 cups sugar
5 eggs
3 cups pre-sifted flour
1 cup milk
1 tsp. lemon extract
1 tsp. vanilla

Cream shortening, margarine and sugar; add eggs one at a time. Add flour and milk alternately. Add lemon and vanilla. Pour into lightly greased and floured tube pan. Place in COLD oven; turn temperature on to 325° and bake 1 hour-WITHOUT opening the door. Raise temperature to 350° and bake 30 minutes longer. DO NOT OPEN OVEN AT ANYTIME. Remove finished cake and let cool in pan.

Donna Hager

+ + + + +

COCONUT POUND CAKE

1 lb. whipped margarine-not solid (6 sticks)
3 cups sugar
3 cups flour
9 eggs
1 (7-oz.) box Angel Flake coconut
1 tsp. vanilla
1 tsp. lemon extract

Cream margarine and sugar. Add flour alternately with eggs. Add other ingredients. Bake in greased and floured tube pan at 325° for 1 hour and 30 minutes.

Evelyn Bromberg

+ + + + +

POUND CAKE

½ cup shortening	½ tsp. baking powder
1 cup butter	1 cup milk
3 cups sugar	1 tsp. vanilla
5 eggs	1 tsp. lemon extract
3 cups flour	

Cream shortening and sugar until light and fluffy. Add eggs one at a time. Add dry ingredients alternately with milk. Add extracts. Bake in greased and floured tube pan at 325° (do not preheat oven) for 1½ hours or longer.

Lynn Vann

MUZZY'S POUND CAKE

1½ cups sugar
5 eggs
1½ cups flour
1 cup margarine or butter

1 tsp. vanilla
1 tbl. flour
½ tsp. baking powder

Beat sugar and eggs together. Beat flour and butter together. Mix egg mixture and butter mixture together. Beat in vanilla. Blend into cake mixture (just enough to mix) the 1 tablespoon of flour and baking powder. Bake in buttered poundcake pan at 325° for 1 hour. Frost with a lemon glaze.

Jude Mariano

VARIATION: Add 1 tsp. almond extract and nuts, if desired. Bake at 350° for 1 hour. Check at 50 minutes to see if it is firm. You can rub powdered sugar on the cake while still hot. May use a tube pan or loaf pans.

Rosemary Priest

+ + + + +

EGGLESS-MILKLESS CAKE

1 cup brown sugar
1¼ cups water
1 cup seeded raisins
1/3 cup shortening
½ tsp. salt

1 tsp. cinnamon
1 tsp. nutmeg
2 cups flour
5 tsps. baking powder

Boil sugar, water, raisins, shortening, salt and spices together in saucepan 3 minutes. Cool. Add flour and baking powder; mix well. Bake in loaf pan at 350° for 45 minutes.

Barbara Herrly

+ + + + +

EGGLESS RAISIN CAKE

1 cup raisins
2 cups water
½ cup butter
1 3/4 cups flour
1 tsp. soda

½ tsp. salt
1 cup sugar
½ tsp. cinnamon
½ tsp. nutmeg
½ cup nuts

Boil raisins with water for 10 minutes. Add butter and let cool. Add rest of ingredients; mix and pour into greased square pan. Bake at 325° for 40 minutes.

Susan Phipps

STRAWBERRY JELLO CAKE

4 eggs
1 sm. pkg. strawberry jello
1 pkg. white cake mix
3/4 cup salad oil
½ cup water
½ pkg. frozen strawberries, drained

Beat eggs, add rest of ingredients. Bake in two 9"
layer pans (or one large 9 x 13" pan) at 325° for
1 hour.
FROSTING:
    ¼ cup margarine
    1 box powdered sugar
    ¼ tsp. vanilla
    Add remaining berries and enough juice to spread.

Barb Taylor, Patty Roth, Nancy Ryan and Kathy Shulman

+ + + + +

LEMON CAKE

1 pkg. lemon cake mix
1 pkg. lemon instant pudding mix
3/4 cup apricot nectar
4 eggs
1/3 cup lemon juice
3/4 cup oil

Mix above ingredients and beat well. Bake at 350°
for 45 minutes in a greased and flour-dusted tube
pan. Sprinkle with powdered sugar.

Carol Hurd

+ + + + +

WALNUT CAKE

1 box yellow cake mix
4 eggs
1 box instant vanilla pudding
1/3 cup salad oil
1 cup chopped walnuts
1 1/3 cup water

Add all ingredients except water. Then gradually
add water and mix together. Bake in angel food
cake pan at 350° for 1 hour.

Julie Schroen

LEMON-GLAZED CHIFFON CAKE

[A delicious lemony-moist cake]

1 pkg. yellow or lemon cake mix
1 sm. pkg. lemon instant pudding or lemon jello
2/3 cup vegetable oil
3/4 cup water
4 eggs

Place all ingredients in a bowl and beat with an
electric mixer for 2 minutes at high speed. Pour
mixture into a greased 9 3/4" tube cake pan or a
9 x 13" pan. Bake at 350° for 55 minutes. Cool
for 10 minutes before removing from pan. Place
cake on a serving plate and prick holes in cake
with a toothpick or fork. Spoon lemon glaze over
cake until all glaze is absorbed.
GLAZE: Mix 1 cup powdered sugar and 2 tablespoons
lemon juice. Drizzle over warm cake.

Nellie Daniels, Bonnie Porter
Linda Bond and Julie Schroen

VARIATION for LIME CAKE: Instead of using lemon
flavored jello or pudding, use lime jello. Glaze
with 2 cups powdered sugar mixed with juice of 2-3
limes after cake has been pricked while still hot.

Alison Brown

+ + + + +

HAPPINESS CAKE

Mix together thoroughly 1 cup good thoughts, 1 cup
kind deeds, 1 cup consideration for others, 2 cups
sacrifice, 2 cups well-beaten faults, 3 cups forgive-
ness. Add tears of joy, sorrow and sympathy; flavor
with love and kindly service. Fold into daily life;
bake well with the warmth of human kindness and
serve with a smile, any time.

Doris Rood

NOBBY APPLE CAKE

[A quick and easy but delicious dessert]

2 cups sugar
1 cup margarine or cooking oil
2 eggs
2 cups flour   1 tsp. salt
2 tsps. soda   1 tsp. vanilla
1 tsp. cinnamon   4 cups chopped apples
1 tsp. nutmeg   1 cup chopped nuts

Cream margarine and sugar. Blend in eggs and vanilla.
Sift dry ingredients and add to sugar mixture. Add
apples and nuts and mix thoroughly. Bake in 9 x 13"
cake pan at 350° for 40-45 minutes.

Billie Thurman, Linda Dillow and Jane Prall
and Doris Rood

+ + + + +

APPLE CAKE

[A favorite moist cake]

1 pkg. spice cake mix
2 eggs
½ tsp. nutmeg
½ cup salad oil
1 tsp. vanilla
1 can apple pie filling
1 cup raisins (or ½ cup raisins and ½ cup cut dates)
½-1 cup nuts

Mix first 5 ingredients by hand. Add rest of ingredients and blend in thoroughly. Bake in 9 x 13" pan
at 350° for 40 minutes. Serve warm or cold with ice
cream or whipped cream.

Midge Piedot

+ + + + +

APPLESAUCE CAKE

2 cups sugar   1 tsp. cloves
1 cup butter   1 tsp. allspice
2½ cups hot applesauce   1 pkg. raisins
4 tsps. soda   (or 2 lbs. of mixed fruit)
Dash of salt   1 cup walnuts
2 tsps. cinnamon   5 cups sifted flour

Cream sugar and butter; add salt. Heat applesauce
and soda; add to creamed mixture along with the
spices, raisins and nuts. Add flour one cup at a
time and mix thoroughly. Bake in large cake pan (or
3 loaf pans) at 350° for 1½ hours.

Barbara Ball

APPLESAUCE DATE CAKE

2 cups flour
2 tsps. baking soda
1 tsp. cinnamon
½ tsp. allspice
¼ tsp. cloves
½ tsp. nutmeg
¼ tsp. salt

2 eggs
1 cup light brown sugar
½ cup butter
2 cups hot applesauce
1 cup chopped dates
3/4 cup coarsely chopped
  walnuts

Sift dry ingredients into large bowl. Add eggs, sugar, butter and 1 cup hot applesauce. Beat at low speed just until combined. Beat at medium speed 2 minutes longer. Add remaining applesauce, dates and nuts. Beat 1 minute. Pour into greased and floured 9" pan. Bake 50 minutes at 350°.
CREAM CHEESE FROSTING:
    1 pkg. (3-oz.) cream cheese
    1 tbl. butter
    1 tsp. vanilla
    2 cups sifted powdered sugar
Beat until fluffy. Frost cooled cake.

                              Marilyn Heavilin

+ + + + +

DELICIOUS DATE NUT CAKE

1 cup boiling water
1 cup cut up dates
2 tsp. baking soda
1 cup sugar
1 cup salad dressing
1 tsp. vanilla
2 cups flour
½ tsp. salt
1 cup nutmeats

Pour boiling water over cut up dates and soda. Let stand until cool. Mix sugar, salad dressing and vanilla. Sift flour and salt; add date and sugar mixtures and mix well. Add nuts. Bake in 7 x 12" glass baking dish at 350° for 40 minutes. When cool, cut into squares. Coat with powdered sugar.
Serves 12
                              Nellie Daniels

ORANGE KISS-ME CAKE

1 large orange	1 tsp. salt
1 cup raisins	½ cup shortening
1/3 cup walnuts	1 cup milk
2 cups flour	2 eggs
1 1/3 cups sugar	1 tsp. cinnamon
1 tsp. soda	¼ cup walnuts

Squeeze orange, reserve juice. Grind together rind of orange, raisins and walnuts, using coarse blade of chopper. Combine flour with 1 cup sugar, soda and salt in large mixing bowl. Add shortening and milk. Blend at lowest speed of mixer for 1½ minutes. Add eggs, beat 1½ minutes more. Stir in orange-raisin mixture. Spread batter in prepared 9 x 13" pan. Bake at 350° for 40-45 minutes. Drizzle orange juice over warm cake. Combine 1/3 cup sugar, cinnamon and chopped nuts. Spread over cake.
(This is a Pillsbury bake-off recipe.)   Joyce Nelson

+ + + + +

BUSY-DAY LEMON CHEESECAKE

1 8-oz. pkg. cream cheese
2 cups milk
1 pkg. Jello Lemon Instant Pudding
1 8" graham cracker crust

Stir cream cheese until very soft, blend in ½ cup milk. Add remaining milk and the pudding mix. Beat slowly with egg beater just until well mixed. Pour at once into graham cracker crust. Sprinkle graham cracker crumbs lightly over top. Chill about 1 hour.
Serves 8
                              Lee Etta Lappen

+ + + + +

CHEESE CAKE

2 (8-oz.) pkg. cream cheese, softened	
1 carton (2 cups) sour cream	
1 cup sugar	Pinch of salt
2 eggs	Graham cracker crust
1 tsp. vanilla	

Combine all ingredients in a bowl and beat until well blended. Pour into crust. Bake at 350° for 20 minutes.
                              Kerry Fix

BLUEBERRY LEMON CAKE

1 can (15-oz.) blueberries
1 pkg. (17-oz.) lemon cake mix
1 cup sour cream
4 eggs

Drain blueberries--reserve syrup for sauce. Combine
dry cake mix, sour cream and eggs in bowl. Blend at
low speed until moistened. Beat 4 minutes at medium
speed. Add 1 tbl. water if too dry. Fold in blueberries. Pour into well-greased, lightly-floured
10" Bundt or tube pan. Bake at 350° for 35-45
minutes. Cool 15 minutes. Remove from pan. Cool
completely. Serve with sauce and whipped cream.
SAUCE: ¼ cup sugar
         1 tbl. corn starch
         Blueberry syrup
Combine sugar and corn starch in sauce pan. Gradually
stir in syrup. Bring to boil on medium heat. Continue stirring until slightly thickened.

Lynn Owen

+ + + + +

SUNSHINE LEMON LOAF

[A 10-minute party cake]

2 pound cakes 6" long x 4½" wide (1 lb. 3 oz. each)
Grated rind of 1 lemon or ¼ tsp. lemon extract
1 can (14-oz.) sweetened condensed milk
½ cup lemon juice
2 egg yolks
1 cup mixed diced candied fruit
1 pkg. (6½-oz.) fluffy white frosting mix
Yellow food coloring
Shredded orange rind
½ cup flaked coconut
½ can (11-oz. size) mandarin oranges, drained

Cut each cake crosswise into 3 layers and set aside.
Add lemon rind to milk with lemon juice and egg yolks
and beat well. Chop candied fruit and stir into mixture; chill. Prepare frosting as directed on the
label, adding a few drops of yellow food coloring
before beating. Set 2 bottom layers of cake end to
end on serving tray to make a long loaf. Spread
with half the filling and repeat with the next 2
layers. Add top layers. Spread top and sides of
cake with frosting. Shred orange rind and add to
coconut to taste. Use with mandarin oranges to
decorate the top of the cake. Makes 12-14 servings.

Lana Jones

CHERRY STREUSEL CAKE

1 cup butter
1 cup sugar
2 eggs
2 cups sifted flour
2 tsps. baking powder
½ tsp. salt
1 can (1 lb. 6-oz.) cherry pie filling
2 tbls. butter
¼ cup sugar
¼ cup flour

Cream butter and sugar until light and fluffy. Add
eggs and beat thoroughly. Add sifted dry ingredients
and mix well. (Batter will be very heavy.) Spread
about 3/4 of batter in a 9 x 13" pan. Pour pie filling down center of batter. Spread filling over batter
gently, using a spatula. Drop remaining batter from
a spoon over filling. Spread gently and swirl over
all. Combine remaining ingredients and sprinkle on
top. Bake at 350° for 45 minutes. Serves 12-16

Barbara Ball

+ + + + +

HAWAIIAN PECAN CAKE

1 pkg. butter pecan coffee cake mix
2 tbls. pineapple yogurt
1/3 cup butter
1 can (13½-oz.) crushed pineapple, drained
1 pkg. (3-oz.) cream cheese
1/3 cup pineapple yogurt
2 eggs

In small sauce pan, combine dry topping mix (from
coffee cake mix), 2 tbls. yogurt, butter and 2 tbls.
pineapple. (Reserve remaining pineapple for cake.)
Boil topping 1 minute, stirring occasionally. Set
aside. In small mixer bowl, blend cream cheese and
1/3 cup yogurt until smooth. Add eggs; blend thoroughly at low speed. Add coffee cake mix and remaining drained pineapple; beat at medium speed about 1
minute, scraping bowl occasionally. Pour into 9"
square or round layer pan which has been floured on
the bottom and sides. Spoon 1/3 cup topping mixture
over batter and swirl. Bake at 350° for 40-45
minutes or until toothpick inserted in center comes
out clean. Spread remaining topping mixture over
warm cake. Serve warm or cold. Serves 9

Carol Carter

JAPANESE CARMAPPLE CAKE

4 eggs
½ cup granulated sugar
½ cup light brown sugar
1 cup Kraft safflower oil
1 cup chopped raisins
¼ cup chopped cherries (maraschino)
1 box Pillsbury applesauce cake mix
1 cup buttermilk
1 cup nuts
3 cups apples, pared, cored, cubed
Juice of ½ fresh lemon
1 tsp. butter flavoring
2 tsps. vanilla

(Have all ingredients at room temperature.) Beat
eggs until frothy in blender, add sugar and oil gradually. Add to this mixture, raisins and cherries, to
be chopped by blender. While this is mixing well, mix
cake mix alternately with buttermilk in mixing bowl.
To cake-buttermilk ingredients, add egg mixture,
followed by nuts, cubed apples, lemon juice, butter
and vanilla flavorings. Put all ingredients into a
greased and floured Bundt Teflon cake pan and bake
at 325° for 1¼ hours. Let cake cool in pan 15-20
minutes before taking it out. Ice while still warm
with the following:
    1 pkg. caramel icing
    ¼ cup butter
    ¼ cup hot apple cider
Dribble hot on above cake.

                    Created by Jane Prall

+ + + + +

CREAMY "BOX" CAKE

1 box Betty Crocker new moist cake (any flavor)
1 cup buttermilk (or sweet milk with 1 tbl. vinegar)
1/3 cup salad oil
3 eggs
1 tsp. butter flavoring
1 tsp. vanilla flavoring
Mix and bake as directed on package.

                    Jane Prall

80

OATMEAL CAKE

1¼ cups boiling water
½ cup margarine
1 cup quick-cooking oatmeal
1 cup brown sugar
1 cup white sugar
2 eggs
½ tsp. salt

1 tsp. soda
1 1/3 cups flour
1 tsp. cinnamon
½ tsp. nutmeg
1 tsp. vanilla

Put oats and butter in bowl and pour hot water over.
Let stand 20 minutes. Add eggs and sugar; stir in
flour, salt, cinnamon and nutmeg sifted together.
Add vanilla. Bake at 350° for 35 minutes. Let set
for 10 minutes; add topping and broil 3-5 minutes.
TOPPING: 6 tbls. butter
           ½ cup sugar
Cream together. Add:
           ½ cup coconut
           ¼ cup cream or canned milk
           1 tsp. vanilla
           1 cup nuts
           Blend.

Nancy Schurle

+ + + + +

ONE BOWL JELLY ROLL

3 eggs, beaten until lemon colored
1 cup sugar -- add gradually to eggs
1 tsp. vanilla -- add to egg mixture
Sift together:
1 cup flour
1 tsp. baking powder
½ tsp. salt
Add to egg mixture on slow speed. Add 1/3 cup hot
water all at once. Spread in 10 x 15" jelly roll
pan. Bake at 375° for 12-14 minutes. Put 2 tablespoons powdered sugar on top of jelly roll. Turn
from pan onto towel and roll up. Place on rack to
cool. Unroll and fill; reroll.
FILLING: Spread 1 3-oz. pkg. cream cheese creamed to
spreading consistency with cream. Then a layer of
blueberry thickened with cornstarch and lemon.

Midge Piedot

FROSTING HINTS:

Adding 1 teaspoon vinegar to grainy frosting makes
it creamy. Dorothy Gregory

When frosting layer cakes, place first layer topside down; then frost. Place top layer on, topside
up. Midge Piedot

+ + + + +

SMOOTH ICING

½ cup butter
½ cup margarine
Beat for 3 minutes. Add:
1 cup granulated sugar. Blend; add:
2/3 cup warm milk
1 tsp. vanilla
Beat 5 minutes.

                              Midge Piedot

+ + + + +

DREAM FROSTING

1 pkg. (3 3/4-oz.) instant vanilla pudding
1 pkg. Dream Whip
1½ cups milk

Mix pudding and Dream Whip in mixing bowl with milk.
Beat at high speed for 5-7 minutes. Enough to cover
large cake.
                              Grace Frick

+ + + + +

FLUFFY FROSTING

2 tbl. flour
½ cup milk
¼ cup shortening
¼ cup butter
½ cup powdered sugar
1 tsp. vanilla

Cook flour and milk together until thick. Cool
slightly. Beat rest of ingredients until very light.
Add flour mixture and beat thoroughly.
                              Midge Piedot

82

FRENCH CREAM FROSTING

½ cup butter or margarine
2¼-2½ cups sifted powdered sugar
1 egg
3 sqs. melted, unsweetened chocolate, cooled
1 tsp. vanilla

Cream butter and powdered sugar. Add egg, mix
thoroughly. Blend in chocolate and vanilla. Beat
to spreading consistency. Thin with milk if necessary. Frosts two 8 or 9" layers.

Nancy Schurle and Kerry Fix

+ + + + +

"NO COOK" MARSHMALLOW FROSTING

¼ tsp. salt
2 egg whites
¼ cup sugar
3/4 cup Karo syrup (Red label)
1¼ tsp. vanilla

Add salt to egg whites and beat until mixture forms
soft peaks. Gradually add sugar and Karo syrup,
beating thoroughly after each addition, until
firmly peaked. Fold in vanilla.

Midge Piedot

+ + + + +

BUTTER ICING

Blend: 1/3 cup butter
         3 cups powdered sugar
         1 egg yolk
Stir in:
         3 tbls. cream
         1½ tsps. vanilla
Spread on cake.

Sandy Buell

+ + + + +

COCOA FROSTING

3½ cups powdered sugar
½ tsp. salt
1/3 cup cocoa

1/3 cup butter
1/3 cup hot milk
½ tsp. vanilla

Sift sugar, salt and cocoa together. Cream butter
with half of sugar mixture. Add rest of mixture alternately with milk; beat until smooth. Add vanilla.

Dorothy Brooks

EASY PENUCHE FROSTING

½ cup butter
1 cup brown sugar, packed
¼ cup milk
1 3/4 - 2 cups powdered sugar

Melt butter, add brown sugar. Boil and stir over
low heat 2 minutes. Add milk; bring to boil stirring
constantly. Cool to lukewarm. Gradually add sifted
powdered sugar. Beat until thick enough to spread.
If too thick, add hot water. Good on Spice or White
cake.

Dorothy Brooks

+ + + + +

EASY CARAMEL ICING

Mix together in saucepan:
1½ cups brown sugar, packed
¼ cup top milk
2 tbls. butter
Bring to a boil and boil 3 minutes stirring constantly. Remove from heat. Add 1 teaspoon vanilla and
cool to lukewarm. Beat until creamy and thick
enough to spread. Spread quickly onto cake because
it hardens fast. (Add a little cream if necessary
to thin.)

Midge Piedot

+ + + + +

LEMON BUTTER CREAM FROSTING

1 lb. or about 4 cups sifted powdered sugar
½ cup butter or margarine
1 tsp. grated lemon rind
1/8 tsp. salt
2 egg yolks
2 tbls. (or more) milk

Cream butter with lemon rind. Add salt and part of
the sugar; add egg yolks. Beat in rest of sugar
alternately with milk until creamy. Use half of
this recipe to frost square cake. If desired,
sprinkle with grated rind.

Midge Piedot

FRENCH CREME CANDY BARS

[Creamy, fondant-type filling has delicate coffee flavor undertones.]

¼ cup butter
½ cup sugar
¼ cup dairy ½ and ½
1/8 tsp. salt
½ tsp. instant coffee powder
¼ cup chocolate chips
1 cup miniature marshmallows
2 cups powdered sugar
½ cup whole unblanched almonds (3¼-oz. pkg.)
½ tsp. almond extract or vanilla
Chocolate coating

Combine butter, sugar, ½ and ½, salt and coffee powder in 2-qt. heavy saucepan. Bring to a boil, stirring occasionally; boil 3 minutes. Remove from heat and stir in chocolate chips and marshmallows. Then stir in powdered sugar, almonds and almond extract. Cool until lukewarm. Spread half of choco- late coating on waxed paper to make an 8" square. Slide waxed paper with chocolate onto a baking sheet and place in refrigerator a few minutes, or until chocolate is firm. Remove. Spoon filling several places over the coating. Then carefully spread it evenly to cover coating. (Thin filling if necessary with additional ½ and ½ until creamy and of spreading consistency.) With a metal spatula, smooth top and sides of filling. Spread remaining half of coating over filling to cover. Set aside until candy is firm and until it separates easily from waxed paper. Cut in 2½ x 1" bars, or any size desired. May wrap in- dividually in plastic wrap or aluminum foil. Makes 24 bars.

CHOCOLATE COATING:
        1 (6-oz.) pkg. chocolate chips (1 cup)
        2 tbls. vegetable shortening
Melt chocolate chips and shortening over hot water. Stir until smooth.

                                        Midge Piedot

OATMEAL FUDGE

1 cup white sugar
1 cup brown sugar
2/3 cup milk
¼ cup butter or margarine
3 tsps. Karo white syrup

Bring to a boil slowly. Boil for 1 minute; add ½
cup nutty peanut butter. Add 2 cups chocolate chips.
Stir until dissolved. Finally stir in 3 cups of
quick oatmeal. Spread in large pan and allow to set.

Linda Dillow

+ + + + +

MILE HIGH FUDGE

[If you're on a diet, don't even look at this recipe!]

Combine in a saucepan:
    4½ cups sugar
    Pinch salt
    1 (13-oz.) can evaporated milk
Boil to a soft ball stage (250°) or for 5 minutes
after it comes to a full boil. Put in a bowl:
    12 oz. semi-sweet chocolate
    12 oz. German-sweet chocolate
    1 pint marshmallow cream
    2 cups nuts
Pour first mixture over second mixture which melts
the chocolate. Beat with mixer and pour in a buttered pan. Let set before cutting.

Helen Lovell

+ + + + +

"NO FAIL" CHOCOLATE FUDGE

Prepare in large bowl:
    3 sm. pkgs. chocolate chips (3 cups)
    1 cup butter
    2 cups nuts, chopped
    3 tsps. vanilla
Place in a saucepan:
    4½ cups sugar
    1 large can evaporated milk
Bring sugar and milk to a boil. Boil 6 minutes.
Pour over contents in bowl. Stir rapidly until
smooth. Pour onto a buttered platter. Chill.

Ginger Gabriel

86

MOM MOSHER'S PRALINES

2 cups white sugar
1 cup buttermilk
1 tsp. baking soda
¼ tsp. salt
2 cups pecan (or walnut) halves
2 tbls. margarine

Combine sugar, buttermilk and baking soda in sauce
pan. Bring to boil; add salt. Stir 5 minutes. Add
nuts and margarine. Cook hard for 5 minutes to very
soft ball stage. Remove from heat; cool 5 minutes.
Beat with spoon. Spoon onto wax paper.

Nancy Olsen

+ + + + +

CARAMELS

2 cups sugar
1 cup milk
1 cup carnation milk
½ cup light cream

½ cup butter
1 cup Karo syrup
1½ tsps. salt

Mix all ingredients together and cook over medium
heat until hard-ball stage. Pour into greased
(buttered) pan and cool. Cut in small cubes and
wrap individually in wax paper.

Julie Schroen

+ + + + +

DANDY SNAP CANDY

½ cup molasses
½ cup butter
1 tsp. ginger

1/8 tsp. salt
1 cup flour
2/3 cup sugar

Heat molasses to boiling point, add butter then
other ingredients which have been sifted. Drop
by half teaspoonfuls onto greased baking sheets
at 2-3" intervals. Bake at 325° for 10 minutes.
Cool slightly. Pick up and roll over wooden sticks.

Donna Lou Gaunt

BROWN SUGAR CANDY

1½ cups brown sugar   1 tbl. Karo white syrup
1½ cups white sugar   3 tbls. butter
1 cup half and half cream   1 cup chopped nuts

Mix first four ingredients in saucepan and cook to
soft ball stage. Add vanilla and about 3-4 tbls.
butter. Beat until the color changes and it can be
poured easily. Add nuts and pour on greased platter.

Bailey Marks

+ + + + +

SPICED MIXED NUTS

3/4 cup sugar
3/4 tsp. salt
1 tsp. cinnamon
½ tsp. cloves
¼ tsp. allspice
¼ tsp. nutmeg
1 egg white
2½ tbls. water
1 cup walnut halves
1 cup pecan halves
1 cup Brazil nuts

Heat oven to 275º. Combine spices and sugar. Stir
in slightly beaten egg white and water. Add nuts,
½ cup at a time. Stir with fork until coated. Lift
out and place on greased cookie sheet. Bake 45
minutes.

Lee Etta Lappen

+ + + + +

PEANUT POPCORN

Melt equal parts butter and peanut butter and pour
over popped corn.

Dorothy Gregory

+ + + + +

POPPYCOCK

Prepare 2 quarts popcorn
Combine in saucepan:
1 1/3 cups sugar
1 cup butter
1 tsp. vanilla
½ cup light Karo

Combine sugar, butter, vanilla and Karo syrup in
saucepan. Stir over medium heat until caramel-brown
color (about 10 minutes after it comes to a boil).
While hot, pour over popcorn, coating as much as
possible. Especially good if you add 2/3 cups
almonds and 1 1/3 cups pecans to popcorn before
pouring syrup over. Spread in clusters on greased
cookie sheet to cool.

Charlotte Day

+ + + + +

FIDDLE-FADDLE

In a very large and slightly greased bowl, mix 2
quarts of popped corn and 1 or 2 cups of pecans.
(Mixed nuts or peanuts may be used.) In a heavy
pan cook:
1½ cups sugar
½ cup Karo
1 cup butter or margarine
Boil 10-15 minutes stirring constantly to the hard-
crack stage. Remove from heat and add 1 tsp. vanilla.
Pour over corn and nuts. (Place syrup pan in hot
water immediately so candy will not harden onto sides
of pan.) Stir until the mixture sticks together.
Spread mixture in a large flat, slightly greased pan
and cool. Break into pieces and store in tight
containers.

Linda Dillow

+ + + + +

CEREAL SNACK

6 tbls. margarine   2 cups Wheat Chex
4 tsps. Worcestershire sauce 2 cups Rice Chex
2 tsps. seasoned salt   2 cups Corn Chex
3/4 cup nuts

Melt butter. Stir in Worcestershire sauce and
seasoned salt. Add rest of the ingredients and
stir over low heat until well-coated. Bake at
250° for 1 hour, stirring every 15 minutes. Drain
on paper towel.

Suzie Brenneman

AFTER CHURCH SNACK

Combine before church:
    1 jar of "Cheese Whiz"
    ½ cup mayonnaise
    1 sm. can chopped olives
    3-4 strips bacon, fried and crumbled
Spread on split hamburger buns or English muffins.
Broil open faced until brown and bubbly.

Dorothy Gregory

+ + + + +

FUDGY BANANA POPS
[Frozen banana]

8 bananas
Lemon juice
¼ cup butter
¼ cup light corn syrup
2 tbls. water
1 6-oz. pkg. semi-sweet chocolate chips
1 6-oz. pkg. sweet chocolate pieces
Chopped nuts - coconut

Dip peeled bananas in lemon juice. Insert wooden
skewer; freeze. Combine butter, corn syrup and
water in saucepan. Bring to boil - remove from
heat. Add chocolate pieces; stir until smooth.
Dip frozen bananas into chocolate. Spread evenly
and scrape off excess with small spatula. (If mixture becomes too thick, place pan in very hot
water.) Spread with nuts, coconut or small candies.
Place on lightly greased shallow pan. Return to
freezer immediately. Do not allow bananas to soften.
Serve frozen

Dorothy Gregory

+ + + + +

HINTS FOR THE COOKIE JAR:

Make a double batch of your favorite cookie recipe.
Freeze half for later. (Candace Steele)

When baking cookies use powdered sugar in place of
flour when rolling out the dough. They will always
be soft instead of having a tendency to get hard as
they do with too much flour. (Midge Piedot)

Measure basic ingredients in recipes accurately; you
can increase or decrease seasonings and spices.

To measure a part of a cupful of shortening, sub-
tract the amount of shortening desired, and place that
amount of cold water in a cup. Add shortening to the
water, keeping the shortening submerged until the cup
is level full.

Unless otherwise specified in a recipe, cookies
should be placed 2-3 inches apart on a cookie sheet.

For a chewier cookie, bake the minimum of time. For
a crisper cookie, bake a minute or two longer.

If crisp cookies become soft, they can be reheated.

Refrigerator cookies may be stored three weeks before
baking. They may also be frozen. They will keep for
one year. Bake as needed.

To keep drop cookies from spreading, chill dough first.

Your home will be a happy home if your family can
count on finding cookies in the cookie jar!

FINGER KLACHEN

[Cookies with jam in center]

1 cup butter	1 tsp. salt
3/4 cup sugar	Red jelly
3 egg yolks	Powdered sugar
2½ cups sifted flour	Slivered almonds

(Have butter and egg yolks at room temperature.)
Combine butter and sugar. Beat egg yolks and mix
into butter mixture. Add 2½ to 2 5/8 cups flour
sifted with salt. Roll dough into small balls.
Flatten with thumb in the center. Bake at 325°
for about 20 minutes until light brown. While hot,
place a dab of red jelly in the center of each
cookie. Sprinkle with powdered sugar. Top with
1 unblanched slivered almond.

Dottie Larson and Norma Galyon

+ + + + +

YUM-YUMS

½ cup butter	1 tsp. baking powder	1 egg white
1 cup sugar	½ tsp. salt	1 cup brown
2 eggs	Vanilla	sugar
1½ cups flour	1 cup chopped nuts	

Cream butter, add sugar, then well-beaten eggs.
Add flour, baking powder and salt. Add vanilla.
Spread on cookie sheet. Sprinkle nuts on batter.
Beat egg white until stiff. Gradually add brown sugar
and spread over nuts. Bake at 350° for 30 minutes.

Nancy Scott

+ + + + +

LACE COOKIES

½ cup sugar	6 tbls. butter, melted
½ cup flour	2 tbls. cream (or milk)
½ cup dry oatmeal	1 tbl. vanilla
¼ tsp. baking powder	3 tbls. dark Karo syrup

Mix all ingredients together. Drop by half teaspoon onto ungreased cookie sheet. Bake at 375°
for 6-7 minutes. Let stand a minute, then remove.

Alison Brown

STARLIGHT MINT SURPRISE COOKIES

1 cup butter or margarine
1 cup sugar
½ cup firmly packed brown sugar
2 eggs
1 tsp. vanilla
3 cups flour
1 tsp. soda
½ tsp. salt
½ pkg. mint-chocolate wafers

Cream butter gradually adding sugars. Add eggs,
water and vanilla. Sift dry ingredients together
and blend in, mixing thoroughly. Cover and chill
at least 2 hours. Enclose each chocolate wafer in
about 1 tbl. of chilled dough. (Flatten out each
tbl. of dough with your hands, then bring the dough
up over the top of each mint.) Top each with a walnut. Bake at 375º for 10-12 minutes. Makes 4½ dozen.

Lee Etta Lappen

+ + + + +

HERSHEY BARS

[A real quickie that even children love to make.]

Melt: Mix in:
3/4 cup butter   3 cups oatmeal
3/4 cup brown sugar

Spread in square cake pan. Bake at 375º for 15 minutes. While hot, spread with 8 Hershey bars.
(These may also be baked in a larger pan.)

Andre' Rabe

+ + + + +

UNCOOKED COOKIES

2 cups oatmeal, quick   ½ cup butter
1 cup chocolate chips   2 cups sugar
½ cup coconut   ½ cup milk
½ cup chopped nuts   1 tsp. vanilla

Mix first four ingredients in large bowl. Mix in
saucepan the butter, sugar and milk. Bring to rolling boil over low heat. Remove from heat and stir in
vanilla. Pour this mixture over oatmeal mixture.
Drop from teaspoon on wax paper. Makes 18

Connie Whitmore

HELLO DOLLIES!

1 cup graham cracker crumbs
3/4 stick (6 tbls.) butter
Melt butter; add crumbs. Press into bottom of pan.
Add in layers the following in order:
1 cup coconut
1 cup chocolate chips
1 cup chopped pecans
Over this pour 1 can Eagle Brand sweetened condensed milk.
Bake at 375° for 20-30 minutes. Cool. Cut into squares.

Joyce Pierce

+ + + + +

SAN DIEGO SPECIAL

1 cup Borden's sweetened condensed milk
1 pkg. graham crackers (16)
1 sm. pkg. chocolate chips
½ cup nuts, opt.

Crush graham crackers and add remaining ingredients.
Press into a well greased 9" pan. Bake at 350° for
15-20 minutes until golden brown. Cool 10 minutes.
Cut into bars and remove immediately; roll in powdered sugar.

Leslie Lewis

+ + + + +

BUTTERSCOTCH GRAHAMS

[Rich! Rich! Rich!!]

1 cup butter or margarine
1 cup brown sugar
1 cup chopped nuts
Whole graham crackers

Boil butter and sugar together for 3 minutes. Fold
in chopped nuts. Place whole graham crackers on
buttered 9 x 13" pan. Spread mixture over crackers.
Bake at 325° for 10 minutes. Cut into bars while
still warm.

+ + + + +

"GOOD-FOR-YOU" COOKIES

2 beaten eggs
2 cups brown sugar
1 cup oil
¼ cup buttermilk
1 cup raisins (seedless)
½ cup almonds, chopped
1 6-oz. pkg. butterscotch chips
1 cup flour
1 cup wheat germ
1 cup whole wheat or graham flour
2 cups oatmeal
3/4 tsp. salt
1 tsp. soda
½ tsp. baking powder
½ tsp. vanilla

Combine ingredients in order listed. Drop onto greased baking sheet. Bake at 350° until light brown. Makes 4-5 dozen

Nan Green

+ + + + +

RAISING WHOOPEE COOKIES

[Healthy, raisin cookies]

1 cup seedless raisins
1 cup shredded coconut
1 cup whole wheat flakes
1 cup quick-cooking oats
2 cups whole wheat flour
3/4 cup granulated sugar
½ tsp. baking powder
½ tsp. soda
½ tsp. salt
3/4 cup soft shortening
3/4 cup brown sugar, packed
2 eggs
1 tsp. vanilla

Mix raisins with coconut, cereal flakes, oats, whole wheat flour, baking powder, soda and salt. Beat shortening with sugar. Beat in eggs and vanilla. Add dry ingredients working in with hands to form firm dough. Shape into large balls and place on lightly greased baking sheet. Flatten with palm of hand. Bake at 375° for 10-12 minutes. Remove cookies to cooling rack. Makes 2 dozen

Lana Jones

PINEAPPLE DROP COOKIES

½ cup shortening
½ cup brown sugar
½ cup white sugar
½ cup crushed pineapple
1 egg, well beaten
2 cups flour

¼ tsp. salt
¼ tsp. soda
1 tsp. baking powder
½ cup chopped nuts
1 tsp. vanilla

Cream shortening and sugars. Add drained pineapple and egg. Sift dry ingredients and mix in. Drop by teaspoonful onto cookie sheet. Bake at 375° for 10-20 minutes. Makes 3 dozen

+ + + + +

OATMEAL COOKIES

½ cup butter
½ cup margarine
½ cup sugar

1 cup flour
1½ cups quick oatmeal

Cream butters and sugar. Add flour and oatmeal. Shape into balls and flatten with bottom of glass dipped in flour. Bake at 350° for 15-20 minutes. Sprinkle with powdered sugar.

Barbara Ball

+ + + + +

PEANUT BUTTER COOKIES

1 cup butter
1 cup granulated sugar
1 cup brown sugar
1 tsp. soda
1 tsp. baking powder

Dash of salt
3 cups flour
2 eggs
1 cup peanut butter
1 tsp. vanilla

Cream butter, sugar; add peanut butter and lightly beaten eggs. Sift dry ingredients and mix in thoroughly. Roll in balls the size of walnuts and press down with fork in two directions. Bake at 375° for 10-12 minutes or until light brown.

Carol Williams

VARIATION: Roll dough into balls and place on greased pan. Put thumb print in center of each. Bake 5 minutes, then put chocolate candy kisses in center of each and bake 5-7 minutes more.

Lynn Noble

LEMON COOKIES

½ cup butter
1 cup flour
½ cup powdered sugar
Pinch salt

Mix with hands and pack into a 9 x 13" glass pan.
Bake at 350° for 5 minutes. Place baking dish on
cookie sheet (to keep from scorching on bottom)
and bake 10 minutes longer.
TOPPING:
1 cup sugar
2 eggs
2 tbls. lemon juice
½ tsp. baking powder
2 tbls. flour

Beat and pour over cookies. Bake 25 minutes or
until done.

Barbara Ball

+ + + + +

WHEAT-GERM COOKIES

1/3 tsp. salt
1 tbl. honey
10 tbls. vegetable oil
1 cup sugar
3 eggs, well-beaten
1 tsp. vanilla
1 1/3 cups raisins
1 cup chopped nuts
2 cups wheat germ
1½ cups flour (unbleached)

Add the salt and honey to the oil and work together
in a bowl. Add the sugar gradually and cream the
mixture until white and light. Add well-beaten eggs
and vanilla and mix. Add raisins, nuts, wheat
germ and flour. Mix lightly (by hand) and press off
from side of spoon onto oiled baking sheet. Bake
at 375° until a delicate brown. Makes 2½ dozen

Charlotte Melcher

RANGER COOKIES

1 cup brown sugar	½ tsp. soda
2/3 cup shortening	½ tsp. salt
1 egg, well beaten	1 tsp. vanilla
1 cup flour	3/4 cup rolled oats
¼ tsp. baking powder	½ cup pecans

Cream sugar and shortening; add egg, vanilla and oats. Sift flour, baking powder, soda and salt. Add to mixture; mix in nuts. Drop on greased cookie sheet; bake at 350° for 10-12 minutes.

Vonette Bright

+ + + + +

OATMEAL CRISPIES

1 cup melted margarine	1½ cups flour
1 cup brown sugar	1 tsp. salt
1 cup white sugar	1 tsp. soda
2 eggs, well beaten	3 cups quick cooking oats
1 tsp. vanilla	

Thoroughly cream shortening and sugars; add eggs and vanilla; beat well. Add sifted dry ingredients. Add oatmeal and nuts if desired; mix well. Bake at 350° for 10 minutes. Makes about 5 dozen.
VARIATION: Shape in a roll, wrap in wax paper; chill. Slice and bake.

Jacquie Tanner

+ + + + +

GUM DROP COOKIES

1 cup shortening	1 tsp. baking powder
1 cup brown sugar	1 tsp. vanilla
1 cup white sugar	1 cup coconut
2 eggs	1 cup chopped nuts
2 cups flour	1 cup cut-up gum drops
1 tsp. soda	2 cups oatmeal
½ tsp. salt	

Cream shortening and sugar. Add eggs. Sift dry ingredients and add to mixture. Add vanilla and other ingredients; mix. Chill and form into small balls on a cookie sheet. Flatten slightly with back of a teaspoon dipped in canned milk. Bake at 375° for 7 minutes.

Vonette Bright

SUGAR COOKIES

[Good and easily done without a mixer]

1 cup sugar
3/4 cup salad oil
1 egg, beaten
2 cups flour
½ tsp. cream of tartar
½ tsp. soda
½ tsp. salt
½ to 1 tsp. vanilla

Mix sugar, oil and egg. Sift together dry ingredients and add to sugar mixture. Add vanilla. Roll
in balls and flatten a little. Put on cookie sheet
and flatten with a fork cris-crossing the fork
design. Bake at 350° for 10 minutes. Sprinkle the
top with sugar.

Roselyn Shaver

+ + + + +

WHITE SUGAR COOKIES

3 cups flour
2 tsps. baking powder
1 tsp. soda
½ tsp. nutmeg
½ tsp. salt

1 cup shortening
2 eggs
1 cup sugar
¼ cup milk

Combine dry ingredients. Cut in shortening. Beat
eggs, sugar and milk together. Add to first mixture. Roll out on floured surface; cut with cookie
cutters and bake at 350° for 8-10 minutes.

Kerry Fix

+ + + + +

BON BON COOKIES

1 cup butter
1½ cups sifted powdered sugar
1 egg, well beaten
½ tsp. vanilla

½ tsp. almond extract
2½ cups sifted flour
1 tsp. soda
1 tsp. cream of tartar

Thoroughly cream butter and sugar. Beat in eggs
and extracts. Sift dry ingredients, add to creamed
mixture. Mix thoroughly; chill one hour. Form in
small balls. Place on greased cookie sheet. Flatten slightly and center with blanched almonds or
frost after baking. Bake at 375° for 10-12 minutes.

Kerry Fix

CHINESE ALMOND COOKIES

3 cups sifted flour   1 cup shortening
1 cup sugar   1 egg, well beaten
1 tsp. baking soda   1 tbl. almond extract
¼ tsp. salt   1 cup blanched almonds

Sift together flour, sugar, soda and salt. Cut
shortening into dry ingredients until mixture resembles cornmeal. Add egg and flavoring. If mixture seems very dry, add another egg. Mix well.
Knead 6-8 times. Break off dough and roll into
balls the size of walnuts. Flatten with the heel
of your hand and place on cookie sheet. Place an
almond on top of each cookie. Bake at 350° for
15 minutes. Makes 5 dozen   (These may be frozen.)

Lana Jones and Helen Lovell

+ + + + +

SNICKERDOODLES

Mix: 1 cup shortening
       1½ cups sugar
       2 eggs
Stir in:
       2 3/4 cups flour
       2 tsps. cream of tartar
       1 tsp. soda
       ¼ tsp. salt

Roll into balls about the size of a walnut. Roll
balls in mixture of 2 tbls. sugar and 2 tbls. cinnamon. Bake on ungreased cookie sheet at 400° for
8-10 minutes.   Jude Mariano and Sandy Buell

+ + + + +

SKILLET COOKIES

Mix: 2 eggs   ½ cup margarine
       1 cup sugar   3 cups Rice Krispies
       1 cup chopped dates 3/4 cup chopped nuts

Place first four ingredients in skillet over low
heat. Stir constantly. Cook 15 minutes. Remove
from heat. Add Rice Krispies and nuts. When cool
make into balls. (Or shape like strawberries, roll
in red colored sugar, use green icing decorator and
make a stem and leaf on end.)   Nancy Scott

PUMPKIN COOKIES

1 cup brown sugar
1 cup cooked or canned pumpkin
½ cup oil
1 tsp. vanilla   ½ tsp. cinnamon
2 cups sifted flour   ½ tsp. nutmeg
1 tsp. soda   ¼ tsp. ginger
1 tsp. baking powder   1 cup raisins
½ tsp. salt   ½ cup chopped nuts

Beat sugar, pumpkin, oil and vanilla together. Sift
dry ingredients together; add and stir until smooth.
Blend in raisins and nuts. Drop by spoonfuls onto
greased baking sheets. Bake at 350° for 12-15 minutes. Makes 3-4 dozen

                              Bonnie Porter

+ + + + +

SWEDISH GINGER COOKIES

3/4 cup shortening   3 tsp. soda
1 cup sugar   1 tsp. ginger
1 egg   1 tsp. cloves
4 tbls. molasses   1 tsp. cinnamon
2 cups flour   ½ tsp. salt

Mix in order given. Chill overnight, roll in balls
the size of marbles. Roll in sugar. Bake at 325°
about 10 minutes until lightly browned. Do not pat
down, but leave in balls. Cookies will round as
they bake.

                              Nellie Daniels

+ + + + +

ICEBOX COOKIES

[Great to freeze and have on hand for emergencies]

4 cups brown sugar   1 cup butter
4 eggs   6 cups flour
1 tsp. soda   1 tsp. salt
1 tsp. cream of tartar 1 tsp. vanilla

Mix sugar, shortening, flour, soda, salt and cream of
tartar; add nuts, vanilla and eggs. When mixed well,
roll into 4 rolls; chill; slice and bake at 375° for
10-15 minutes.

                              Karen Kuhne

LUSCIOUS APRICOT BARS

2/3 cup dried apricots
½ cup butter or margarine
¼ cup white sugar
1 cup flour, sifted
1/3 cup flour, sifted
½ tsp. baking powder
¼ tsp. salt
1 cup brown sugar

2 eggs, well beaten
½ tsp. vanilla
½ cup chopped nuts
Powdered sugar

Rinse apricots, cover with water, boil 10 minutes. Drain, cool, chop. Combine butter, white sugar and 1 cup flour until crumbly. Pack into 8" square, greased pan. Bake at 350° for 25 minutes or until lightly browned. Sift rest of dry ingredients together. Gradually beat brown sugar into eggs. Add flour mixture. Mix in vanilla, apricots and nuts. Spread over baked layer. Bake 30 minutes more at 350°. Cool in pan. Cut and roll bars in powdered sugar. Makes 2½ dozen

Barbara Ball

+ + + + +

FRUIT BARS

[Very rich and good]

½ cup dried prunes, finely diced
½ cup dried apricots, finely diced
1 cup white sugar
½ cup orange juice
¼ cup water
1 cup chopped nuts
1 tsp. grated lemon peel
1 tsp. grated orange peel
5 tbls. lemon juice
1½ cups flour
1 tsp. baking soda
¼ tsp. salt
1 cup dark brown sugar
1 3/4 cups quick cooking rolled oats
3/4 cups butter

Mix fruit, sugar, orange juice and water and bring to a boil. Simmer 10 minutes until thick. Remove from heat and add nuts, peels and lemon juice. Cool. Mix other dry ingredients with butter and press half in a 9" greased and floured pan. Spread with fruit mixture and top with rest of flour mixture. Bake at 350° for 15-20 minutes.

Paula Carter

BUTTER CHEWS

[A rich bar cookie]

1½ cups margarine
½ cup sugar
3 cups flour
Mix together until crumbly. Press into 9 x 13"
pan. Bake at 375º for 15 minutes, until slightly
brown.
6 egg yolks, beaten
2 cups coconut
1 cup chopped nuts
4 cups (1 box) brown sugar

Mix together. Beat 6 egg whites until stiff - fold
into egg yolk mixture. Pour on top of butter crust
and bake 25 minutes longer until brown. Cool and
cut into bars.

Midge Piedot

+ + + + +

SCOTCH BARS

1 cup flour
½ tsp. baking powder
1/8 tsp. baking soda
½ tsp. salt
1/3 cup shortening, melted
1 cup brown sugar
1 tbl. water
1 egg
1 tsp. vanilla
½ cup chocolate chips

Sift flour, baking powder, soda and salt together.
Melt shortening in saucepan. Add brown sugar and
water; mix well. Cool slightly. Add egg and vanilla
and blend. Add flour mixture, a small amount at a
time. Turn into a 9" square pan. Sprinkle chocolate
chips over top. Bake at 350º for 20-25 minutes. Do
not overbake. Cool in pan. Makes about 2 dozen.

Jeanne Johnson

+ + + + +

DREAM BARS

½ cup sugar
2 cups flour
1 cup butter
Pinch of salt
Mix above ingredients together and pack into 9 x 12"
pan. Prepare:
2 cups brown sugar
½ cup coconut
1 cup chopped nuts
2 eggs
1 tsp. baking powder
2 tbls. flour
Spread over butter layer. Bake at 350° for 30 minutes. (Frost with butter frosting, if desired.)

Joan Kendall

+ + + + +

SWEDISH TOSCAS

[A yummy little tart to serve with coffee or tea]

SHELL:
6 tbls. butter or margarine
½ cup sugar
1 cup sifted flour

Cream butter and gradually add sugar, creaming well.
Blend in flour. Divide into 12 small ungreased muffin
cups. Press into bottoms and halfway up sides of
cups. Bake at 350° for 10 minutes.
FILLING:
1/3 cup slivered almonds
¼ cup sugar
2 tbls. butter
1½ tbls. cream
2 tsps. flour
Combine filling ingredients in saucepan. Cook over
medium heat, stirring constantly until mixture boils.
Remove from heat. Divide into partially baked cookie
shells. Bake at 350° for 10 more minutes until light
brown. Cool 5 minutes, then carefully remove from
pan. Makes 1 dozen

Midge Piedot

+ + + + +

"CAMELBACK INN" BARS

[A rich, "something special" dessert; good for a coffee or tea]

½ cup butter
½ cup sugar
1 egg
4 tbls. cocoa
2 cups graham cracker crumbs
1 cup coconut
½ cup chopped nuts

Mix butter, sugar, egg and cocoa in double boiler over boiling water. Stir until mixture resembles custard. Combine crumbs, coconut and nuts. Blend well with custard mixture. Spread and press tightly in 9" pan.

¼ cup butter
3 tbls. milk
2 tbls. vanilla instant pudding
2 cups sifted powdered sugar

Cream above ingredients. Spread over mixture in pan. Melt 4 squares semi-sweet chocolate and 1 tbl. butter. Blend well and spread on top. Let set.

                    Kerry Fix and Bonnie Porter

                    + + + + +

TOFFEE BARS

½ cup brown sugar   2 tsps. vanilla
½ cup white sugar   1 cup rolled oats
1 cup shortening   1 tsp. salt
1 cup flour   1 6-oz. pkg. chocolate chips
2 eggs

Cream shortening with sugars. Add vanilla and eggs. Blend in sifted dry ingredients and oats. Spread in a 9 x 12" baking pan. Bake at 350º for about 20 minutes. Cool for a few minutes and spread with melted chocolate chips. Sprinkle with chopped nuts. Cut into squares when cold. Makes about 32 bars.

                         Karen Kuhne

                    + + + + +

CHOCOLATE CHIP BAR COOKIES

2/3 cup shortening
1 cup white sugar
1 tsp. salt
4 tsps. water
2 eggs
1 cup coconut
1 6-oz. pkg. chocolate chips
Nuts
1 cup brown sugar
2 cups flour
2½ tsps. baking powder
2 tsps. vanilla

Melt shortening in saucepan, remove from heat, add
sugars and mix; add eggs; add dry ingredients last
with coconut, nuts and chips. Bake in large cake
pan at 350° for about 20 minutes.

Karen Kuhne

+ + + + +

CHINESE TREAT

1 small pkg. chocolate chips
1 small pkg. lemon custard chips
1 cup cashew nuts, opt.

Melt chips in top of double boiler. Add 1 large
can Chinese noodles. Drop by clusters onto wax
paper. Cool.

Dorothy Gregory

+ + + + +

CHOCOLATE NUT WAFERS

½ cup shortening
1 cup sugar
1 egg
1 tsp. vanilla
2 sqs. bitter chocolate

3/4 cup flour
3/4 tsp. salt
3/4 cup finely chopped
nuts

Mix shortening, sugar and egg. Stir in vanilla and melted chocolate. Sift together flour and salt and stir in. Add nuts. Drop teaspoonfuls of dough 2" apart onto greased baking sheet. Flatten with bottom of a glass covered with a slightly dampened cloth. Bake at 325° for 10-12 minutes. Makes 3-4 dozen cookies.

Jeanette Belcher

+ + + + +

COCOA DROP COOKIES

1½ cups sugar
½ cup cocoa
3/4 cup melted butter
1 egg, well beaten
1 cup nuts, opt.

½ tsp. baking soda
¼ tsp. cream of tartar
3/4 cup sour milk
2 tsps. vanilla
Flour

Cream sugar, cocoa and butter. Add egg. Dissolve baking soda and cream of tartar in sour milk. Add vanilla. Mix together. Add enough flour to make dough of firm enough consistency to retain shape when dropped from teaspoon onto cookie sheet. Bake at 375° for 5-7 minutes.

Nancy Schurle

+ + + + +

DROPPED WALNUT COOKIES

½ cup shortening
½ cup brown sugar
½ cup honey
1 3/4 cups flour

¼ tsp. salt
½ tsp. soda
½ tsp. cinnamon
½ cup chopped walnuts

Cream shortening and sugar; add honey. Sift dry ingredients and add to creamed mixture. Add nuts; bake at 375° for 12 minutes. Makes 3 dozen

Andre' Rabe

CHOCOLATE CHIPPERS

½ cup shortening (margarine)
¼ cup brown sugar
½ cup sugar
1 egg
1 tsp. vanilla

1 cup flour
½ tsp. soda
3/4 tsp. salt
1 6-oz. pkg. chocolate
   chips (1 cup)
½ cup walnuts

Cream margarine, sugars, egg and vanilla until very fluffy. Sift together dry ingredients; stir into creamed mixture. Stir in the chips and nuts. Refrigerate until well chilled. Drop from teaspoonfuls 2" apart onto a cool, greased baking sheet. Bake at 375° for 8-10 minutes. Makes 3 dozen

Jeanne Schuetz

+ + + + +

TOLL HOUSE KOOKIE BRITTLE

1 cup margarine
1½ tsps. vanilla
1 tsp. salt
1 cup sugar

2 cups flour
½ cup finely chopped nuts
1 6-oz. pkg. chocolate chips

Combine margarine, vanilla and salt in bowl and blend well. Gradually beat in sugar. Add flour and chocolate chips; mix well. Press evenly into ungreased 15 x 10 x 1" pan. Sprinkle nuts over top and press in. Bake at 375° for 25 minutes. Cool, then break into irregular pieces.

Susan Phipps

+ + + + +

CHOCOLATE CHIP BISQUICK COOKIES

¼ cup soft butter
3/4 cup brown sugar
1 egg

1 1/3 cups Bisquick
½ cup chopped nuts
6-oz. semi-sweet chocolate
   chips

Mix butter, sugar and egg well. Stir in Bisquick, nuts, chocolate chips. Drop with teaspoon 2" apart on ungreased baking sheet. Bake at 375° for 10 minutes until light brown.

Jane Prall

108

MOIST BROWNIES

½ cup margarine
1 cup sugar
4 eggs
1 #1 can chocolate syrup
½ tsp. salt
1 tsp. vanilla
1 cup flour
1 cup nuts

Cream margarine, sugar and eggs. Add syrup and
vanilla. Beat well. Add dry ingredients. Stir
in nuts. Pour into greased 9 x 13" pan. Bake at
350° for 30 minutes.

Lynn Vann

+ + + + +

BROWNIES

½ cup butter
½ cup margarine
2 cups sugar
½ cup cocoa (add ½ cup boiling water to form
        a smooth paste)
4 eggs
2 cups sifted cake flour
1 tsp. vanilla
½ cup milk
1 cup nutmeats

Cream butters. Add sugar and beat well. Add cocoa
and beat well. Add eggs at once and beat 3 minutes.
Add flour alternately with milk and add vanilla.
Fold in nuts. Put in greased jelly roll pan. Bake
at 350° for 40-50 minutes. Top with chocolate lemon
frosting.
CHOCOLATE-LEMON FROSTING:
Melt 1½ squares unsweetened chocolate with ¼ cup
butter. Add ¼ tsp. salt and cool. Add 1 egg, beaten,
1 tsp. vanilla, 2 tsp. lemon juice and 1 1/3 cup
sifted powdered sugar. Mix in ½ cup finely chopped
nuts. Spread over cake.

Barbara Ball

COOKIE MIX

[Store at room temperature, tightly covered and you
can make a variety of cookies in a matter of minutes.]

4 cups sifted flour	1 cup brown sugar
2 tsps. soda	4 cups quick rolled oats
2 tsps. salt	2 cups shortening
2½ cups white sugar	

Sift flour, soda, salt and white sugar together into
mixing bowl. Add brown sugar, oats and shortening.
Mix together with pastry blender until in fine crumbs.
To make cookies, measure out 3 cups of mix. Beat one
egg slightly with ¼ cup milk, add 1 tsp. vanilla (or
preferred flavoring); stir into mix. Now you can let
your imagination go -- add shredded coconut, chopped
nuts, candied orange peel, chocolate or butterscotch
pieces, cut dates or raisins. Drop by teaspoonfuls
on greased cookie sheet. Bake at 375° for 12 minutes
or until light brown. Three cups of mix makes about
24 cookies.

Dorothy Gregory

+ + + + +

PVM BROWNIES
(Protein, Vitamin, Mineral)

[These will take a trip to the Health-food store for
most of the ingredients.]

1 cup soy granules
2 envs. unflavored gelatin
4 tbls. dietetic cocoa (carob flour)
Sweetening equal to 1 cup sugar (3/4 cup honey)
½ cup wheat germ
½ cup lecithin
½ cup whole hulled sunflower seeds
4 cups water
1 tsp. vanilla
Pinch of salt
Sprinkle of cinnamon

Boil water; add seeds to soften. Add soy granules
gradually. Dissolve gelatin in a little cold water.
Add to mixture. Boil for 10 minutes. Remove from
heat and add other ingredients. Beat well. Pour into
a flat pan and refrigerate. When cool, cut into small
squares.

Judy Anderson

HURRY-UP COOKIES

The following recipes are quickies made from cake
mixes using suitable variations. Great for College
Life meetings, Cub Scouts, picnics, or just to fill
the cookie jar.

CHOCOLATE DROPS

1 pkg. chocolate cake mix   2 eggs
½ cup cooking oil

Mix all ingredients well and drop on ungreased baking
sheet. If desired, top each with a nut. Bake at
350° for 10-12 minutes. Makes 4-5 dozen.

APPLE SAUCE RAISIN COOKIES

I pkg. Applesauce raisin cake mix
2 tbls. water   1 egg
2 tbls. cooking oil   ½ cup chopped nuts

Mix all together; drop on greased cookie sheet.
Bake at 375° for 10 minutes. Makes 2½ to 3 dozen.

TROPICAL BANANA COOKIES

1 pkg. Banana cake mix   3/4 cup mashed ripe bananas
¼ cup cooking oil   (2 medium)
1 egg   Pecan halves (if desired)

Combine all ingredients and drop on ungreased baking
sheet and top with nuts. Bake at 350° for 10-12
minutes. Makes 4 dozen.

PEANUT BUTTER COOKIES

1 pkg. Yellow cake mix   2 tbls. water
1 cup peanut butter   2 eggs
½ cup cooking oil

Mix well and drop on ungreased baking sheet. Press
crossways with fork. Bake at 350° for 10-12 minutes.
Makes 4-5 dozen.

CHERRY DROP COOKIES

1 pkg. Cherry cake mix   2 eggs
½ cup cooking oil   Few drops of red food
2 tbls. water   color (if desired)
1 cup chopped nuts   Maraschino cherries

Mix all ingredients but cherries and drop on ungreased baking sheet. Top with quartered cherries
and bake at 350° for 10-12 minutes. Makes 4-5
dozen.

Nan McCullough

You can hold your family in the hollow of your spoon...with a good dessert. Choose a dessert that fits the meal--a light dessert for a heavy meal; a richer dessert for a lighter meal.

Include fruit in the dessert if it is not in any other part of the meal or the day's meals. Crushed pineapple is just right to use in molded desserts; tidbits for fruit cups; chunks are all purpose; spears for fruits; and slices to put in, under, or over desserts.

You are never too full for jello! Dissolve fruit-flavored gelatin in 1 cup boiling water; add 10 ice cubes, stirring constantly 2 minutes. Remove unmelted ice. Let stand 5 minutes; add remaining ingredients. Before unmolding gelatin, rinse platter or plate with cold water so mold will slide on it.

When serving frozen desserts, remove from freezer 15 to 20 minutes before serving. When whipping cream for desserts, chill cream, bowl and beater for more volume. (Midge Piedot)

Use crushed peanut brittle in whipped cream as topping for angel food cake. (Dorothy Gregory)

Buy a can of red tart cherries and add 2 tablespoons of cornstarch to the juice, ½ cup sugar, 4-5 drops red food coloring and ½ tsp. cinnamon. Thicken them yourself to make a cherry topping. Better than the more expensive prepared type topping.

One easy and economical prepared dessert mix you can always make in a jiffy is the Jello or Royal Cheesecake mix. All you need is in the box except for milk, sugar and margarine. You can top the cheesecake with the cherries or stir in leftover cream cheese and fresh orange and date pieces for a delicious dessert all done with no baking. (Nan Green)

A favorite lemon meringue pie and hot chocolate fudge sauce are both recipes from the inside label of Borden's Eagle Brand sweetened condensed milk. They always bring raves and "how did you do it?" (Paula Carter)

LEMON SPONGE CUSTARD CUPS

3 tbls. butter
1 cup sugar
3 eggs, separated
¼ cup lemon juice
5 tbls. flour
1 cup milk

Cream butter and sugar. Add beaten egg yolks and
lemon juice and stir. Add flour, mix and add milk;
blend. Fold in egg whites, beaten stiff. Pour into
greased custard cups. Set in pan of hot water.
Bake at 350° for 30 minutes. (Baking dish may be
used - bake 35 minutes.)

                                            Jane Prall

+ + + + +

LEMON-LIME CHIFFON DESSERT

1 pkg. lemon pie filling
¼ cup sugar
2 cups water
2 eggs, separated
1 sm. pkg. lime jello
2 cups water
¼ cup sugar
Graham cracker crust

Mix in saucepan the lemon pie filling, sugar and ¼ cup
water. Add 2 egg yolks, well beaten and 1 3/4 cups
water. Cook and stir over medium heat until it comes
to a full boil and is thickened (about 5 minutes).
Meanwhile, dissolve lime jello in 1 cup hot water;
add 1 cup cold water. Add gradually to pudding mixture, blending well. Beat egg whites until foamy.
Add ¼ cup sugar gradually, beating until mixture
stands in stiff peaks. Fold into cooled lemon-
lime mixture. Turn into graham cracker crust and
chill until firm.
CRUST: Combine 1¼ cups graham cracker crumbs (24
crackers), ¼ cup finely chopped nuts (opt.), 2 tbls.
sugar. Add 1/3 cup melted butter. Mix well and
press firmly on bottom of 8 x 12" pan. Chill.

                                        Nancy Robinson

LEMON SNOW

[Great for entertaining and parties]

1 can Eagle Brand sweetened condensed milk
2 eggs, separated
2 lemons, juiced and grated
1 box vanilla wafers
12 coconut cookies
¼ cup margarine, melted

Roll wafers and coconut cookies into crumbs. Blend in margarine. Press into 9" pan. Bake at 350° for 10 minutes. Cool. Blend condensed milk, eggs and lemon together. Pour into crumb crust. Sprinkle additional crumbs on top. Refrigerate overnight.

Joyce Pierce

+ + + + +

LEMON SOUFFLE'

2 pkgs. lemon pie filling
2/3 cup sugar
3 eggs, separated
½ cup heavy cream

Add sugar and egg yolks to lemon pie filling. Cook according to pkg. directions. Allow to cool. Beat egg whites until stiff but not dry. Slowly fold into cooled pudding mixture. Pour into 1½-qt. dish. Chill 4 hours or more. Serve with chocolate mint cookies or petit fours. Serves 10-12

+ + + + +

LEMON DELICACY A LA DELAWARE

2 tbls. butter
3/4 cup sugar
Juice of 1 lemon
Rind of ½ lemon
2 eggs, separated
1 cup milk
2 tbls. flour

Cream butter; add sugar gradually and mix well. Add well beaten egg yolks, flour, lemon juice and rind. Mix thoroughly. Add milk and fold in stiffly beaten egg whites. Pour into greased baking dish. Set in pan of hot water and bake at 350° for 45 minutes. Serves 4

Ruth Jones

114

FRENCH APPLE COBBLER

FILLING:
5 cups apples, tart, sliced
3/4 cup sugar
2 tbls. flour
½ tsp. cinnamon
¼ tsp. salt
1 tsp. vanilla
1 tbl. butter

Combine apples, sugar, flour, cinnamon, salt, vanilla
and ¼ cup water in medium bowl. Turn into 9" pan.
Dot with butter.

BATTER:
½ cup flour
½ cup sugar
½ tsp. baking powder
¼ tsp. salt
2 tbls. butter
1 egg, slightly beaten

Combine all ingredients in medium bowl. Beat until
smooth. Drop batter in 9 portions onto apple mixture. Bake at 375° for 35-40 minutes. Serve warm
with ice cream.

Mary Lou Lyon

+ + + + +

APPLE CRISP

4 cups thinly sliced cooking apples
1 tbl. lemon juice
1/3 cup sifted flour
1 cup oatmeal, uncooked
½ cup brown sugar
½ tsp. salt
1 tsp. cinnamon
1/3 cup melted margarine

Place apples in greased, shallow baking dish.
Sprinkle with lemon juice. Combine dry ingredients;
add melted butter, mixing until crumbly. Sprinkle
crumb mixture over apples. Bake at 375° for 30 minutes or until apples are tender.

Kerry Fix

BERRY COBBLER

1½ cups flour
2 tsps. baking powder
½ tsp. salt
1 cup sugar
1 egg, well beaten
3 tbls. butter, melted
1 cup milk
Fresh berries
1 cup sugar
1 cup water

Mix flour, baking powder, salt and 1 cup sugar in a
bowl. Slowly add egg, butter and milk. Pour batter
into a greased, shallow baking pan and cover thickly
with berries. Over the fruit pour a syrup made by
combining the sugar and water. Bake at 375° about
45 minutes. (As the cobbler bakes, the batter will
rise to the top of the pan.) Allow to cool thoroughly before serving. (Sliced peaches or apricots
sprinkled with lemon juice may also be used.)

Midge Piedot

+ + + + +

RHUBARB COBBLER

[This is so fast to prepare, yet everyone thinks
you've been cooking all day!]

3-5 cups rhubarb
1 cup sugar
3 tbls. butter
Mix and place in 9" sq. pan. Top with the following
        mixture:
1½ cups flour
¼ tsp. salt
3 tsps. baking powder
½ cup milk
3/4 cup sugar
¼ cup shortening
1 egg
Bake at 350° for 35 minutes. (Apples mixed with
        cinnamon may be substituted for the rhubarb.)

Karen Kuhne

FRESH FRUIT COBBLER

1/3 cup margarine
1 cup sugar
1½ cups flour
2 tsps. baking powder
¼ tsp. salt
1 cup milk

Mix above ingredients and spread batter in 9" greased
baking pan.   Cover with any fruit desired. Sprinkle
with 1 cup more sugar; dot with extra butter. Pour
1 cup of boiling water over top.   Bake at 350° for
1 hour. (If fresh fruit is used, more sugar will be
needed.)

Midge Piedot

+ + + + +

RASPBERRY DELIGHT

1 cup vanilla wafer crumbs
1 cup butter
1½ cups powdered sugar
2 eggs
1 cup whipping cream
1 pkg. frozen raspberries (do not thaw)
½ cup nuts
¼ tsp. vanilla

Line 9" sq. pan with crumbs. Cream butter and sugar.
Add eggs one at a time. Spread over crumbs. Whip
cream; fold in raspberries, nuts and vanilla. Spread
over butter and sprinkle a few nuts over the top.
Chill overnight. Serves 9

Jeanne Lawrence

+ + + + +

PEACH MELBA

Peach halves, canned
Ice cream
Frozen raspberries
1 tbl. cornstarch

Thaw raspberries; heat with cornstarch until thickened. Cool and chill.   For each individual serving
use: 2 peach halves; fill with a scoop of ice cream;
pour raspberry sauce over top. Serve immediately.

Barbara Ball

CHERRY CRUNCH

1 pkg. yellow cake mix
½ cup butter or margarine
½ cup chopped pecans or almonds
2 cans cherry pie filling (or 1 can pie filling and
    1 can crushed pineapple)

Cut cake mix and butter together. Resrve about 1/3
for top and mix this with ½ cup chopped nuts. Put
2/3 of the mixture in bottom of large greased cake
pan. Cover with fruit filling. Then sprinkle top
with the nut-crumb mixture. Bake at 350° for 35-40
minutes. Serve warm topped with ice cream or whipped
cream.

                    Linda Ewing and Doris Ryen

+ + + + +

CHERRY CRISP

1 cup sugar   1 tsp. baking powder
¼ tsp. salt   1 can cherry pie filling
1 egg   ½ cup butter
1 cup flour

Place cherry filling in deep pie dish. Mix in a bowl
sugar, flour, salt, baking powder and egg until
crumbly. Pour evenly over cherry filling. Melt
butter and pour over crumbs. Bake at 350° for 35
minutes.
                          Ralph Weitz

+ + + + +

CRANBERRY DESSERT

1 lb. cranberries
1½ cup water
2 cups sugar
1 pkg. Dream Whip (or whipping cream)
3 slices sour dough bread

Cook cranberries with 1½ cups water and sugar together about 10 minutes until thick. Toast bread
in 250° oven (until crispy). Whip cream. Alternate
layer of crumbs, whipped cream and cranberries in
a baking dish. Finish with the whipped cream and
sprinkle a few bread crumbs on top. Chill 2 hours
in refrigerator. Serve immediatly because it
won't keep!
                          Gail Peterson

COCONUT-CHERRY CRUNCH

[A real quickie!]

¼ cup sugar
½ cup butter
1 can coconut
1½ cups flour
1 can cherry pie filling

Mix first 4 ingredients. Put half of mixture on bottom of greased 8" sq. pan. Pour cherries over. Cover with remaining crumbs. Sprinkle coconut over the top. Bake at 400° for 30 minutes.

Julie Schroen

+ + + + +

QUICKIE DESSERT

1 pkg. Jiffy cake mix
1 can cherry pie filling
½ cup margarine
Chopped nuts

Empty pie filling into 8" sq. baking dish. Cover with dry cake mix directly from the box. Melt margarine and pour over contents in dish; sprinkle with nuts. Bake at 350° for 50-55 minutes.

Jan Stevens

+ + + + +

CHERRY DESSERT

1 yellow cake mix
2 eggs
½ cup melted butter
1 large can cherry pie filling
1 box almond-coconut frosting mix

Mix cake mix with eggs and melted butter. Pat on bottom of greased 9 x 13" pan. Cover with pie filling. Mix frosting mix with enough melted butter to make it crumbly; spread on top of cherries. Bake at 350° for 30 minutes. Top with whipped cream.

Nancy Robinson

ALMOND STRAWBERRY CREPES

Filling:
2 cups cottage cheese
1 tsp. grated lemon rind
½ tsp. salt
3 tbls. honey
½ tsp. vanilla

Crepes:
3/4 cup sifted flour
2 tbls. sugar
½ tsp. salt
3 eggs
1 cup milk
1 tbl. butter, melted

Combine all ingredients for filling in a bowl and mix
well. For crepes: beat eggs until thick. Sift dry
ingredients together over eggs; beat just until
smooth; stir in milk and butter. Heat a 6" heavy
frying pan over low heat; test temperature with a
few drops of water. When drops bounce, temperature
is right. Lightly grease pan with butter. Pour in
a scant ¼ cup batter at a time; fry until crepe top
appears dry and underside is golden; turn; brown
other side. Repeat, lightly greasing pan before
each frying. (Makes 12 crepes.) Spoon about 2 tbls.
filling into center of each crepe when it is cooked;
roll up and place, seam side down, in shallow baking
pan; keep warm in 250° oven. (Crepes may be made and
filled ahead, chilled and then reheated at 350° for
10 minutes just before serving.)
Sauce: Combine ¼ cup sugar, 1 tbl. cornstarch and
1 cup water in pan; cook, stirring constantly until
sauce thickens and boils 3 minutes. Stir in 2 10-oz.
pkgs. frozen sliced strawberries, slightly thawed;
heat just to boiling. Arrange crepes on serving
dish; spoon hot sauce over; sprinkle with almonds.

Lois Mackey

+ + + + +

BIG BERRY CREAM

1 qt. vanilla ice cream
1 pkg. slightly thawed frozen strawberries

Mix strawberries into softened ice cream. Serve
immediately or refreeze. An extra touch: melt
strawberry jelly (not jam) and pour over the ice
cream/fruit mixture in partait glasses.

Marilyn Ehle

STRAWBERRY BLINTZES

1¼ cup Bisquick   3 eggs
2 cups milk   ¼ cup melted butter

Beat ingredients with rotary beater until smooth.
For each pancake spoon 2-3 tablespoons batter onto
lightly greased griddle. Spread with back of spoon.
Bake until small bubbles appear, then loosen edges
gently; turn and brown other side.
FILLING:
1 cup cottage cheese   1 pkg. frozen strawberries
1 3-oz. pkg. cream cheese 1 tbl. lemon juice
1½ tbls. lemon rind   ¼ tsp. almond flavoring
3 tbls. lemon juice
¼ cup sugar

Whip cheeses, lemon and sugar until creamy. Place
¼ cup filling on each pancake. Roll up. Put in
7 x 11" baking dish. Bake at 400° for 10 minutes.
Thaw berries; heat with 1 tbl. lemon juice and almond flavoring. Serve on rolled pancakes. Serve
with a dab of sour cream if desired. Makes 15-20

                                        Lois Mackey

                    + + + + +

STRAWBERRY ANGEL-BAVARIAN

2 sm. pkg. strawberry jello
1 cup sugar
2 cups hot water
Juice from drained strawberries and
    cold water to make 1½ cups
1 Angel food cake
3-4 boxes of strawberries (fresh or frozen)
1 cup whipping cream

Add sugar to jello, dissolve in hot water; mix well
with 1½ cups juice. Let set enough to whip (of egg-
white consistency). Add angel food cake broken in
small pieces; add drained fruit, fold in whipped
cream. Mold; place in refrigerator until firm. May
serve with whipped cream.
VARIATION: Slice an oblong angel food cake into 3
layers horizontally. Then put mixture between and
over cake instead of breaking cake up and putting
it in the mixture.
                                        Alice Gurtler

FROSTED FRUIT COCKTAIL

[Great served with Mexican food.   Keeps in freezer
to have on hand for emergencies]

3 med. ripe bananas, mashed
1 cup sugar
1 can (2 cups) crushed pineapple and juice
2 lemons, juice and strained
2 cups orange juice
2 cups ginger ale

Mix in order given. Freeze in a clean ½-gal. milk
carton. Scoop out portion desired about ½ hour before serving. Serve when mushy in sherbet dishes
or at a pot-luck in small dixie cups. Serves 24

Gwen Martin

+ + + + +

FROSTY AMBROSIA

1 can (13½-oz.) pineapple chunks
2 sliced bananas
1½ cups diced, pared oranges
3/4 cup coconut

Freeze pineapple chunks; partially thaw. Toss with
bananas, oranges and flaked coconut. Serve while
pineapple is frosty.

Joan Kendall

+ + + + +

CHOCOLATE FROZEN DESSERT

1 cup softened butter
4 sq. melted, unsweetened chocolate
2 cups sifted powdered sugar
4 eggs
3/4 tsp. peppermint flavoring
2 tsps. vanilla

Mix butter, chocolate and sugar. Add eggs, beating
well after each one. Blend in flavorings. Fill 14
small souffle' cups. Freeze. Garnish with whipped
cream or chopped nuts before serving. Serves 14

Paula Carter

122

DOUBLE RASPBERRY PARFAIT

[Quick and easy]

1 pkg. (10-oz.) frozen raspberries
1 pkg. raspberry flavor self-layering dessert mix
Boiling water

Thaw raspberries. Drain into 2-cup measuring cup.
Add water to syrup to make 1 1/3 cups. Spoon drained
raspberries into 4 parfait glasses. (Save 4 berries
for top.) Prepare dessert mix with boiling water
according to directions. Use prepared syrup mixture
in place of cold water. Spoon over raspberries.
Chill for 3 hours. Top with reserved berries and
Dream Whip. Serves 4

Cinny Hicks

+ + + + +

CHERRIES IN THE SNOW

1 pkg. Dream Whip or 1 cup whipped cream
1 8-oz. pkg. cream cheese
2 cans red tart cherries
4 tbls. cornstarch
½ cup sugar (or 3/4 cup)
½ tsp. cinnamon
6 drops red food coloring
Graham cracker crust

Spread graham cracker crust in 9 x 13" cake pan.
Mix together the whipped cream and cream cheese.
Thicken the cherry juice with cornstarch, sugar,
cinnamon and food coloring. Pour half the cherry
filling on crust, spread on cream mixture, then top
with remaining cherries. Freeze for 2 hours. Set
out one half hour before serving. Serves 15

Nan Green

+ + + + +

FROZEN MACAROON DELITE

1 pkg. coconut macaroons, crumbled
2 pints lime sherbet   1 cup chopped nuts
2 pints raspberry sherbet   1 tsp. vanilla
1 pint whipped cream   ¼ cup powdered sugar

Add crumbled macaroons to whipped cream with nuts,
vanilla and sugar. Put half of macaroon mixture in
9 x 13" cake pan. Spoon sherbets by spoonfuls over
crumbs--alternating colors. Spread remaining crumb
mixture over sherbet. Freeze at least 24 hours.
Serves 16   Suzie Brenneman and Judy Anderson

YOGURT

Bring 1 quart milk (may use part canned milk)
to boil or 198°. Cool to 125°-130°.
Blend 2 tbls. yogurt culture (left from previous
batch) with a little of the cooled milk.
Stir back into the remaining milk. Transfer quickly
to smaller covered pan.
Wrap up tightly in newspaper. Let stand for 5 hours
in a warm place (up to 200°) until solid.
Refrigerate. Eat plain or add fruit or flavoring to
taste.

Louise Shukarian and Arlene Dennison

+ + + + +

ICE CREAM

2 large cans evaporated milk
6 eggs, well beaten
1 1/3 cups sugar
2 cups milk
2 tbls. vanilla

Combine ingredients which makes a custard. Pour into
ice cream maker and fill with extra rich milk or
cream. Turn.

Nancy Schurle

+ + + + +

ICE CREAM

1 quart whipping cream
½ gal. milk
6 eggs
3 cups sugar
¼ cup vanilla

Beat together and freeze in a hand-crank or electric
freezer. Makes 6 quarts

Kerry Fix

MOONSHINE GINGERBREAD

2 cups flour
1 cup sugar
½ cup butter (scant)
1 tsp. baking powder
3/4 cup sour milk

½ tsp. ginger
½ tsp. soda
½ tsp. cinnamon
1 egg, well beaten
¼ tsp. nutmeg

Mix flour, sugar and butter. Reserve one cupful.
Add rest of ingredients to remaining crumb mixture.
Sprinkle ½ cup crumbs on bottom of baking pan, then
batter, then rest of crumbs on top. Bake at 350°
for 35 minutes. Serve hot, topped with vanilla ice
cream, whipped cream or vanilla custard sauce.

Lee Etta Lappen

+ + + + +

GINGER PEACHY CAKE

¼ cup margarine
½ cup brown sugar
1/3 cup maraschino cherry halves
1 can (1-lb.) peach slices
Gingerbread mix

Melt margarine in 9" sq. pan. Blend in brown sugar;
spread in pan. Add cherries and peaches. Pour
gingerbread mix over top. Bake at 350° for 40-45
minutes. Serve warm with whipped cream.

Kerry Fix

+ + + + +

FROSTED CREAMS

1 cup shortening
1 cup sugar
1 cup hot water
1 cup light molasses
3 cups sifted flour
1 tsp. vanilla

3 eggs, separated
1 tsp. soda
Pinch salt
1 rounded tsp. cinnamon
1 tsp. ginger

Add spices to flour and sift together. Cream shortening and sugar. Add egg yolks and molasses. Gradually add dry ingredients alternately with hot water
in which soda has been dissolved. Fold in egg whites
which have been beaten until stiff. Turn into 16 x
12" pan and bake at 350° for 30 minutes. When completely cool, spread with medium frosting: 2 cups
powdered sugar blended with enough milk to make
right consistency. Cut in squares.

Barbara Ball

SUGAR PLUM PUDDING

2 cups sifted flour	1 tsp. cinnamon
2½ tsps. baking powder	3/4 cup salad oil
½ tsp. salt	3 eggs
1½ cups sugar	1 cup buttermilk
1¼ tsps. soda	1 cup chopped prunes
1 tsp. nutmeg	1 cup chopped nuts
1 tsp. allspice	

Sift dry ingredients including sugar. Stir in other
ingredients in order given. Pour into 3 1-qt. jello
molds. Bake at 325° for 50 minutes. Glaze: Combine
1 cup sugar, ½ cup buttermilk, 2 tsps. lemon extract;
1 tbl. white corn syrup, ½ cup margarine. Bring to
a boil and pour over hot puddings.

                                        Marilyn Heavilin

+ + + + +

STEAMED HOLIDAY PUDDING

1½ cups sifted flour
1½ tsps. soda
1½ cups sugar
1½ tsps. cloves
1½ tsps. cinnamon
1½ tsps. nutmeg
3/4 tsp. salt
3 tbls. butter, melted
3 eggs, beaten
1½ cups grated potato, raw
1½ cups grated carrots, raw
1 cup chopped nut meats
1½ cups raisins

Sift flour with soda, sugar and spices. Beat eggs and
gradually add melted butter in large bowl. Prepare
nuts, raisins, potato and carrots and add to the egg
and butter mixture. Add the dry ingredients and stir
well. May be baked in an angel food cake pan or two
tall coffee cans (1 lb. size). Cover with foil and
tie a string tightly around top of pan or can. Be
sure there are no breaks in the foil. Place pudding
in large kettle that has a rack in the bottom. Put
water in kettle until it comes half way up. Bring to
boil; turn down to simmer and cook for 2½ hours.

                                        Jane Prall

FUDGE-FUDGE PUDDING

¼ cup butter
1 pkg. fudge cake mix
1 1/3 cups hot water
¼ cup chopped walnuts or pecans
1 pkg. buttercream fudge or walnut fudge frosting mix
2½ cups boiling water

Melt butter in a 9 x 13" cake pan in oven. Remove
from oven; add dry cake mix and hot water. Stir with
fork until smooth. Spread evenly in pan. Sprinkle
with walnuts. Sprinkle dry frosting mix over all.
Gently pour 2½ cups boiling water over frosting mix.
Bake at 350º for 30-35 minutes until crust is shiny
and cake starts to pull away from sides of pan.
Serve warm, saucy side up, with whipped cream or ice
cream.

Carol Carter

+ + + + +

DATE PUDDING

Mix: 1 cup brown sugar   ½ cup flour
      ½ tsp. salt   ½ cup milk
      1 tsp. baking powder
Mix: 1 cup dates, chopped
      ½ cup flour

Add dates and flour to first dry mixture, stirring
well. Pour into a greased 8" sq. pan. Sprinkle with
chopped nuts. Cook the following sauce and pour
over the above: 1 cup brown sugar, 1 tbl. butter and
1 cup water. Boil together. Bake at 350º for 20-25
minutes. Serve warm with whipped cream.

Patty Roth

+ + + + +

DATE AND NUT TORTE

4 eggs, well beaten   1 tsp. baking powder
1 cup sugar   2 cups cut up dates
1 cup fine, dry bread crumbs 1 cup chopped walnuts

Beat sugar gradually into eggs, then stir in and mix
together the bread crumbs and baking powder. Add
dates and nuts last and spread in an 8" sq. well-
greased pan. Bake at 350º for 35 minutes until set.
Serve with whipped cream or ice cream.

Vonette Bright

CHOCOLATE DESSERT

2 cups powdered sugar
½ cup butter
2 sqs. melted chocolate
1 tsp. vanilla
½ cup pecans
3 beaten egg yolks
Vanilla wafers
½ gal. vanilla ice cream

Cream sugar and butter together. Add melted chocolate. Beat egg yolks and add to chocolate mixture.
Fold in stiffly beaten egg whites. Line 9 x 13"
pan with ½ box vanilla wafers. Pour chocolate mixture over wafers. Spread ice cream (softened) on
top of chocolate mixture. Sprinkle with crumbs and
pecans. Cover with foil and freeze.

Barbara Ball

+ + + + +

HOT FUDGY PUDDING

[Delicious! and no eggs!]

1 cup flour
2 tsps. baking powder
1 tsp. salt
2/3 cup sugar
2 tbls. cocoa
½ cup milk
2 tbls. melted shortening
1 tsp. vanilla
½ cup chopped pecans
1 cup brown sugar
4 tbls. cocoa
1½ cups boiling water

Sift dry ingredients together. Add milk, shortening,
vanilla and mix only until smooth. Add ½ cup chopped
pecans. Pour into greased 1-qt. casserole. Mix
brown sugar and cocoa and sprinkle over dough. Pour
boiling water on top. Bake at 350° for 40 minutes.
Serve hot with whipped cream or milk.

Linda Skulte

128

STRAWBERRY SWIRL

1 cup graham cracker crumbs	1 cup boiling water
1 tbl. sugar	½ lb. marshmallows
¼ cup melted butter	½ cup milk
2 cups fresh strawberries	1 cup whipping cream
1 3-oz. pkg. strawberry jello	

Mix crumbs, sugar and butter. Press firmly over
bottom of 9" square baking dish. Chill until set.
Sprinkle 2 tbls. sugar over fresh berries--let stand
½ hour. Dissolve jello in boiling water. Drain
berries, reserving juice. Add water to juice to
make 1 cup, add to jello. Chill until partially
set. Meanwhile, combine marshmallows and milk.
Heat and stir until marshmallows melt. Cool thoroughly, then fold in whipped cream. Add berries to
jello, then swirl in marshmallow mixture to marble.
Pour into crust. Chill until set.

                                        Barbara Ball

+ + + + +

RICH'S STRAWBERRY DELIGHT
[A strawberry cheese cake dessert]

Prepare graham cracker crust:
    1½ cups graham cracker crumbs (8 full crackers)
    ¼ cup sugar
    ½ cup melted butter or margarine
Mix well, press into 8" square pan. Refrigerate
until firm.
Cheesecake filling:
    1 8-oz. pkg. cream cheese (slightly softened)
    1 cup powdered sugar
Mix together. Then fold in 2 cups (1 pkg.) prepared
Dream Whip topping. Place filling over firm graham
cracker crust. Refrigerate while making the straw-
berry glaze.
Strawberry Glaze:
    1 pkg. (sm.) strawberry jello
    1 cup boiling water
    1 pkg. (10 oz.) frozen strawberries
Dissolve jello in boiling water. Add frozen straw-
berries and stir until berries separate and mixture
thickens. Spoon over top of cheesecake filling.
Chill until glaze is firm--about 1 hour or more.
Serves 9 generously

                                        Bonnie Skinner

APRICOT-ORANGE CHEESECAKE

1 crumb crust
1 pkg. (8-oz.) cream cheese
1 can (15-oz.) sweetened condensed milk
1/3 cup lemon juice
½ tsp. orange extract
8 canned whole apricots, well drained; reserve syrup

Beat cheese until fluffy. Gradually add condensed
milk, beating until well blended. Beat in lemon
juice and flavoring. Pour into 9" crumb shell and
chill 2-3 hours. Arrange apricots on top of cake and
cover with glaze. Chill 1-2 hours.
GLAZE: In small saucepan mix ¼ cup sugar, 1½ tbls.
cornstarch and dash of salt. Stir in ½ cup each
apricot syrup and strained orange juice. Mix until
smooth. Cook, stirring, until thick and clear; cool.

+ + + + +

CHERRY-CHEESE DELIGHT

16 graham crackers, crushed
 (or 1½ cups graham cracker crumbs)
¼ cup powdered sugar
1/3 cup butter or margarine, melted

Mix together and press on bottom and sides of 8 x 12"
baking dish. Place in refrigerator until firm.
FILLING:
1 8-oz. pkg. cream cheese
1 cup powdered sugar
1 envelope Dream Whip, whipped as directed on pkg.

Soften cheese and beat in sugar. Add Dream Whip and
beat until creamy. Spread on crust. Refrigerate for
24 hours. Before serving, spread with Comstock
Cherry Pie Filling (or strawberry or blueberry pie
filling may be used).
                                    Suzie Brenneman

DELICIOUS CHEESECAKE TARTS

2 8-oz. pkg. cream cheese
½ cup sugar
2 eggs
1 tsp. vanilla
Fruit pie filling

Blend cream cheese with sugar, eggs and vanilla.
Beat until smooth. Place a vanilla wafer in each
paper muffin cup. Fill cups 2/3 full with cream
cheese mixture. Bake at 400° for 10 minutes. After
cool, top with fruit pie filling. Refrigerate.
(if you don't have vanilla wafers, use 1½ cups
graham cracker crumbs mixed with ¼ cup butter,
melted. Put one teaspoonful in each muffin cup.)

Donna Lou Gaunt

+ + + + +

BLUEBERRY CHEESE SQUARES

1 roll prepared cookie dough   1 egg
  (lemon, butterscotch, etc.) ½ tsp. vanilla
8-oz. cream cheese   1 can blueberry pie
1 cup sour cream   filling
¼ cup sugar

Slice cookies in ¼" slices. Overlap in bottom of
9 x 13" ungreased pan. Bake at 375° for 12-15 minutes. Allow to cool a few minutes. Meanwhile,
combine cream cheese, sour cream, sugar, egg and
vanilla. Beat until smooth. Pour pie filling over
cookie crust. Pour cream mixture over berries and
bake 25-30 minutes more. Serves 12

Lois Mackey

+ + + + +

CHERRY CHEESE CAKE

1/3 lb. graham crackers   ½ cup butter, melted
¼ cup sugar   2 pkgs. whip cream mix
11 oz. cream cheese   3/4 cup sugar
2 cans cherry pie filling

Roll crackers until fine; mix crumbs, sugar and
butter; line bottom of oblong Pyrex dish. Prepare
whip cream mix according to directions. Soften
cream cheese, add 3/4 cup sugar and beat well; fold
into whipped mix. Pour over cracker layer and chill
until firm. Top with cherry pie filling, refrigerate
until served.

Laurie Killingsworth

KARL DENNISON'S FAVORITE CHEESE CAKE

Prepare crust:
- 1 cup graham crackers
- 3 tbls. butter
- 2 tbls. sugar

Press into pie plate and bake at 350° for 5 minutes.
Filling:
- 3 eggs
- 1 lb. cream cheese
- ½ cup honey

Blend in electric beater or blender. Pour into
crust. Bake at 350° for 30 minutes. Sprinkle
with 2 tsps. cinnamon and cover with topping:
1 cup sour cream mixed with 2 tsps. sugar and 2 tsps.
vanilla. Bake 5 minutes more.

Ginger Gabriel

+ + + + +

MIRACLE CHEESE CAKE

1 sm. pkg. lemon jello
1 cup boiling water
3 tbls. lemon juice
1 8-oz. pkg. cream cheese
1 cup sugar
1 tsp. vanilla
1 can chilled Topic

Graham cracker crust: Mix about 1 3/4 cups crushed
crackers and ¼ cup margarine with 1 tbl. water and
½ tsp. cinnamon.

Dissolve gelatin in boiling water. Add lemon juice.
Cool. Cream together cream cheese, sugar and vanilla.
Add gelatin and mix well. Fold whipped Topic into
gelatin mixture. Pack 2/3 of crust into 9 x 13"
pan, add filling and sprinkle on remaining crumbs.
Chill several hours.

Linda Bond

GLAMOROUS ANGEL FOOD CAKE DESSERT

1 cup powdered sugar
1 can (16 oz.) crushed pineapple, drained
1 can (2½ cups) fruit cocktail, drained
(reserve juice)
2 envelopes plain gelatin
½ cup cold water
3 beaten egg whites
1 pt. whipping cream or 1 large Dream Whip
Marschino cherries and nuts if desired

Combine powdered sugar, drained pineapple and drained
fruit cocktail. Dissolve gelatin in cold water and
add heated fruit cocktail juice. Cool. When it
starts to thicken, fold in beaten egg whites and
whipped cream. Add drained fruit and marschino cherries and nut meats. Cut or tear large angel food
cake, place in large pan and add above mixture over
cake pieces, stirring lightly. Leave in refrigerator
2 hours. Cut in squares. Use large Pyrex dish to
refrigerate.

Nellie Daniels

+ + + + +

ORANGE CHARLOTTE

[A lovely, light dessert especially delicious after
a heavy dinner]

1 cup boiling water
1 env. Knox gelatin
4 tbls. cold water
1 cup sugar
1 cup orange juice
Juice of one lemon
1 pint whipping cream
1 angel food cake, broken in bite-size pieces

Dissolve gelatin in cold water. Pour boiling water
over it. Add sugar, orange juice and lemon juice
while hot. Mix thoroughly. Set in refrigerator or
freezer until it is quite stiff. Whip cream; fold
into gelatin mixture along with the pieces of cake.
Pour into 9 x 12" pan. Set in refrigerator at least
1 hour. The longer it sets, the better it is.
Serves 12

Kathy Shulman

SNOWBALL CAKE

[All the men love this one!]

2 envelopes Knox gelatin
½ cup cold water
1 cup boiling water
1 cup sugar
1 can (#2) crushed pineapple
8-10 oz. marschino cherries
3 pkgs. Dream Whip
1 Angel Food Cake
1 pkg. fresh or frozen coconut

Dissolve gelatin in cold water; add boiling water and sugar, stirring until completely dissolved. Add crushed pineapple and cherries (cut in halves). Refrigerate until mixture begins to thicken (but not firm). Whip 2 pkgs. Dream Whip. When gelatin mixture begins to thicken, fold in Dream Whip. Break cake into small pieces and place in greased tube pan alternately with the gelatin mixture, beginning with gelatin mixture and ending with cake. Return to refrigerator until cake has become firm (preferably overnight). Turn cake out and top with third pkg. of Dream Whip and coconut. Serve.

Sherri Sykula

ORANGE ANGEL FOOD DESSERT

1 loaf angel food cake
1 sm. pkg. orange jello
1 pint orange sherbet
1 cup whipping cream
2 sm. cans Mandarin oranges
1 can Angel Flake coconut

Dissolve jello in 1 cup hot water, add juice from 1 can oranges, chill until cool but not set. Add sherbet, stir until mushy. Refrigerate while whipping cream. Combine whipped cream and drained oranges. Place a layer of cake in a 9 x 13" Pyrex pan. Add jello mixture, then whipped cream mixture. Top with coconut and refrigerate several hours before serving. May be made a day ahead. Serves 10-12

Connie Van Maanen

134

CREAM PUFFS

½ cup water   ½ cup sifted flour
¼ cup margarine   2 eggs

Put water and margarine into heavy 1-qt. saucepan.
Heat to boiling, melting margarine; reduce heat to
very low. Add flour all at once. Stir until mixture leaves sides of pan, looks dry and forms a
ball. Remove from heat; cool 10 minutes. Add eggs,
one at a time; beat well after each addition. Beat
until mixture is smooth. Drop from tablespoon onto
ungreased baking sheet. Bake at 400° for 40-45 minutes until puffs are dry. Carefully cut off top of
each puff. When cool, fill with cream filling.
Sprinkle top with powdered sugar, chocolate sauce,
or whipped cream, etc. Makes 4 large or 6 medium
puffs.

CREAM PUFF FILLING

1/3 cup sugar   1 egg yolk
¼ cup flour   ½ tsp. vanilla
1/8 tsp. salt   ¼ cup whipping cream
1 cup milk

Combine dry ingredients in heavy 1-qt. saucepan. Stir
in milk gradually; cook over medium heat. Stir constantly until mixture thickens and boils. Stir some
hot mixture into slightly beaten egg yolk. Pour back
into remaining hot mixture. Cook, stirring, over low
heat 1 minute. Cool, covered; add vanilla; fold in
whipped cream. Fill cooled puffs. Enough filling
for 6 medium cream puffs.

Denise Kiser

+ + + + +

LEFSE
(Scandinavian)

5 large potatoes   3 tbls. butter
½ cup sweet cream   2½ cups flour
1 tsp. salt

Boil potatoes, mash very fine and add cream, butter
and salt. Beat until light and let cool. Add flour.
Roll a piece of dough as for pie crust, rolling as
thin as possible. Bake on top of stove or on a pancake griddle until light brown, turning frequently
to prevent scorching. Use moderate heat. When baked,
place between a clean cloth to keep from becoming
dry. The next day, spread butter on crusts, sprinkle
with sugar and roll up. Or may serve immediately
after removing from stove. (Best this way.)

Gail Palmquist

EGG CUSTARD

[Great to make the day before for a nutritious quick breakfast!]

4 eggs, separated
1/3 cup sugar
¼ tsp. salt
2 cups milk, scalded
1 tsp. vanilla

Beat egg yolks, sugar and salt slightly to mix.
Stir in scalded milk. Add vanilla. Bake in 1½-qt.
baking dish in a pan of hot water. Sprinkle nutmeg
on top. Bake at 350⁰ for 45-50 minutes or until edge
is set. Whip egg whites until stiff and glossy.
Add 1/3 to 1/2 cup sugar and 1 tsp. vanilla. Spread
over custard. Bake at 400⁰ until brown. Cool away
from drafts.

Sue Smith

+ + + + +

DANISH CREME

1½ cups milk
¼ cup sugar
½ tsp. salt
2/3 cup minute rice
1 tsp. vanilla
¼ cup chopped almonds
½ cup whipping cream
Bing cherry sauce

Boil milk, sugar, salt and minute rice uncovered for
8 minutes. Fluff rice occasionally. Remove from
heat, cover tightly. Let stand 10 minutes. Add
almonds and vanilla. Cover and chill. Whip cream,
fold into rice mixture. Serve with sauce: Drain
1 can (17-oz.) pitted cherries. Add enough water to
syrup to make 1½ cups. Blend syrup, 2 tbls. cornstarch and a dash of salt. Cook and stir until
thickened and clear. Add cherries, 1 tsp. lemon
juice and if desired, ½ tsp. almond extract.
Serves 6

+ + + + +

PINK CLOUD DESSERT

1 sm. pkg. strawberry gelatin
1½ cups boiling water
2 tbls. lemon juice
1 cup evaporated milk, chilled icy cold
2 cups (4-oz.) miniature marshmallows
¼ cup chopped walnuts
¼ cup sliced maraschino cherries
1 cup graham cracker crumbs
2 tbls. butter, melted

Stir gelatin into boiling water until completely
dissolved. Cool until consistency of unbeaten egg
white. Pour chilled milk into deep bowl and whip
until stiff. Fold whipped milk into gelatin.
Carefully fold in marshmallows, nuts and cherries.
Mix crumbs with melted butter. Spread half of crumb
mixture over bottom of 8 or 9" square pan. Carefully
spoon in gelatin mixture. Sprinkle remaining crumbs
over top. Chill until set--1-2 hours.

Sue Smith

+ + + + +

CARAMEL FLAN

1¼ cups sugar   2 cans (13-oz.) evaporated milk
6 tbls. water   2 tsp. vanilla
6 eggs

Combine ½ cup sugar and water in small saucepan over
medium heat, stirring constantly until sugar dis-
solves. Continue cooking until syrup turns golden
brown. Pour into 8-cup ring mold. Quickly turn and
tip mold to coat bottom and sides. Beat eggs slightly in bowl, stir in remaining 3/4 cup sugar, evaporated milk, vanilla. Strain into prepared mold.
Set mold in baking pan on oven shelf--pour boiling
water in pan to depth of 1 inch. Bake at 350° for
1 hour or until custard is set. Remove at once from
pan of water. Cool. Chill 3 hours. When ready to
serve, loosen custard around edge and center ring
with knife. Cover with serving plate - turn upside
down, let it stand several minutes until syrup runs
down. (This can be doubled and baked in large
Bundt pan.)

Barbara Ball

CHINESE ALMOND JELLY

2 pkgs. unflavored gelatin   2/3 cup sugar
1 cup water   1 tsp. almond extract
2 cups scalded milk

Soften gelatin in water. Dissolve sugar in scalded
milk; add to gelatin mixture. Stir in almond extract. Chill until firm. Cut into ½" cubes and
serve with chilled fruit cocktail as topping.
Serves 6

                                    Lana Jones

+ + + + +

FRENCH CREME

ANGEL CRUST:
      6 egg whites, beaten stiff
      2 cups sugar, add gradually to egg whites and
          continue beating
Add: 2 tsps. vinegar
      2 tsps. baking powder
      2 tsps. vanilla
Fold in:
      24 double soda crackers, crushed
      ½ cup chopped nuts
Pour into buttered 9 x 13" pan. Bake at 350° until
browned, about 20-30 minutes.
FILLING: Beat 1 8-oz. pkg. cream cheese with 1 cup
powdered sugar. Add 1 pkg. Dream Whip, prepared
according to directions on box. Beat until it holds
shape. Spread on cooled Angel Crust. Spread 1 can
prepared pie filling (cherry, raspberry, or blueberry) over cream mixture. Refrigerate. Serves 10-12

                              Charlotte Melcher

+ + + + +

CHOCOLATE MINT DESSERT

[A favorite company dessert - guys love it!]

20 Oreo cookies, crushed 3 drops peppermint flavoring
25 large marshmallows   1 cup whipping cream
½ cup milk   Green or pink food coloring
½ tsp. vanilla

Melt marshmallows and milk in sauce pan. Add mint and
coloring. Cool. Whip cream, add vanilla. Fold
marshmallow mixture into whipped cream. Pour mixture
over half the Oreos in bottom of 8" square pan.
Sprinkle rest of Oreos on top. Chill.

                              Carole Samms

FORGOTTEN CAKE

[Really a meringue shell filled with fruit]

5 egg whites
½ tsp. cream of tartar
1/8 tsp. salt
1½ cups sugar
1 tsp. vanilla

Beat whites, cream of tartar and salt until whites
hold peaks. Gradually add sugar, then vanilla.
Grease and flour 8" Pyrex baking dish and pour in
mixture. Pre-heat oven to 450°; place meringue in
oven, turn oven off and leave overnight. Three or
four hours before serving, whip 1½ cups whipping
cream and spread over meringue. Refrigerate. Serve
topped with your favorite fresh or frozen fruit.

Vonette Bright

+ + + + +

JELLO-PUDDING BOSTON CREAM PIE

[A yummy, easy dessert for entertaining]

1 (5-oz.) pkg. vanilla or banana cream pudding mix
2 1/3 cups milk
1 sq. unsweetened chocolate
½ cup prepared Dream Whip
    (or ¼ cup heavy cream, whipped)
1 baked, cooled 8 or 9" yellow cake layer

Combine pudding mix and milk in saucepan. Cook,
stirring over medium heat until full boil. Remove
from heat. Combine 1 cup hot pudding with chocolate
and butter, stirring until melted. Cover surface of
both chocolate and plain pudding with plastic wrap
and chill. Beat plain pudding until smooth, then
blend in whipped cream. Split layer cake in half to
make 2 layers. Place one on plate, spread with plain
pudding; top with second layer. Beat chocolate
pudding until smooth. Spread over top of cake. Chill
1 hour.

Nan McCullough

MINT SAUCE FOR MELON BALLS

[Good for melon-ball cocktail or summer dessert]

½ cup sugar
3/4 tbl. cornstarch
½ cup boiling water
1 tbl. butter
1½ tsps. chopped mint leaves
1/8 tsp. salt

Mix sugar, cornstarch and salt. Add boiling water,
butter, and mint leaves. Cook, stirring until smooth
and clear. Add a few drops of green food coloring.
Chill. Combine with melon balls just before serving.
Garnish with sprig of mint. The sauce will keep
refrigerated for several weeks. It will become
thick but you may add a little water to thin before
serving.

Charlotte Day

+ + + + +

FRESH FRUIT SAUCE

[For apple, peach, pear, plum or rhubarb sauce]

4 cups washed, peeled, cut-up fruit
1 cup boiling water
½ cup to 1 cup sugar
Dash salt
½ tsp. lemon juice
¼ tsp. grated lemon rind
1/8 tsp. cinnamon or nutmeg

Prepare fruit and add to boiling water in saucepan.
Simmer until nearly tender. Stir in sugar, salt, also
(if desired) lemon juice, grated lemon rind and spice.
Cook until fruit is tender.

Doris Rood

+ + + + +

LEMON SAUCE

1 cup sugar   1 well-beaten egg
½ cup butter   3 tbls. lemon juice
¼ cup water   1 tbl. grated lemon peel

Mix together and cook, stirring constantly until
mixture comes to a boil. (Reserve extra, refrigerate
and use as a topping on toast!)

Barbara Edwards

FUDGE SAUCE

½ cup butter
2¼ cups powdered sugar
2/3 cup evaporated milk
3 sqs. bitter chocolate

Mix butter and sugar in top of double boiler. Add milk and chocolate. Cook over hot water for 30 minutes. Do not stir while cooking. Remove from heat and beat. It may be stored in refrigerator and reheated as needed. Thin with cream.

Carol Williams

+ + + + +

CHOCOLATE SAUCE

[Very good, but not good for you!]

1 cup sugar
1 sm. can evaporated milk
¼ cup margarine
Boil above mixture together for 1 minute. Add:
2 sqs. unsweetened chocolate
½ tsp. vanilla
Dash salt
Beat until smooth. Good over ice cream.

Patty Roth

+ + + + +

ALMOND PRALINE SAUCE

3 tbls. butter
2 tbls. slivered almonds
1 cup brown sugar
¼ cup light corn syrup
Dash of salt
½ cup evaporated milk

Melt 1 tablespoon butter in saucepan. Add almonds. Saute' until lightly browned. Add 2 tablespoons butter, sugar, corn syrup and salt. Cook over low heat stirring constantly until sugar is thoroughly dissolved. Slowly blend in evaporated milk. Cool. Serve over coffee ice cream and orange sherbet.

Judy Anderson

FOR HEALTHIER EATING HABITS:

"Know ye not that your body is the temple of the Holy
Ghost which is in you, which ye have of God, and ye
are not your own? For ye are bought with a price;
therefore glorify God in your body, and in your
spirit which are God's" (I Corinthians 6:19-20).

Use liquid shortening (cooking oil) as much as
possible rather than the hydrogenated (solid) short-
enings.

Add approximately ¼ cup wheat germ to cold cereal, and
all batters - muffins, pancakes, waffles, bread, etc.
using slightly less flour than recipe calls for.

Use whole wheat bread exclusively. White bread short-
changes you on vitamins and minerals, even though
enriched.

If serving cold cereal for breakfast (this is almost
"empty" of nutrition, except for the milk,of course),
serve cheese toast with it (a square of cheese on
bread, heated under the broiler). This really "holds"
the kids until lunch.

Use non-hydrogenated peanut butter. One nutritionist
says the hydrogenation process makes the protein
unavailable to your body. Laura Scudders is a good
brand - "peanuts and salt, that's all." (Gwen Martin)

"Pleasant words are like a honeycomb, sweet to the
soul and health to the bones" (Proverbs 16:24).

Serve eggs every other day for breakfast - cuts down
on cholesterol. Have cooked cereal; very hearty and
economical. Oro wheat makes a seven-grain cereal
that even the fussiest man will eat! Oatmeal with
raisins or dates is delicious. If you use cold
cereal, Wheat Chex is a good one.   (Nan Green)

Adding non-fat dry milk to casseroles is an inexpensive way of supplying added protein to the diet.

Pork is full of good nutrition. In addition to pro-
tein, it is a major source of iron and vitamin B.
Fish is a high-quality protein food, with plenty of
B vitamins and vitamin D.

To meet necessary calcium requirements, serve children
3-4 glasses of milk a day, teenagers 4 glasses, and
adults 2 glasses.   (Candace Steele)

142

MORE HEALTH HINTS:

Use honey for sweetening all fruits, also in tea and
coffee and in cereal. Use honey butter on toast,
pancakes, rolls, etc. Make honey butter by combining
butter, honey and wheat germ. Blend until smooth.
(Sandy Davis)

Add extra eggs and powdered milk to pancakes or
waffle recipes to give added nutritional value.

Add a tablespoon of vinegar to the soup as the
vinegar draws the calcium out of the soup bone into
the soup stock. The acid in tomatoes, if added,
will do the same.   (Diane Willis)

On a diet? A pinch of salt will intensify sweetness.
Substitute slightly sweetened sour cream for whipped
cream for dessert topping. Fewer calories.
(Dorothy Gregory)

"If you are willing and obedient, you shall eat the
good of the land" (Isaiah 1:19).

A DIET LIST

The rivers eat away their banks,
The tides devour the sand,
The morning sun drinks up the mists,
The ocean eats the land;
Taxes eat up property,
And pride eats out the soul,—
But moths the diet record hold,
Because they eat a hole!

The following pages of recipes are considered low-
calorie recipes or at least, less fattening than the
average recipe.

"O Lord...Remove far from me falsehood and lies,
give me neither poverty nor riches; feed me with the
food that is needful for me" (Proverbs 30:8).

THINK THIN CANAPES

Clean 8 to 12 carrots and slice them crosswise,
using the portion that will give a good sized disc.
Cover with water and store in refrigerator for a
few hours before using.
TOPPING:
½ cup cottage cheese
2 tsps. sour cream
1 tsp. chives

Keep the cheese at room temperature for an hour
and then put it through a sieve or blender so that
it is creamed. Blend the cheese, sour cream and
chives thoroughly. Spread this mixture on the
carrot discs and top each disc with a dram of caviar,
a caper, a rolled anchovy or just some seasoned
salt. Calorie content: negligible!

Lana Jones

+ + + + +

THINK THIN SANDWICHES

Instead of bread, use cheese - however, leave the
cheese uncovered in the refrigerator so that it
dries out and becomes firm. Then for a carbohydrate-
free sandwich you can use the following fillers:

Swiss cheese with ham, mustard, tomato and
lettuce - 335 calories.

Sweet Muenster cheese with chicken brushed with
Russian dressing, dill pickle and lettuce -
300 calories

American cheese brushed with mayonnaise, sliced
egg, capers, lettuce and tomato - 280 calories

Swiss cheese with ½ tart apple, peeled and sliced
250 calories

Edam cheese with English mustard (DiJon), sliced
meat loaf and lettuce - 350 **calories**

American cheese with cottage cheese with seasoned salt, sliced bermuda onion, tomato, cucumber, green pepper slivers and lettuce - 250
calories

Sweet Muenster cheese with tuna fish salad,
sliced radishes and lettuce - 300 calories

Swiss cheese with roast beef, sliced pickled
beets, bermuda onion and lettuce - 300 calories

Lana Jones

STUFFED PEPPERS

1 cup canned tomatoes
2 eggs
1 cup okra, cooked
2 cups cooked ground meat
1 cup raw celery
¼ cup raw cabbage, finely diced
1 onion, chopped
Salt
6 bell peppers

Steam peppers until tender; place in cold water to
chill. Remove stems and seeds. Stuff with the
remaining mixture and bake 20 minutes at 400° without covering.

Evelyn Bromberg

+ + + + +

STUFFED CABBAGE

1 large head of cabbage
3 onions
Veal knuckles or beef bones
1 can (#2½) tomatoes
1 lb. ground beef (lean)
3 tsps. salt
1 egg, beaten
4 tbls. lemon juice
1 tsp. sucaryl (liquid)

Cover cabbage with water, bring to a boil and cook
10 minutes. Drain carefully; separate 12 leaves.
Slice 2 onions and combine in a heavy saucepan with
the bones, tomatoes and sucaryl. Cook over medium
heat while preparing the cabbage rolls. Grate the
remaining onion and combine with beef. Add egg,
salt and pepper. Mix well. Place heaping tablespoon
of mixture on each cabbage leaf. Roll up and hold
with tooth pick. Arrange in tomato mixture. Cook
over low heat 1 hour. 100 calories per roll.

Evelyn Bromberg

SHRIMP CREOLE

3 med.-sized onions, peeled and sliced
½ cup chopped green peppers
1 can (3/4-oz.) chopped mushrooms
½ tsp. salt
¼ tsp. paprika
¼ tsp. curry powder
1/8 tsp. pepper
1 can stewed tomatoes (1 lb.)
Non calorie sweetener to equal 2 tsps. sugar
3 cans (5-oz. each) deveined shrimp

Put all ingredients in large frying pan (except
shrimp). Heat slowly, stirring constantly to boiling; simmer 10 minutes more, stir in shrimp, simmer
10 minutes more or until heated through.

Evelyn Bromberg

+ + + + +

CHOP SUEY

6 oz. of beef, chicken or shrimp
2 med. tomatoes
1 finely chopped onion
4 large celery sticks cut in squares (use generously)
½ chopped green pepper
2 cups bean sprouts (use generously)

Slice meat thin. Brown it in a dry pan. Add
tomatoes, onions, celery, green pepper and very
little water. Parboil bean sprouts in separate pan
and add these last. Flavor with soy sauce, but no
extra seasoning. Enough for 2 servings

Dorothy Gregory

+ + + + +

VEAL ALA BASIL

8 oz. veal cutlets
1/8 tsp. pepper
2 tbls. lemon juice
½ tsp. basil leaves
½ tsp. salt
2 tbls. vinegar
1 tbl. parsley flakes

Season veal with salt and pepper. Brown meat in pan
over high heat, using no fat. Add remaining ingredients. Cover. Simmer over low heat until meat is
tender, about 6 minutes.

Evelyn Bromberg

GROUND BEEF CASSEROLE

1 lb. ground round, lean
5 tomatoes, quartered
½ lb. string beans, cut up
1 large green pepper
6 stalks celery, chopped
¼ lb. mushrooms
1 medium head cabbage, red, white, or mixed, chopped

Cook all ingredients until tender. Season with salt substitute and Accent. One cup = approximately 200 calories

Evelyn Bromberg

+ + + + +

BARBECUE SAUCE

2 cups tomato juice
6 tsps. Worcestershire sauce
5 tbls. soy sauce
2-4 packets of artificial sugar

Simmer all ingredients until thickened - about 20 minutes. Good on fish, chicken or to marinate roasts. For hamburger too!

Evelyn Bromberg

+ + + + +

CELERY SAUCE
[for meat or vegetables]

2 cups celery
Water
1 pkg. chicken bouillon
1 pkg. onion bouillon
Dash salt and pepper

Cut celery with leaves into 1" pieces to yield 2 cups. Cover with water in large saucepan. Cook uncovered until celery is tender and liquid reduced to 1 cup. A few minutes before removing from heat, add bouillon. Blend and season to taste.

Dorothy Gregory

+ + + + +

MUSHROOM SOUP

1/3 cup skim milk
1 cup water
1 beef bouillon
Salt and pepper
1 can Mushrooms with liquid

Mix ingredients and heat.

Dorothy Gregory

BAKED APPLES

Wash and core apples. Slit and peel 1/3 of the way
down. Place apples in a Pyrex dish and pour non-
caloric black cherry soda over them. Sprinkle with
cinnamon and artificial sweetener and bake in moderate oven at 375⁰ until apples are tender - about
50 minutes.

Evelyn Bromberg

+ + + + +

THOUSAND ISLAND DRESSING

½ cup lemon juice
¼ cup V-8 juice
¼ cup water
1/8 tsp. vinegar
2 tsps. diced dill pickles
½ tsp. tabasco sauce
1 egg yolk
1 egg white

Beat egg yolk; add all other ingredients but the egg
white. Cook until almost thick and add slightly
beaten egg white. Mix and store in refrigerator.
If too tart, add non-caloric sweetener.

Evelyn Bromberg

+ + + + +

YOGURT DRESSING FOR REDUCERS

½ cup yogurt
½ cup tomato juice
Few drops honey
Few drops lemon juice
Pinch of salt

Beat all ingredients together. Serve with any raw
or cooked vegetable salad. Vary by including chopped
green olives, watercress, chives, dill, parsley or
minced garlic. Serves 8-10

+ + + + +

DIET ICE CREAM

2 cans condensed milk
1 can water
Any type fresh fruit or flavoring

Mix together and pour in freezer tray. Fill remaining space to 3/4 full with whole milk. (This recipe doesn't call for sugar or eggs, therefore isn't as rich as some. It is sweet enough with condensed milk.)

Dorothy Gregory

+ + + + +

LO-CAL SHERBET

Put one layer of frozen, unsweetened berries, (strawberries, boysenberries, blueberries) into ice cube tray; pour buttermilk over berries, almost covering. Sprinkle artificial sweetener on top (to taste) and a few drops vanilla. Freeze only 30 minutes. (Do not freeze longer - it will become too hard.) Mash it up and eat! Delish!

Diane Willis

+ + + + +

DIETARY JELLO DESSERT

Mix:
Any diet jello (except cherry)
With any diet fruit (except cherries)
Fold in D-Zerta whipped topping

Diane Willis

+ + + + +

TAPIOCA PUDDING

1 egg
Artificial sweetener to equal 1/3 cup sugar
3 tbls. quick tapioca
1/8 tsp. salt
2 3/4 cup milk (made from non-fat powdered)
1 tsp. vanilla

Mix together and let stand 5 minutes. Cook over medium heat, stirring constantly until thick. Remove and add vanilla.

Dorothy Gregory

MILK SHAKE

1/3 cup powdered non-fat milk
1/3 cup water
½ capful flavoring extract
2-3 packets granulated sugar substitute (to taste)
½ tray ice cubes

Place milk, water, extract and sweetener in blender.
Add ice cubes one at a time. When ice is crushed,
blend on low speed for 5 minutes.

Evelyn Bromberg

+ + + + +

SWITZEL

A refreshing drink for hot weather is old-fashioned
Switzel, made by adding a small amount (½ - 2 tsps.)
apple cider vinegar and a pinch of ginger to a
glass of cold water. In the "olden days" this was
used as a very cooling summertime drink and often
carried to the harvesters working in the fields.
A good rule to follow in the use of Switzel is:
if it tastes good to you, drink it. [This was copied
word for word from an old Moody Cookbook.]

Dorothy Gregory

+ + + + +

HINTS FOR THE MEAT DEPARTMENT

"It is God's gift to man that every one should eat and drink and take pleasure in all his toil" (Ecclesiastes 3:13).

Some stores have a budget-priced section in which they have 20% markdowns on meat that was out on the counter the previous day. This is an especially good way to buy beefsteaks as the "day of aging" improves it. Often ground round or chuck can be found and if still pink- ish, it's fine. Just make it into patties, put in plastic and freeze immediately. Poul- try is never marked down and is unwise to buy old. Other finds may include liverwurst, beef roasts, and beef short ribs or soup bones and sometimes lamb chops. (Nan Green)

Store poultry in coldest part of refrigerator, and for safety's sake cook within 24 hours after purchasing. Wash under cold water and rewrap before refrigeration. (Candace Steele)

Instead of greasing a skillet for hamburgers, sprinkle the bottom lightly with salt and the hamburgers will fry in their own juices. (Midge Piedot)

For time-saving convenience make two meat loaves. Freeze one for later; use in sand- wiches or a "lazy-day" lunch. (Candace Steele)

Since you spend a good part of your food money on meat, it will help to know as much as you can about choosing it, storing it and prepar- ing it. As far as the amount of meat you'll need goes, use this is a guide:

Per serving:
boneless meat (e.g. ground beef), 1/4 lb.
bone-in meat (e.g. chops), 1/2 lb.
boney meat (e.g. spareribs), 3/4 to 1 lb.
When you're trying to figure out the best value, work it out to cost per serving rather than cost per pound.

Purchase a roast with 2 days' meals in mind-- that's thrifty buying! Chuck steak is a good buy any time. When buying ready-to-cook tur-

keys under 12 lb., allow 3/4 to 1 lb. per
serving. Buy a 6-8 lb. turkey to serve 6-10
people. (Candace Steele)

Don't waste molasses, honey or syrups in measuring. Grease the measuring cup lightly and
every drop will pour out. (Dorothy Gregory)

Price isn't everything. You can add variety
to your meals by looking for cuts such as
chuck or flank which are just as nutritious as
the more expensive cuts. They can also be as
tender and flavorsome. It's all in how you
cook them, slowly, simmering in a delicious
sauce.

Fish for compliments. Remember that fish is a
good low-cost source of protein. For best results, use a moderate temperature and don't
overcook it. Since fish deteriorates rapidly,
it should be cooked as soon as possible after
you buy it.

Poultry, which you can get all year round,
always is a good buy. When buying chicken or
turkey, figure on 1/4 to 1/2 pound per serving,
depending on the size of your family's appe-
tite.

Experiment with noodles, all shapes and sizes.
They can give you good variety and they help
share the cost of meat.

Every once in a while use cheese, nuts or eggs
instead of meat. According to nutritionists
you can do this without sacrifice to a balanced
diet.

If you have the freezer capacity, buy ground
beef at bulk special prices. Divide into two
serving packages or hamburger patties and
freeze.

BEEF HINTS: Beef-vegetable soup or stew is
very hearty and economical. Buy beef short
ribs or neck bones rather than a soup bone.
The cost is only slightly higher and there is
more meat and flavor. If pieces are quite

meaty, stew can be made from them. Cut-up stew meat is very expensive--do it yourself with a chuck roast or with the above. For a delicious, tender roast, buy a cheaper cut, salt it, add onion slices and wrap air-tight in foil. Bake in low temperature oven for several hours. An hour and a half before dinner, you can add potatoes and carrots and a small amount of liquid if needed. Move temperature to 350°. The secret is baking it slowly in its own juices. The same procedure can be used for pork and lamb roasts.

CHICKEN HINTS: Look for chicken on sale and buy several. Cut them up that day and place the number of pieces needed for one meal in a plastic bag and freeze. Place the back, ribs and necks in plastic bags and use for soup. Cook in 1-2 quarts of salted water until tender, cool, cut off pieces into broth, add noodles or rice, seasonings such as poultry seasoning and celery salt, diced onion, celery and carrots. Simmer until done. (Uncooked items can be added, if chicken is taken out to cool, to cook at a faster pace.) Very good soup, economical with no fillers or preservatives! Note--white looking chickens are usually from out of state and have been packed in a chemical which makes them white. Look for plump, yellow chickens and buy the heaviest ones. (Bone size is usually the same, and heavy ones contain more meat.) Chicken livers are one of the highest sources for iron and protein of all liver. They are very economical because there is no bone or waste. Fry 2 slices of bacon in pan, then add chicken livers and brown. Salt and simmer for a short time; don't overcook. Delicious!

PORK HINTS: Pork is plentiful, therefore it is usually a good buy. Buy pork loin roast when it's on special. Chop it into pork chops yourself. This is cheaper than having the butcher do it for you.

Buy ham when the price is relatively low for the shank portion. Look for a small bone and an average size you can use up in 2 weeks; it

is smoked and will keep in the refrigerator.
Freezing loses some flavor. Use slab for
baking, use chunks for New England boiled dinner (very easy, colorful and tasty), cubes in
eggs, slices for sandwiches and the bone with
small amount of meat on it for delicious split
pea soup or navy bean soup. These hearty
soups can also be made with bacon or economical ham seasoning pieces you may find. Carrots
and celery are good with the pea soup and
celery with the bean--both having onion and
celery salt.

PORK HINTS (continued): Buy pork roast when
it is reasonably priced for a loin or rib
portion. Ask the butcher to slice part of the
roast into the number of pork chops your family needs and use the other part for a pork
roast. You can also have additional slices
made to cut up for chop suey meat. Packaged
chop suey meat and pork chops are very expensive. Simply cut up the meat and place in
plastic bag for future chop suey and likewise
package pork chops and roast section--put in
freezer. When making chop suey, buy bean
sprouts canned or fresh and water chestnuts.
Water chestnuts add a lot and can be found in
a 6-oz. can (part of them can be used and the
rest frozen). Add onion and celery--much more
economical than buying chop suey vegetables.
By the way, brown rice is delicious and much
better for you as is the use of whole wheat
bread, whole wheat flour and brown sugar.

LAMB shoulder roast can be found at a reasonable price and is delicious when baked slowly
in foil. Cheaper cuts of lamb make delicious
stew.

CHICKEN CASSEROLE

1 pint jar chicken
1 sm. pkg. Creamettes macaroni (uncooked)
½ lb. Velveeta cheese
3 hard cooked eggs (cut up)
1 pint milk
2 cups mushroom soup
1 sm. onion (minced)
Salt and pepper to taste
Buttered bread crumbs

Mix together. Sprinkle buttered bread crumbs on top
and bake 1 hour at 350°. Serves 10

Nellie Daniels

+ + + + +

MENNONITE CHICKEN BAKED IN SOUR CREAM

¼ cup margarine
¼ cup flour
1 tsp. salt
Dash pepper
1-2 lb. chicken
Paprika
Pepper
3 tbls. water
1 tbl. flour
¼ tsp. pepper
½ cup sour cream

Place butter in shallow pan; heat to melt butter.
Combine ¼ cup flour, salt and pepper; roll chicken in
mixture until coated. Dip chicken in melted butter
and arrange skin side up in baking pan. Sprinkle with
paprika. Bake at 325° for 1¼ hours until chicken is
tender and nicely browned. Remove chicken from pan
and keep warm. Add water to pan drippings; mix well.
Blend in 1 tbl. flour, ¼ tsp. salt, dash each of
pepper and paprika and ½ cup sour cream. Bring to
a boil, stirring constantly. Remove from heat and
serve over chicken.

Kerry Fix

OLD-COUNTRY CHICKEN AND RICE

1 cut-up frying chicken	1 tsp. salt
1 tbl. margarine	Dash pepper
1 heaping tbl. paprika	1 cup rice (not Minute)
1 sm. onion, chopped	2 tsp. parsley flakes

Wash chicken; put in a saucepan. Barely cover with
water. After it begins to boil, skim the scum from
top. Simmer for 10 minutes. Saute' onions in margarine; add paprika (DO NOT BURN). Place in casserole
dish. Add 2 cups liquid from the boiled chicken.
Add rice, salt, pepper and parsley. Arrange chicken
on top. Bake at 350° for 1 hour or until liquid is
taken up. Serves 4

Nancy Olsen

+ + + + +

CHICKEN-RICE SUPREME

1 cup rice, uncooked
1 can cream of chicken, celery, or mushroom soup
1 can water
1 pkg. dry onion soup mix
1 chicken, cut-up
    OR 4 halved chicken breasts
½ cup almonds (opt.)

Combine rice, soup, water and onion mix in large
casserole dish. Brown chicken and place on top.
Cover and bake for 1½ hours at 350°. Sprinkle with
almonds. Serves 4

Juanita Sander, Carole Wormser and Betty Marquez

VARIATION: Pour 1 can golden mushroom soup on top.
Bake 2 hours covered, ½ hour uncovered at 350°.

Nancy Robinson

VARIATION: Use 1 2/3 cups uncooked Minute rice instead of 1 cup raw rice. Add chopped green pepper for
color.

Jacquie Tanner

VARIATION: Use milk instead of water. Do not brown
chicken. Season chicken and arrange skin side up on
rice mixture. Brush with 3 tbls. melted margarine.
Bake uncovered at 325° for 1 hour. Sprinkle with
Parmesan cheese during last half hour. You may want
to add diced celery, or carrots and peas for color.
Cranberry salad and hot rolls go perfectly with
this dish.

Jan Scholes

CHICKEN FLORENTINE

12 drumsticks or thighs, 6 breasts
1 pkg. Shake 'N Bake or similar mix
2 pkgs. frozen chopped spinach
2 tbls. butter or margarine
1 cup sour cream
½ cup Parmesan cheese
½ cup grated cheddar cheese

Toss chicken in seasoned mix and bake 30-40 minutes
at 400°. Meanwhile, cook spinach until thawed.
Drain very well and toss with margarine. Place chick-
en on top of spinach in baking dish. Spoon over top
the blended sour cream and cheeses. Place under
broiler about 5 minutes until bubbly and golden.
Serves 6

+ + + + +

FLORENTINE TURKEY

[From the Good Housekeeping Cook Book]

1 (10-oz.) pkg. frozen chopped spinach
Butter or margarine
3 tbls. flour
1 tsp. M.S.G.
1 tsp. salt
Dash cayenne pepper
1½ cups milk
¼ cup Parmesan cheese, grated
½ cup light cream
2 cups cooked turkey or chicken in chunks
¼ cup dried bread crumbs

Cook spinach according to label; drain well; arrange
in 1½-qt. casserole. Melt 2 tbls. butter. Stir in
flour, MSG, salt and pepper. Gradually stir in milk.
Boil until thickened, stirring constantly. Add cheese
and cream. Stir over low heat until cheese melts.
Add meat and pour over spinach. Sprinkle with crumbs.
Refrigerate several hours. Dot casserole with butter.
Bake at 350° for 15 minutes. Set under broiler to
lightly brown top. Serves 4

Linda Skulte

CHICKEN DIVAN

1 frying chicken (about 2½ lbs.) split
2 cups water
Salt and pepper
1 pkg. (10-oz.) frozen broccoli spears
2 tbls. butter
3 tbls. flour
Milk
Grated Parmesan cheese

Wash chicken. Simmer chicken, covered, in water with
1 tsp. salt for 45 minutes or until very tender.
Save broth. Remove meat from bones in large pieces;
cut into long slices. Cook broccoli until just
tender; drain and put in shallow casserole. Melt
butter in top part of double boiler; stir in flour.
Measure chicken broth and add enough milk to make
2 cups. Gradually stir into butter and flour. Cook
over boiling water, stirring constantly until thickened. Add seasoning. Cover broccoli with chicken,
then with sauce. Sprinkle with cheese. Bake at 400°
for about 12 minutes. Makes 4 servings.

Diane Yancy

+ + + + +

PINEAPPLE CHICKEN

2 cups uncooked chicken filets (1 x 1" pieces)
½ tsp. salt
1 egg
½ tsp. soy sauce

Mix above ingredients, then dust lightly with cornstarch. Heat 4 tbls. oil in skillet to sizzling
point. Add chicken and deep dry until brown. Drain
on toweling. Drain oil from skillet. In same skillet
place: ½ cup vinegar
       ½ cup sugar
       ¼ tsp. salt
       1/3 cup catsup
       4 drops hot sauce (tabasco)

Cook on medium heat to boiling point, then thicken
with cornstarch paste until medium thick. Add:
       1 cup pineapple chunks
       ½ cup green pepper, sliced (1 x 1" pieces)
       Browned chicken
Toss and mix thoroughly until chicken is heated
through. Serves 4

Rose Marie Obien

CHICKEN SOUFFLE'

[This is a "Southern Living" recipe and is very
good.]

8 slices day-old bread
2 cups (or more) cooked chicken
½ cup mayonnaise
1 cup diced celery
3/4 cup finely chopped onion
3/4 cup finely chopped green pepper
Salt and pepper to taste
4 eggs, beaten
3 cups milk (may use part chicken broth)
1 cup cream of mushroom soup
1 cup grated cheese

Cut 4 slices of the bread into cubes, remove crusts
from other 4 slices. Line bottom of 7 x 10" baking
dish with bread cubes. Combine chicken, mayonnaise,
celery, onion, and pepper--season to taste. Spread
this mixture over bread cubes. Cover with bread
slices. Combine beaten eggs and milk and pour over
bread slices. Cover and place in refrigerator overnight or for several hours. Bake souffle' at 350°
for 15 minutes. Pour undiluted soup over mixture and
bake 30 minutes more. Sprinkle with grated cheese and
bake 15 minutes more. Serve immediately.
10-12 servings

Jeanette Belcher

+ + + + +

GOURMET CHICKEN

3 breasts, split
3 drumsticks
3 thighs
1 can (1-lb.) whole purple plums
Juice of 1 lemon
1 med. onion, chopped
¼ cup chili sauce
¼ cup soy sauce
1 tbl. Worcestershire sauce
1 tsp. ginger
2 tsp. prepared mustard
2 drops tabasco

Arrange chicken in a single layer in a 9 x 13" baking
pan. Seed and puree plums and add to remaining ingredients to make a sauce, and pour over chicken.
Bake at 350° for 1¼ hours. Serves 6

Judy DeBoer

OVEN FRIED CHICKEN

Chicken breasts, halved
Flour
Dixie fry
Salt and pepper
¼ cup margarine, melted
Paprika
1 can cream of mushroom soup
1 can cream of chicken soup
½-1 can half and half or milk

Dip washed chicken into a mixture of equal amounts
of flour and Dixie fry with salt and pepper. Place
on a greased cookie sheet and brush with melted margarine. Sprinkle with paprika. Bake at 325° for 1
hour. Combine rest of ingredients to make a quick
gravy; heat and serve over rice or chicken.

Vonette Bright

+ + + + +

COUNTRY CAPTAIN

2 cans stewed tomatoes
1 can tomato sauce
1 can tomato soup (opt.)
½ cup chopped onion
3/4 cup chopped green pepper
2 sm. jars mushrooms
3/4 tsp. salt
1 tsp. parsley flakes
½ tsp. pepper
½ tsp. curry powder
Fried chicken pieces
3-4 cups cooked rice (rice pilaf)

Combine ingredients and allow to simmer over low heat
approximately 30 minutes to 1 hour. Spread rice over
large serving tray or dish. Place chicken pieces over
rice. Pour tomato sauce over chicken and rice.
Sprinkle 3/4 cup cashew nuts over sauce. Serve hot.
Serves 4-6

Nancy Dordigan

+ + + + +

CRUNCHY, MUNCHY BAKED CHICKEN

Cut up 1 frying chicken; dip pieces in melted butter
or margarine. Roll in crushed potato chips. Bake on
foil-lined baking pan for 1 hour at 350°.

Karla Crawford

CHICKEN MONTE CARLO

5 large chicken breasts
4 pkgs. frozen broccoli
2 cans mushrooms, saute'd in 4 tbls. butter
Parmesan cheese
Pimiento pieces

SAUCE: 2/3 cup melted butter
        1 cup flour
        3 cups chicken broth
        1 tsp. poultry seasoning
        1 tsp. salt
        1½ cups cream or condensed milk

Cook sauce until thickened. Stir often. Partially cook broccoli. Cook chicken until tender; save broth. Remove bones. Place a layer of broccoli on bottom of buttered 2-3 qt. casserole dish. Pour over 1/3 of the sauce, sprinkle with Parmesan cheese. Spread mushrooms over. Add chicken pieces on top. Pour remaining sauce over all. Sprinkle Parmesan cheese on top. Dot with butter and pimiento pieces. Bake at 350° for 1 hour. Serves 8
                                    Louise Shukarian

+ + + + +

FRIED CHICKEN IN MUSHROOM SAUCE

1 2½-lb. fryer, cut up
Salt and pepper
½ cup diced celery
¼ cup green pepper, chopped
1 can cream of mushroom soup
1 can water
¼ cup shortening

Wash and dry fryer, sprinkle with salt and pepper. Brown on all sides in hot shortening. Arrange in baking pan; pour mushroom soup mixture (mixed to smooth consistency with water) over all. Add the celery and green pepper. Bake uncovered at 425° for 1 hour or until tender, basting occasionally with gravy in the pan. Serves 4
                                    Connie Burnside

CHICKEN ITALIANO

2 lbs. chicken parts
2 tbls. shortening
1 can (11-oz.) cheese soup
1 can (8-oz.) tomatoes
2 tbls. chopped onion
1 small, minced garlic clove
1/8 tsp. oregano

Brown chicken. Pour off excess grease. Add all
remaining ingredients. Cover and simmer 45 minutes
or until the chicken is tender. Uncover the last
5 minutes to thicken the sauce. Serves 4

Diane Yancy

+ + + + +

ZIPPY HONEYED CHICKEN

1/3 cup butter   4 tsps. curry powder
½ to 3/4 cup liquid honey   1 fryer cut up or breasts
¼ cup mustard

Melt butter in large shallow pan in oven. Remove from
oven and add honey, mustard and curry; blend well.
Roll chicken in mixture and place meaty side down in
pan. Bake at 375° for 45 minutes, basting; turn and
bake 15 minutes more or until chicken is tender.

+ + + + +

SWEET AND SOUR CHICKEN

Cut-up chicken pieces
½ cup crushed pineapple, including juice
1½ cups brown sugar
½ cup catsup
½ cup vinegar with garlic (or plain vinegar)
2 green peppers, chopped
1 medium onion, chopped
3 stalks celery, chopped

Flour and brown chicken. Put in casserole dish.
Cook onion, celery and green pepper until tender and
crisp. Add pineapple, catsup, sugar and vinegar.
Pour over chicken, cover and cook at 350° until
chicken is tender-approximately 1 hour.

Billie Thurman

CHICKEN TORTILLA CASSEROLE

[This is delicious and can be made several days ahead]

4 chicken breasts, (cook in foil 1 hour at 400°, then skin, bone and sliver
1 can cream of mushroom soup
1 can cream of chicken soup
1 cup milk
2 cans Ortega green chili salsa
½ grated onion (opt.)
8-12 tortillas snipped in small pieces
1 lb. grated sharp cheese

Butter a 9 x 13" pan. Pour a little chicken liquid in bottom of pan. Layer bottom with half of the snipped tortillas. Pour half of the chicken - soup - chili mixture over. Add a layer of half of the cheese. Repeat layers ending with cheese. Refrigerate 24 hours or overnight. Bake at 350° for 45 minutes covered and 30 minutes uncovered. Serves 8

Paula Carter

+ + + + +

CHICKEN SUPREME-TORTILLAS

[A chicken dish guys love!]

1 hen or 2 fryers
1 dozen tortillas (frozen)
1 can cream of mushroom soup
1 can cream of chicken soup
1 tall can evaporated milk
½ cup butter
1 med. onion
1 cup sharp cheese, grated
1 tall can mild chili peppers
Sprinkle with paprika

Cook chicken until tender; cool and tear apart. Saute' onion in butter, adding soups, milk, onions and chilies. Drop tortillas in chicken stock, 2 at a time and soak 2 minutes. Line bottom of sheet cake pan, using 6 tortillas. Put layer of chicken and another layer of tortillas and the rest of chicken. Pour soup mixture over top of all. Lift tortillas lightly to allow mixture to dribble through all the pan. Add grated cheese, sprinkle with paprika. Bake at 325° for 45 minutes.

Bobi Baker

MEXICAN CHICKEN IN ORANGE JUICE

[An excellent company dish]

1 large fryer, disjointed
Salt and pepper
3 tbls. margarine
½ cup sliced almonds
1/3 cup seeded golden raisins
1 cup crushed pineapple, with liquid
1/8 tsp. ground cinnamon
1/8 tsp. ground cloves
2 cups orange juice
1 tbl. flour
2 tbls. cold water
Avocado slice for garnish

Sprinkle the chicken with salt and pepper. Melt
margarine in a large skillet, add chicken and saute'
until the pieces are brown on all sides. Add almonds,
raisins, pineapple, cinnamon, cloves and orange juice.
Cover the skillet tightly and simmer for 45 minutes
or until the chicken is fork tender. Mix the flour
with 2 tbls. cold water to make a smooth paste. Stir
into the pan juice after removing chicken to a warmed
platter. Pour a little of the sauce over the chicken
and serve the remainder in a gravy bowl. Garnish
the chicken platter with slices of avocado and serve
with fluffy rice. Serves 4 (This is a very simple
recipe to quadruple for a buffet supper. Use a dutch
oven instead of a skillet.)
                                    Carol Williams

+ + + + +

FIESTA FRIED CHICKEN

1 young chicken   3/4 tsp. celery salt
1 cup sour cream   ½ tsp. paprika
1 tbl. lemon juice   1 tsp. Worcestershire sauce
2 cloves garlic, crushed   1½ cups flour
½ tsp. salt   ½ cup shortening
3/4 tsp. pepper

Place chicken in Pyrex dish. Combine remaining
ingredients (except flour and shortening) and heat.
Pour over chicken, covering all pieces. Cover dish
and let stand overnight in refrigerator. Drain.
Dredge chicken in flour. Cook uncovered in hot shortening about 40 minutes. Sprinkle with chopped parsley. 4 servings
                                    Lynn Noble

CHICKEN 'N HAM SUPREME

8 slices ¼" ham, cooked
8 pieces chicken breasts, boned
1 cup sour cream
½-1 cup milk
1 can cream of mushroom soup
Pinch salt
Dash pepper
1/8 tsp. garlic salt
1 cup crushed corn flakes
1 cup grated sharp cheese

Place chicken in baking pan on top of ham slices.
Combine rest of ingredients and pour over chicken
and ham. Cover with foil. Bake at 350° for 1 hour.
Sprinkle with cheese and crushed corn flakes. Bake
10 more minutes.

Barbara Ball

+ + + + +

CHICKEN CASSEROLE

3 eggs
1 can chicken noodle soup
1 can cream of chicken soup
1 can cream of mushroom soup
½ cup butter, melted
10 slices white bread, cubed
4 chicken breasts, cooked and cubed

Beat eggs, add soups and melted butter. Add bread and
chicken. Pour into greased 9 x 13" casserole. Bake
at 300° for 1¼ hours. Serves 8

Lynn Vann

+ + + + +

CURRIED BROCCOLI CHICKEN

1 pkg. frozen broccoli
½ can cream of chicken soup
½ cup mayonnaise
2 tbls. lemon juice
½ tsp. curry powder
3 cups chicken, cooked and cut up

Boil broccoli; cover with chicken. Mix soup, mayonnaise, lemon juice and curry powder in saucepan; cook
until creamy and smooth. Pour over chicken and broccoli; heat through and serve.

Sandy Buell

JAVANESE DINNER

[Great for serving to a crowd. Serve as a buffet in order given]

On each dinner plate place:
> Steamed rice (a large serving patted down)
> 2 tbls. stewed chicken pieces in clear chicken
> gravy (flavored with chicken bouillon and
> spices to suite your taste such as celery
> soup, mushroom soup and curry powder)
> 1 handful chow mein noodles
> 1 tbl. green onions (finely cut up)
> 1 tbl. celery (finely cut up)
> 2 tbls. cheese (grated American)
> 2 tbls. shredded coconut
> 2 tbls. crushed pineapple
> 2 tbls. blanched almonds (chopped big)
> Cover with chicken gravy

Place helpings one on top of the other and eat down through the food. No salad or bread is needed. Serve with tea. For dessert serve Chinese cookies with pineapple sherbet, coconut ice cream or Frosted Fruit Cocktail.

To serve 40 prepare the following quantities:
> 5 stewed chickens in clear gravy
> 1¼ gal. fried noodles or rice
> 2 cups onions
> 3 cups celery
> 5 cups cheese
> 5 cups coconut
> 5 cups pineapple
> 5 cups almonds

Vonette Bright

+ + + + +

BAKED CHICKEN BREASTS

4 or more chicken breasts
1 sm. pkg. chipped beef
4 slices bacon
1 cup sour cream
1 can cream of mushroom soup

Break up chipped beef and place in bottom of baking dish. Place chicken on top. Salt and pepper. Place a slice of bacon on top of each chicken breast. Mix together sour cream and mushroom soup. Pour over chicken. Bake uncovered at 250° for 3 hours.

Becky Ward

AUTHENTIC CURRY DINNER

Onions
Peppers
Carrots, grated
Tomato wedges
Cheese in small chunks
Raisins
Bananas
Oranges
Grapefruit
Peanuts
Coconut
Pineapple chunks
Hard-cooked eggs, sliced

Arrange as many of these on rice as you desire or
serve separately. Make lots of rice and your own
curry to suit your taste--but be sure to make plenty.
(May use curry-seasoned gravy.) Serve with chicken,
hamburger or stew meat. Chicken is preferred.

Candace Steele

+ + + + +

BASIC CURRY RECIPE

Chop 4 onions very fine and fry very slowly. When
    onions are dark brown add:
2 tsps. turmeric
2 tsps. paprika
½ tsp. cinnamon
1 tbl. red chilies (hot)
Black pepper

Fry for a few more minutes. Then add:
Chicken (or beef)
Garbonzo peas or kidney beans or other vegetables.
Fry slowly until dark brown. Add water. Be patient--
meat will probably have to fry at least 30 minutes.
Serve hot with rice.

Barbara Ball

ITALIAN TUNA CASSEROLE

1 can (12-oz.) tuna fish
1 can (6-oz.) evaporated milk
1/3 cup Parmesan cheese
¼ cup onion, chopped
1 can cream of mushroom soup
1 can chopped ripe olives (2½-oz.)
1 can mushrooms (2½-oz.)
1 tbl. real lemon juice
4 oz. egg noodles (thin type)

Cook noodles in boiling water. Drain. Heat soup,
add onion, cheese and milk. Bring to a slow boil.
Add to noodles. Keep burner on low heat and add
remaining ingredients. Heat, stirring, for 3 minutes.
Place in casserole dish and bake at 375º for 22
minutes.

Gene Selander

+ + + + +

TUNA CREOLE

1 10-oz. pkg. frozen Brussels Sprouts

1 10-oz. pkg. frozen peas
2 6½ or 7-oz. cans tuna
1 med. onion, sliced thin
1 cup diagonally sliced celery
1 med. green pepper, slivered
2 8-oz. cans tomato sauce with cheese
½ tsp. salt
¼ tsp. chili powder
¼ tsp. thyme
1 tsp. sugar
¼ tsp. tabasco
1 3-oz. can sliced mushrooms
4 cups hot fluffy rice

Prepare rice. Cook Brussels sprouts and peas as
package label direct. Drain; season to taste and
keep warm. Drain oil from tuna into large skillet;
in it saute' onion, celery and green pepper until
tender crisp. Stir in tomato sauce with cheese,
salt, chili powder, thyme, sugar, tabasco and undrained sliced mushrooms. Simmer, uncovered, for 10
minutes. Add tuna (in large pieces) and heat. Pack
cooked rice into a buttered 5½-cup ring mold. Unmold
onto a heated serving dish. Fill center of ring
with hot tuna mixture. Around outside spoon Brussels
sprouts and peas. Serve at once. Serves 6

Barbara Edwards

TUNA CASSEROLE

1 cup raw rice
1½ cups grated cheddar cheese
1 med. size can tuna, drained
1 tsp. salt
White sauce (medium
   consistency

Cook rice in 2½ cups water and 1 tsp. salt for 25
minutes. While rice is cooking, grate cheese and
make white sauce. When rice is cooked, layer ingredients in a 1½-2-qt. casserole dish. Layer rice,
cheese, tuna; then repeat once. Pour white sauce
over all. Stir slightly so white sauce will sink
down. Bake at 350° for 30 minutes.

Nancy McIntosh

+ + + + +

TUNA CASSEROLE WITH CHINESE FLAVOR

2 (7-oz.) cans tuna
2 sm. or 1 large can Chinese noodles
2 cans cream of mushroom soup
1 med. onion, chopped
4-5 celery stalks, chopped on a slant
Cashew or almonds (opt.)
½ tsp. salt
½ tsp. pepper
½ cup water

Mix all ingredients together. Place in casserole and
bake at 350° for 1 hour. Serve with soy sauce. May
also top with crushed potato chips.

Dorothy Brooks

+ + + + +

CRUNCHIE TUNA BAKE

1 (10½-oz.) can cream of vegetable soup or any
   cream soup
2 cups cooked peas
1 cup shredded cheese (American or cheddar)
½ cup milk
¼ cup chopped ripe olives
2 tbls. chopped pimiento
1 (6½-oz. or 9¼-oz.) can flaked tuna, drained
2 cups chow mein noodles

Combine soup, peas, cheese, milk, olives and pimiento
in greased 1½-qt. casserole. Add tuna and chow mein
noodles. Toss lightly. Bake at 350° for 15-20 minutes or until cheese begins to bubble. Serves 6-8

Paula Carter and Diane Yancy

TUNA ROLLS

[An inexpensive quickie snack]

Prepare baking powder biscuits. Roll out on floured surface; cut into squares. Place filling on squares and roll up. Bake at 400° for 10-15 minutes.
FILLING:
1 can tuna fish
½ cup chopped celery
1 egg, beaten

Thin one can cream of mushroom soup with milk and heat. Serve as a sauce over the baked rolls.

Karen Kuhne

+ + + + +

PROTEIN CASSEROLE

[Good and quick!]

1 #2½ can green beans, cut or whole, partly drained
1 (6½-oz.) can tuna fish, drained
4-6 slices Velveeta cheese (or any melting cheese)

Mix all together in saucepan on top of stove. When heated, cheese melts and forms a sauce. Add Lawry's seasoning salt and black pepper. If desired, sprinkle nuts or sesame seeds on top before serving. Serve with buttered whole wheat bread, big glasses of milk and fresh fruit for dessert.

Shirley VanDeraa

+ + + + +

BECKY'S SHRIMP DELIGHT

¼ cup chopped onion
¼ cup diced green pepper
1 can (4-oz.) sliced mushrooms, drained
1 tbl. chopped pimiento
2 tbls. butter or margarine
1 can (10-oz.) frozen condensed cream of shrimp soup
½ cup milk
1 cup diced cooked shrimp (may use canned)
¼ cup shredded cheddar cheese

Cook onion, mushrooms, green pepper in butter until tender. Add soup, milk and shrimp. Heat until soup is thawed; stir often. Add pimiento and cheese; stir. Serve piping hot with 4 slices of toast or 3 cups cooked rice. Serves 4

Becky Rieke

SHRIMP-TUNA DISH

[Good for a simple luncheon]

8 slices white bread, buttered
1 can (7-oz.) tuna, drained
¼ lb. Swiss cheese, grated
2 tbls. chopped parsley
1 tbl. grated onion
1 cup milk
1 can frozen condensed cream of shrimp soup
3 eggs

Line pan with 4 slices of buttered bread. Combine
tuna, cheese, parsley and onion. Pour over bread.
Top with 4 slices of bread. Heat milk and soup until
melted. Beat eggs and stir into soup. Pour over
dish, cover and chill 4 hours or overnight. Bake uncovered. Start in cold oven 350° for 1 hour or until
puffed up.

Barbara Ball

+ + + + +

SALMON-SHRIMP CASSEROLE

2 tbls. butter
2 tbls. flour
1 can condensed frozen cream of shrimp soup, thawed
1 cup milk
2 oz. sharp American cheese, shredded -- ½ cup
1 can (16-oz.) red salmon, drained and broken into
    large chunks
1 cup frozen peas (½ of 10-oz. pkg.)

Melt butter in saucepan, stir in flour. Add soup and
milk all at once. Cook and stir until thick. Remove
from heat; add cheese, stir until melted. Gently
stir in salmon and peas. Put in 2½-qt. baking dish
and cool. (Can line the dish with foil and freeze.
When frozen, lift the foil from dish, wrap food well
and freeze until ready to use. When you are ready to
serve, unwrap foil, drop food into casserole and bake
at 425° for 40-45 minutes. Stir frequently.) Also,
biscuits (refrigerator type or mix) may be dropped
on top for the last 15 minutes.

Libby Trest

DISHWATER FISH

(Try this for a novelty conversation piece).

WHOLE SALMON -
Stuff salmon with chopped celery, sprinkle with seasoned salt, garlic salt and dot with butter. (Lay
out flat with dressing on top.) Wrap in three layers
of foil, sealing it tightly. Put it through two
cycles of the DISHWASHER (along with the dishes if
you wish!). It's a great way to cook fish when the
oven is small. It takes 2 hours and 5 minutes in a
2-cycle wash but the dishes are clean too! It's a
wonderful way to cook during warm weather when you
don't want to use the range or oven. Besides, you
don't get any fishy odors because the fish is completely sealed and protected in the DISHWASHER.

SMALL FISH -
Select a small fish large enough for each guest to
have plenty. Season well with salt and pepper.
Wrap in three layers of foil, sealing it tightly.
Place on a flat shelf in DISHWASHER to avoid any
punctures and put it through the sani-heat cycle,
using no detergent. The fish will come out excep-
tionally moist and tender.

VEGETABLES -
You may also want to try cooking vegetables this way
wrapped in three layers of foil and tightly sealed.
They will cook to crisp-tender doneness with full
flavor of the seasonings added.

Serve above three items with a tossed salad.

Rita Harvey

+ + + + +

BEEF STROGANOFF

2½-3 lbs. boneless chuck or round steak
3 tbls. flour
3 tbls. salad oil
2 tbls. butter
1 onion, chopped
1 6-oz. can mushrooms (or fresh mushrooms are cheaper
    than canned)
1/3 cup vinegar mixed with 2 tbls. water
1 can tomato soup
2 tbls. Worcestershire sauce
2 cups sour cream

Sprinkle tenderizer on meat. Cut into strips ½"
thick, ½" wide, 2" long. Roll meat in flour. Heat
2 tablespoons oil and butter in Dutch oven (or deep
skillet) over medium-high heat. Brown meat quickly
on all sides. Remove meat. Add rest of oil and reduce heat to moderate. Add onion and saute'. (If
using fresh mushrooms, add more butter and saute'
them also.) If using canned mushrooms, add them with
their liquid and the vinegar mixture to skillet.
Stir to loosen the particles on bottom. Return meat
to pan and bring to a boil. Combine soup, Worcestershire sauce, sour cream and blend well. Pour over
meat and stir. Cover and simmer over low heat for
2 hours, stirring occasionally, until meat is fork-
tender. Serve over hot rice. Serves 6

Lynn Owen

+ + + + +

EASY BEEF STROGANOFF

3 tbls. flour   1 4-oz. can mushrooms
1½ tsps. salt   1 cup sour cream
¼ tsp. pepper
1 lb. beef tenderloin (or hamburger)
1 clove garlic, grated
½ cup minced onion
¼ cup water
1 cup undiluted cream of chicken soup

Combine flour, salt and pepper. Rub both sides with
garlic. Pound flour mixture into both sides of meat.
Cut into 1½ x 1" strips. Brown. Add onion. Saute'
until golden. Add water; stir. Add soup and mushrooms. Cook uncovered over low heat, stirring occasionally until thick and meat is tender--about 20
minutes. Just before serving, stir in cream, heat,
but do not boil. Serve with rice, potatoes or
noodles. Serves 4-6

Judy DeBoer

STUFFED FLANK OR ROUND STEAK

1½-2 lbs. flank or round steak
Beat 1 minute:
1 cup milk
1 egg
1 tsp. sage
½ tsp. salt
2 slices onion
½ cup diced celery
Add ½ cup walnuts
Add ingredients to 3 cups bread crumbs. Mix well
and arrange stuffing in strips on steak. Roll and
fasten with toothpicks. Bake in a well-greased
covered baking dish at 350° for 1½ hours. Serves 6-8

Marilyn Klein

+ + + + +

CHINESE BEEF CURRY

1 medium onion, sliced
2 tbls. oil
1 tbl. curry powder
1 pound round steak, sliced thin across grain
   (Hint: Steak is easier to slice if partially
          frozen)

Cook onion 1 minute in oil.· Stir in curry powder.
Add meat; cook 3 minutes, stirring constantly.
Combine: 1 envelope au jus gravy mix
          1 cup water
          1 tbl. cornstarch
          1 tbl. soy sauce
Pour over meat mixture and cook until thickened.
Serve over hot cooked rice. Serves 4

Peggy Jones

FOIL WRAPPED STEAK SUPPER

Heavy aluminum foil
1½ lbs. chuck steak 1" thick
1 envelope onion soup mix
4 med. carrots, quartered
2 stalks celery, cut in sticks
3 med. potatoes, halved
2 tbls. margarine
½ tsp. salt

Place meat in center of large piece of foil, sprinkle
with onion soup mix, cover with vegetables. Dot with
margarine and sprinkle with salt. Fold foil over
and securely seal to hold in juices. Place on baking
sheet. Bake at 450° for 1-1½ hours. Serves 4

Gail Palmquist

+ + + + +

EARLE'S SPECIALTY ROAST

2-3 lbs. chuck roast
1 pkg. dry onion soup mix

Put meat on large sheet of aluminum foil. Sprinkle
meat with dry onion soup mix and a half cup of water.
Wrap securely and cook in electric skillet or place
in casserole and bake in oven at 350° for 1½-2 hours.
This may also be done with pork chops, chicken or
any other meat.

Judy Carpenter

+ + + + +

NORWEGIAN POT ROAST

3-4 lbs. beef arm or blade pot roast
1 8-oz. can seasoned tomato sauce
1 cup water
1 envelope onion soup mix
2 tsps. caraway seeds
2 bay leaves

Trim off excess fat. Roll meat in flour; brown slowly on all sides in a little hot fat. Mix and add remaining ingredients. Cover; cook slowly 2½ hours or
until tender. Remove to warm platter. Make thickened gravy from roast liquid and serve.

Lois Mackey

ORIENTAL CHARCOAL BROILED ROAST

5 ozs. soy sauce
2 cups tomato juice
Juice of 2 lemons
1 tbl. dehydrated onion
Chuck roast cut about 2" thick

Combine marinade. Marinate roast for several hours or overnight. Grill over hot charcoal until desired doneness. Cut into thin slices to serve. Serves 6

Marilyn Heavilin

+ + + + +

BEEF POT ROAST A LA PROVINCE

3 lbs. pot roast
¼ cup butter
3 carrots, chopped
3 stalks celery, chopped
1 med. onion, chopped
1 clove garlic

Brown meat in butter. Add rest of ingredients and cook until golden, stirring occasionally. Add one can (6-oz.) undrained mushrooms.
Blend together and add:
    1 can condensed beef consomme
    1 cup sour cream
    1/3 cup red wine vinegar
    2 tbls. water
    2 tbls. brown sugar
    1 tbl. drained capers
    ½ tsp. paprika
    1 tsp. salt
    1/8 tsp. pepper

Cover and simmer 2-3 hours until meat is tender. Gravy may be thickened with flour. Serve over the meat.

Patty Roth

+ + + + +

5-HOUR STEW

2 lbs. stew meat	2 tsps. salt
2 large carrots, cut in large pieces	Dash pepper
1 large onion, in rings	1 can mush-
2 med. potatoes, quartered	room soup
½ pkg. frozen peas &/or corn	1 can water

Do NOT brown meat. Place everything raw in large
casserole or roaster and cook covered at 275° for
5 hours. Serves 4

Nancy Robinson

+ + + + +

SIX-HOUR STEW

1 can tomatoes (#2)
3 tbls. tapioca
½ tsp. basil
½ tsp. oregano
¼ tsp. marjoram
2 tbls. and 2 tsps. Worcestershire
2 tsps. salt
4 ribs celery (cut in large pieces)
1 large onion (cut in large pieces)
4 or 5 carrots (in large pieces)
4 or 5 new potatoes (large pieces)
2 lbs. boneless beef stew meat
1 bay leaf (almond size)

Place all ingredients in large roaster. Cover and
place in pre-heated oven, 250° for 6 hours.

Evelyn Bromberg

+ + + + +

HOMEMADE BEEF STEW

[A 1-course meal that you can put in the oven at
noon and go off to campus, Bible studies, etc. yet
still have supper ready.]

2 lbs. stew meat, frozen
1 can cream of mushroom soup, undiluted
Carrots, cut up to size and quantity desired
Potatoes, quartered (enough to go around)
1 pkg. dry onion soup mix

Place all ingredients in a pot; cover tightly, place
in oven at 250° for 5 hours. The last 45 minutes add
a package of frozen peas.

Bobbi Aker

ARMENIAN SH-KEBAB

½ lb. filet of beef, mutton or lamb
1 med. onion
Pinch of thyme
2 cups broth

Cut meat in walnut-sized pieces. Chop onion very fine
and mix with thyme; spread over meat; salt and pepper
to taste. Allow meat to stand 3 hours. Arrange meat
on iron skewers and broil over hot fire. Have a hot
broth in which to place the broiled kebabs. When
broiling is finished, place vessel containing the
broth and kebabs over a slow fire and allow to simmer
for 15-20 minutes. Serve hot.

Rita Harvey

+ + + + +

178

ORIENTAL SKILLET SUPPER

[Very filling]

½ cup green pepper strips
1/3 cup bias-cut celery slices
1 tbl. salad oil
1 large or 2 sm. minute steaks, cut into ¼" strips
1/3 cup cold water
1 tbl. soy sauce
2 tsps. cornstarch
½ tsp. sugar
¼ tsp. salt
1 med. tomato, peeled and cut in wedges
1 cup hot cooked rice
¼ tsp. ground ginger

In heavy skillet, quickly cook green pepper and celery
in oil until crisp-tender. Remove and set aside.
Add meat to hot skillet; brown quickly. Combine
water, soy sauce, cornstarch, sugar and salt; add to
skillet. Cook and stir until mixture thickens and
bubbles. Add celery, green pepper and tomato; heat
through. Serve over ginger rice: toss rice with
ginger. Pass additional soy sauce. Makes 2 healthy
servings.

Karla Crawford

+ + + + +

CHINESE SKILLET BEEF

[Good for using leftover beef]

2 tbls. salad oil
1 med. head cauliflower in flowerettes
¼ cup water
1 can undiluted consomme'
1½ tbls. cornstarch
2 tbls. soy sauce
2 tbls. lemon juice
2 scallions, diced fine
2 cups left over beef cut in strips
1 10-oz. pkg. frozen peas
1 tsp. salt
Chinese noodles

Saute' cauliflower in hot oil for 3 minutes, stirring
constantly. Do not brown. Reduce heat, add water,
cover and let steam for 2-3 minutes. Mix together
consomme', cornstarch, soy sauce, lemon juice and
scallions; stir well and pour over cauliflower.
Add beef, peas, salt and stir well. Cook over medium
heat until steaming hot and sauce is thickened.
Serve with Chinese noodles.

Mary Lou Lyon

MEAT PIN WHEELS

1 cup Bisquick mix
1/3 cup milk
2 tbls. melted butter
3 tbls. catsup
2 tsps. prepared mustard
1 tsp. instant minced onion
1 lb. ground beef, browned, seasoned
1 pkg. mushroom gravy and 1 cup water
    OR grated cheese

Mix Bisquick mix in a small bowl with milk to form a
soft dough. Roll out to 12" square. Mix butter,
catsup, mustard and onion together. Spread evenly
over dough. Crumble ground beef evenly over onion
mixture. Roll up and cut into 8 slices. Bake at
450° for 12-15 minutes on greased baking sheet.
Cover with either gravy or cheese according to taste.

Lynn Noble

+ + + + +

DOUBLE CHEESE MEAT ROLL

2 lbs. lean ground beef
1 egg
3/4 cup cracker crumbs
½ cup finely chopped onion
2 8-oz. cans Hunt's tomato sauce with cheese
1 tsp. salt
1/8 tsp. pepper
½ tsp. oregano
2 cups shredded Mozzarella or cheddar cheese

Combine the meat, egg, cracker crumbs, onion, 1/3 cup
tomato sauce, salt, oregano and pepper. Mix well and
shape into a flat rectangle about 10 x 12" on wax
paper. Sprinkle cheese evenly over meat mixture.
Roll up like a jelly roll and press ends to seal.
Bake in a shallow baking dish at 350° for 1 hour.
Drain excess grease. Pour remaining tomato sauce
over roll and bake an additional 15 minutes.
Serves 4-6

Kerry Fix and Connie Burnside

DOMATELLI

[A whole meal in one dish!]

2 med. onions, chopped
1½ lbs. ground beef
2 cloves garlic, minced
1 green pepper, chopped
1 med. can tomatoes
2 tbls. Parmesan cheese
¼ tsp. thyme (opt.)
1/3 pkg. shell macaroni, cooked
½ lb. cheddar cheese, cut into 8 sticks

Saute' onion, garlic and pepper until soft; add meat
and cook until brown. Drain off grease. Add tomatoes, cheese, thyme and macaroni. Place in 2½-qt.
casserole, stick pieces of cheddar cheese down
through mixture and sprinkle with a little more
Parmesan cheese. Bake at 350° for 25-30 minutes.
(Turkey or chicken may be used.)

Dorothy Brooks

+ + + + +

SPANISH RICE PRONTO

¼ cup bacon drippings
1 onion, chopped
½ green pepper, diced
1 1/3 cups minute rice, uncooked
1 3/4 cups hot water
2 cans tomato sauce
1 tsp. salt
Dash pepper
1 tsp. prepared mustard (opt.)

Brown onion, green pepper and rice together in bacon
drippings. Add hot water, tomato sauce and seasonings, mixing well. Bring quickly to a boil, cover
tightly and simmer 10 minutes. Serves 4-6
VARIATION: Brown ½ lb. ground beef with onions.
    OR add 1 cup (4-oz. can) mushrooms.
    OR stir in ½ cup grated cheese just before
       serving and sprinkle top with another ½
       cup cheese.
    OR add 4 sliced frankfurters or 1½ cups diced
       leftover beef or pork.

Dorothy Brooks

+ + + + +

HAMBURGER HEAVEN

1 lb. ground beef
½ lb. American cheese, sliced
1 cup chopped celery
1 sm. can ripe olives, sliced
2 cups fine, dry noodles
1 can stew-tomatoes
¼ cup water (rinse out can)
Salt and pepper

Brown meat in skillet. Season. Arrange the remaining ingredients in layers in electric skillet or heavy pan. Pour the ¼ cup of water over all. Season. Bring to a boil; reduce heat and cook for 30 minutes.
VARIATION: Leave out olives and celery. Prepare meat in skillet then add Chinese noodles (they cook quicker). Top with sliced cheese. Pour on stewed tomatoes and add about 1 cup water (or half can full). Bring to boil and reduce heat. Cover tightly and simmer slowly for 30 minutes or until noodles are done. If water gets low, add more when cooking to keep from burning.

Howard VanCleave

+ + + + +

BEEF 'N CHEESE PIE

1 lb. ground beef
1 cup soft bread crumbs
½ cup instant dry milk
1½ tsps. minced onion
1 tsp. salt
Dash pepper
½ tsp. Worcestershire sauce
1 8-oz. can tomato sauce
¼ lb. cheddar cheese (1 cup) shredded
2 cups seasoned, mashed potatoes

Mix all ingredients except cheese and potatoes with ½ can of the tomato sauce. Press onto bottom of 9" pie or cake pan. Bake at 350° for 25 minutes. Remove from oven. Sprinkle with cheese. Pour remaining tomato sauce over cheese. Spread mashed potatoes over top. Place 4-5 inches from broiler for 3-4 minutes to heat potatoes and melt cheese. Serves 5-6

Sue Smith

BEEF-ZUCCHINI CASSEROLE

1 lb. ground beef
1 med. onion, chopped
1½ lbs. cooked zucchini
½ lb. grated cheese
1 can cream of mushroom soup
Cracker crumbs

Saute' onion and beef together in skillet. Season
to taste. Arrange cooked zucchini, sliced, with
meat mixture and grated cheese in alternate layers
in casserole. Pour mushroom soup over top and top
with cracker crumbs. Bake at 350° for 1 hour. May
be prepared a day ahead and reheated at 350° for 45
minutes. It usually tastes better reheated.

Dorothy Brooks

+ + + + +

DINNER IN A SKILLET

2 med. zucchini (or summer) squash
1 large tomato
½ med. onion
½ cup grated cheese
Salt and pepper
1 lb. ground beef

Brown ground beef in skillet. Drain excess grease.
Dice squash, tomato and onion; add to meat. Season
to taste. Simmer until vegetables are tender.
Sprinkle with cheese and serve.

Pat Turanski

+ + + + +

"SHEPHERD'S PIE"

1 onion, chopped
1 lb. ground beef, browned
1 can green beans, drained
1 can tomato soup

Brown meat with onion and season with salt and pepper.
Place meat in layers with remaining ingredients in
2½-qt. casserole. Top with 3 or 4 servings of prepared instant mashed potatoes. Bake at 350° for 30
minutes.

Edith Vanderveen

GERMAN CABBAGE ROLLS

1 head of cabbage
1½ lbs. ground beef
1 (10½-oz.) can tomato soup
3/4 can of water
½ onion, chopped
½ cup uncooked rice

Peel off leaves from cabbage and cook in boiling water
for 5 minutes (about 10-12 leaves). Mix together
meat, rice and onion in a bowl. Drain cabbage leaves.
One by one fill each leaf with meat mixture. Form
into oblong ball and do not pat meat too hard. Roll
up and seal with 1 or 2 toothpicks. Place leaves
in casserole and add can of soup and water. Cover
and bake at 400° for 1½ hours. (This will make its
own gravy so all you need to add is potatoes to complete your meal. They taste best if, after cooking,
they are left to marinate for 24 hours in the gravy.)

Evelyn Nickel

+ + + + +

SWEDISH CABBAGE ROLLS

1 egg
1 tsp. salt
Dash of pepper
1 tsp. Worcestershire sauce
¼ cup finely chopped onion
2/3 cup milk
½ lb. ground beef
½ lb. ground pork
3/4 cup rice, cooked
6 large cabbage leaves
1 can tomato soup, condensed
1 tbl. brown sugar
1 tbl. lemon juice

Combine first 6 ingredients in a bowl; mix well. Add
ground meat and rice; beat together with a fork.
Immerse cabbage leaves in boiling water for 3 minutes or until limp; drain. (Heavy center vein of
leaf may be slit about 2½".) Place ½ cup meat mixture on each leaf; fold in sides and roll ends over
meat. Place rolls in 7 x 12" baking dish. Blend
soup, sugar and lemon juice; pour over cabbage rolls.
Bake at 350° for 1¼ hours. Baste once or twice with
sauce. Serves 6

Lana Jones

BACON-WRAPPED BEEF PATTIES

1 lb. ground beef
1 tsp. salt
¼ tsp. pepper
1 egg, beaten
Green onion, chopped
Pepper
Any hamburger seasonings you prefer

Combine ingredients thoroughly. Shape into a roll
three inches in diameter. Lay strips of bacon on a
cutting board. Use one strip for each inch of length
of beef roll. Place roll in center of row of bacon
slices. Fold ends of bacon up over roll and secure
with toothpick. Wrap in wax paper or foil if it isn't
time to cook the patties and store in refrigerator.
At cooking time, unwrap the roll. Slice between
strips of bacon. Place patties on hot broiler rack
in broiler pan. Broil 3" from heat source about 5
minutes. Turn and broil until well browned.

+ + + + +

CHEESEBURGER TURNOVERS

½ lb. ground beef
1 tbl. chopped onion
½ tsp. salt
Dash of pepper
1 can oven-ready biscuits
5 Kraft deluxe slices pasteurized process American
    cheese

Combine meat, onion, salt and pepper. Cook over low
heat 5 minutes or until lightly browned. For each
turnover, place 2 biscuits, slightly overlapping on
well-floured surface. Roll until each biscuit forms
an oval about 5" long. Place about 3 tbls. of meat
mixture on 1 biscuit and top with 2 half slices of
cheese. Moisten edges with water, fold the second
biscuit over the meat and cheese, and seal with fork.
Prick top. Bake at 425° for 8-10 minutes until golden
brown. Serve as a hot sandwich, or top with mustard
or catsup.

                                        Jane Prall

QUICK LASAGNA

Brown together:
      1 lb. ground beef
      1 clove garlic, chopped
Pour off grease. Add:
      1 6-oz. can tomato paste
      1 #2½ can tomatoes
      1 tsp. salt
Simmer for 20 minutes.
Mix: 3/4 lb. cottage cheese
      1 tbl. parsley
      1 tsp. oregano
Let set for flavors to absorb.
Mix: 1 lb. cheddar cheese, grated
      1 lb. Mozzarella cheese, grated
Cook 6 oz. lasagna noodles
Place by layers in very large 2" deep pan:
      Half of tomato-beef sauce
      Layer of cooked noodles
      Half of cottage cheese mixture
      Half of grated cheeses
      Rest of tomato-beef sauce
      Rest of noodles
      Rest of grated cheese
Sprinkle Parmesan cheese on top, if desired. Bake
at 350° for 30 minutes. Serve with tossed green
salad and hot rolls.

                              Jerri Younkman

+ + + + +

CHEESE LASAGNA

1 tbl. oil
1/3 cup onions
1½ tsps. salt
3 (8-oz.) cans tomato sauce
3/4 tsp. oregano
1 (6-oz.) can tomato paste
½ tsp. basil

2 (3-oz.) cans mushroom
      slices
1 (16-oz.) pkg. lasagna
      noodles
2 (8-oz.) pkgs. sliced
      process cheddar cheese
1 (16-oz.) container
      cottage cheese

Cook onions until tender in large saucepan over
medium heat. Stir in tomato sauce, paste, mushrooms
(reserve a few for garnishing), salt, oregano, basil
and 1 cup water. Simmer 15 minutes, stirring occasionally. Cook lasagna; drain. Reserve 4 cheese
slices; cut remaining cheese slices into halves. Layer into greased 9 x 13" baking dish one fourth of the
noodles, sauce and cottage cheese. Also slices of
cheddar cheese. Repeat layers 4 times. Cover and
bake at 375° for 45 minutes.

                              Barbara Ball

MEAT LOAF

1½ lbs. ground beef
½ cup quick oatmeal, uncooked
2 eggs, beaten
¼ cup chopped onion
2 tsps. salt
¼ tsp. pepper
½-1 can tomato soup
½ cup pickle relish
½ cup cheddar cheese, grated

Thoroughly combine all ingredients except relish and
cheese. Pack one half of meat mixture into one
pound loaf pan. Press relish and cheese down through
the center. Add remaining meat. Bake at 350° for
1 hour.

+ + + + +

JUICY MEAT LOAF

1 lb. ground beef   2¼ tbls. chopped onions
2/3 cup evaporated milk   1 tsp. salt
½ cup uncooked rolled oats   1/8 tsp. pepper

Combine all ingredients and shape into loaf with wet
hands. Place into shallow pan and dot top with
1 tablespoon shortening, chili sauce or catsup.
Bake at 350° for 1 hour.

Donna Lou Gaunt

+ + + + +

POT ROAST MEAT LOAF

1 lb. lean ground chuck
3-4 slices whole wheat bread, crumbled in blender
1 cup evaporated milk
1 tbl. catsup
1 tsp. salt
¼ tsp. Worcestershire sauce
¼ tsp. pepper
1 tbl. dried parsley flakes

Mix above ingredients and shape into loaf. Peel and
cut 3 potatoes and 1 lb. carrots into pieces. Place
vegetables around meat and sprinkle with salt. Add
2 tbls. water in bottom of pan. Cover tightly. Bake
at 375° for 1½ hours, uncovering the last 10 minutes
to brown meat. Serves 4

Charlotte Melcher

CHINESE HOT DISH

1 lb. ground round
1 cup diced celery
1 large onion, chopped
1 can mushroom soup
1 can chicken rice soup
1 cup frozen mixed vegetables
3 cups dry Chinese noodles
Soy sauce
Blanched almonds or cashews

Brown beef, celery and onion. Add soups and vegetables. Stir in 1½ cups dry noodles and bake for 30 minutes (covered) at 350°. Sprinkle soy sauce lightly over dish and add remaining noodles. Mix and bake for 30 minutes more. Sprinkle nuts over top and serve. Serves 4-6

Nancy Robinson

+ + + + +

FONDUE-TERIYAKI MEATBALLS

2 tbls. soy sauce
2 tbls. water
3 tsps. sugar
½ tsp. instant minced onion
Dash each: seasoned salt
            ground ginger
            garlic salt
1 lb. ground beef
½ cup fine soft bread crumbs

Combine all ingredients but meat and bread crumbs. Let stand 10 minutes. Combine ground beef and bread crumbs; stir in soy mixture. Shape into 1" meatballs (makes about 40 meatballs). Heat fondue oil to 375°. Transfer to fondue pot to depth of no more than 2". Each meatball takes about 1 minute to cook. Serve meatballs at room temperature.

Sharyn Regier

TAMALE-CHILI STEW

1 lb. ground beef
1 chopped onion
1 (15-oz.) can chili without beans
1 (15-oz.) can tamales, sliced ¼"

Brown meat; drain off grease. Add rest of ingredients and 1 cup water. Simmer until thickened. Serve with crushed Fritos on top.

+ + + + +

TAMALE CASSEROLE

1 lb. ground beef
1 onion, chopped
Small bag Fritos
1 can whole kernel corn
1 can consomme' soup
1 can tomato sauce
1 cup cheddar cheese, grated
½ can ripe sliced olives

Brown meat and onion. Add rest of ingredients and mix well. Put in 2-qt. casserole and bake at 350°
for 1 hour.

Patty Roth

+ + + + +

ENCHILADAS

24 corn tortillas (hand made)
2 lbs. ground meat, browned
1 can black olives, chopped
1 large onion, chopped
1 lb. yellow cheese, grated
1 lb. jack cheese, grated
2 cans enchilada sauce
2 or 3 cans tomato sauce

Brown meat; chop olives and onion. Combine sauces in frying pan or pan large enough to hold tortilla. Heat until simmering. Put tortilla in simmering sauce for a few seconds. Drain slightly on paper towel. Put 2 tbls. meat, 1 tbl. olives, onion to taste and 1 tbl. cheese on tortilla. Roll up. Place edge side down in baking dish (you may vary the ingredients and amounts to suit your own taste). Repeat with all tortillas. Pour remaining sauce over rolled enchiladas in dish. Add remaining onion and olives (if desired) on top with rest of cheese. Bake until cheese bubbles -- about 30 minutes at 325°.

Barbara Ball

TAMALE PIE

2 onions, chopped
2 cloves garlic, minced (opt.)
4-5 tbls. salad oil
1½ lbs. ground beef
1½ tsps. salt
2 tbls. chili powder
1 #2 can tomatoes
1 can corn or Mexi-corn
1½ cup pitted ripe olives, chopped
1 cup seedless raisins (opt.)
2 tsps. salt
2 tsps. chili powder
6 cups boiling water
2 cups yellow cornmeal
½ cup American cheese, grated (opt.)

Brown beef, onions and garlic in salad oil. Add salt, chili powder, tomatoes, corn, olives and raisins. Cook slowly (20-30 minutes) while preparing mush. Add remaining salt and chili powder to water and slowly add corn meal; cook 15 minutes, stirring frequently. Line large greased baking dish with 1" layer of cornmeal mush. Pour in meat filling and spread rest of mush on top. Bake at 350° for 1 hour or more. Sprinkle with grated cheese last 15 minutes. Serves 8.

Dorothy Brooks

+ + + + +

EASY TAMALE PIE

2 pkgs. French's Tamale-Taco mix
2 lbs. hamburger
2 med. onions, chopped
1 med. bell pepper, chopped
½ box of corn bread mix
1 large can whole kernel yellow corn (15-oz.) drained
1½ cans stewed tomatoes, undrained

Brown hamburger, onions, and bell pepper together; drain off excess grease. Add taco mix to hamburger mixture. Add corn and tomatoes; simmer 10-15 minutes stirring occasionally. Place tamale mixture in a 9 x 13" pyrex dish, using a little more canned tomato juice if needed. Follow directions for corn bread. Put this batter on top of tamale mixture. Bake at 350° for 30 minutes. (May sprinkle grated cheese on top.)

Jane Prall

+ + + + +

MOCK ENCHILADAS

1 lb. ground beef
2 tbls. fat (opt.)
½ cup chopped onions
1 tsp. salt
¼ tsp. pepper
½ lb. (1¼ cups) American cheese, diced
1 #1 can (2 cups) chili con carne with beans
1½ oz. pkg. Fritos (1 cup)

Brown meat in hot fat, add onion; cook until golden
brown. Season with salt and pepper. Add chili con
carne. Place a layer of Fritos in greased 1½-qt.
casserole dish. Alternate layers of Fritos, chili
con carne and cheese. Bake at 350° about 10 minutes.
Serves 4

                                        Gail Palmquist

                    + + + + +

ENCHILADAS VERDES

Garlic salt to taste
1 dozen corn tortillas
1 #2 can tomatoes
1 large onion, chopped
1 large can green chilies (Ortegas)
¼ lb. Velveeta cheese
1 cup sour cream

Mix tomatoes, chopped onions, chili peppers, garlic
salt and bring to boil. Simmer 5 minutes. Alternate
layers of tortillas, tomato sauce, cheese and sour
cream. Bake in 2-qt. baking dish at 350° for 30
minutes.

                                        Helen Lovell

                    + + + + +

PIZZA

1 pkg. dry yeast
1 cup warm water
3 cups sifted flour
1½ tsp. soft shortening (or oil)
1 tsp. salt

Add yeast to warm water. Let stand a few minutes, stir to dissolve. Add about half of flour. Beat until smooth. Add shortening and salt with rest of flour. Mix in with spoon or by hand until the flour begins to clean sides of bowl. Beat hard. Turn out dough onto board. Cover with bowl. Let rest 5-10 minutes. Grease pizza pan (a broiler pan works as a good substitute). Gently pat dough to line pan, building up edges to hold filling. Brush with salad oil before adding topping.

TOPPING:
Lay pizza filling over the crust beginning with a layer of grated sharp cheese. Mix 1 #2½ can tomatoes (slightly drained) with 1/8 - 1/4 tsp. garlic powder, ¼ tsp. oregano and ¼ cup finely chopped onions. Pour over the cheese layer. Add mushrooms, hot pepperoni sticks cut in pieces, or ½ - 1 lb. uncooked ground beef and sausage. Top with more grated cheese. Bake at 350° about 1 hour until dough is baked and filling is browned.

Barbara Herrly

+ + + + +

HAMBURG PIZZA

[An inexpensive favorite with students]

1 lb. ground beef
1 tsp. salt
¼ tsp. pepper
¼ cup fine bread crumbs
1 sm. chopped onion
1 clove minced garlic
½ cup water

Mix together and pat into 9" pie pan. Bake for 15 minutes at 375° and pour off grease. Add on top:
1 can (17-oz.) pizza sauce
1 can (8-oz.) mushrooms (opt.)
Sprinkle with grated Mozzarella cheese and oregano. Bake another 15 minutes at 375°. Serves 4-6
Serve with French fries and green salad.

Nan McCullough

SQUARE-MEAL-IN-A-SKILLET

1 lb. ground round
1 tsp. salt
¼ tsp. pepper
½ tsp. garlic salt
1 med. onion, chopped
1 beef bouillon cube
2 cups water
3 vermicilli noodles
1 pkg. (10-oz.) frozen peas and carrots

Brown meat; add onion, salt, pepper and garlic salt.
Boil water with bouillon cube. Add vermicilli to
boiling water; cook until tender (about 7 minutes).
Add to meat mixture. Add cooked peas and carrots.
Serves 4-6

Diane Yancy

+ + + + +

TEXAS HASH

3 sliced onions   1 large ground pepper
3 tbls. shortening   1 lb. ground beef
2 cups tomatoes (#1 can)   ½ cup uncooked rice
1 tsp. chili powder   2 tsps. salt
½ tsp. pepper

Saute' onion and ground pepper in shortening until
onions are yellow. Add meat and brown until mixture
falls apart. Stir in rest of ingredients. Pour into
2-qt. casserole (greased). Cover and bake at 350°
for 3/4 hour; uncover and bake 15 minutes more.
Serves 5-6

Jeanne Johnson

+ + + + +

BEEF CASSEROLE

1 lb. ground beef
1 sm. onion, chopped
½ cup uncooked rice
1 can chicken noodle soup
1 can cream of mushroom soup
1 can water

Brown beef with onion. Add soups, water and washed
rice. Place in casserole and bake at 325° for about
1¼-1½ hours. (This may also be made in a frying pan
and cooked for 15-20 minutes.)

Linda Bond

SWEDISH MEATBALLS

1 lb. ground chuck
1 cup soft bread crumbs
1 cup milk
1 egg, well beaten
1 onion, chopped small
2 tsps. salt
1/8 tsp. pepper
1 cup hot water
1 tbl. flour
2 tbls. cold water

Mix meat, bread crumbs, milk, egg, onion and seasonings in a large bowl. Heat about 2 tbls. shortening
in frying pan over medium heat. Form meat mixture
into small balls--using teaspoon--brown on all sides
a few at a time and keep warm (in the oven on low
temperature). Use more shortening as needed. When
all meat balls are browned, add hot water to drippings
in frying pan and bring to boil. Blend flour (1 to 2
ratio) with cold water and stir into hot mixture.
Cook until thickened. Return meat to frying pan;
cover and cook slowly for 30 minutes or more. Serves
4 (or 2 big eaters!)

Dan Salvesen

+ + + + +

ITALIAN MEAT BALLS

4 slices dry bread, cubed
1 lb. ground beef
2 eggs
½ cup grated cheese
2 tbls. chopped parsley
1 tsp. crushed oregano
1 tsp. salt (onion salt)
Dash pepper

Soak bread in a little water, combine with remaining
ingredients mixing well. Form into small balls and
brown in skillet. Add to Italian Spaghetti Sauce and
cook together. Serve over hot spaghetti. Serves 6

Lois Mackey

(Italian Spaghetti Sauce recipe - page 212)

POLYNESIAN MEAT BALLS

2 lbs. ground beef
½ cup bread crumbs
½ cup milk
1 egg, beaten
2 tsps. salt
½ tsp. garlic salt
½ tsp. pepper

Form above ingredients into balls--brown. Prepare sauce:

    1 can beef bouillon
    ¼ cup wine vinegar
    ½ cup brown sugar
    2 tbls. soy sauce
    ½ tsp. salt
    1 tsp. MSG
    1 med. onion, sliced
    1 med. pepper, sliced
    1 stalk celery
    1 #2 can pineapple tidbits (include syrup)

Blend 2 tbls. flour with ½ cup water to make a thick paste. Add to above mixture. Simmer 15 minutes. Add meat balls and cook 15 minutes more. Serve over rice. Serves 12.

Dorothy Gregory

+ + + + +

SALISBURY STEAK FOR SIX

1 can golden mushroom soup
1½ lbs. ground beef
½ cup fine bread crumbs
1 egg, beaten
¼ cup finely chopped onion
1 tsp. tabasco sauce

Combine ¼ cup soup with ingredients. Shape into 6 oblong loaves. Place in baking dish. Bake at 350° for 45 minutes. Spoon off grease. Add 1/3 cup of water to remaining soup and pour over little loaves; bake 10 minutes longer. (You may want to turn the broiler on for a few minutes to brown loaves before you pour soup over them.)

Nancy Scott

+ + + + +

MEATBALLS

[This recipe comes directly from "Little Italy,"
Westerly, R.I.]

1½ lbs. ground beef
½ lb. veal
½ lb. pork
Mix thoroughly with:
2 cups bread crumbs
1 cup grated cheese
2 eggs
1 tsp. salt
1 tsp. pepper (or to taste)
Use about ½ cup sauce to mix with the meat to make
it moist. Roll into balls and place in sauce to
cook.
SAUCE: 1 large can tomato puree
        2 cans tomato paste
        2 paste cans of water
        1 tsp. sugar
        1 tsp. hot peppercorns (if desired)
        Green peppers and mushrooms, chopped fine
Cook sauce and meatballs together for 2 hours very
slowly on top of range.
VARIATION: Cook hot sausage links in the tomato
sauce along with the meatballs.   Gordon Ainsworth

+ + + + +

TAIPEI SWEET-SOUR BEEF BALLS

1 lb. ground beef
1 egg
1 tsp. salt
¼ tsp. pepper
3 tbls. green onions, diced
3 tbls. cornstarch
1 8-oz. can pineapple wedges
2 green peppers, diced
1 tbl. salad oil
1 tbl. soy sauce
3 tbls. vinegar
1/3 cup sugar
1/3 cup water

Mix beef, egg, salt, pepper, green onions and 1 tbl.
cornstarch together. Shape into marble-sized balls.
Drain pineapple, reserving juice. Heat oil in skillet
and brown meat balls on all sides. Remove meat from
skillet. Mix together the remaining cornstarch, soy
sauce, vinegar, sugar, water and pineapple juice.
Add to the skillet, stirring steadily until thickened.
Add pineapple, green peppers and meat balls. Bring
to boil and cook 3 minutes. Serve over rice.
Serves 4-6
                              Tarver Jo Smith

HAMBURGER-BEAN CASSEROLE

1 lb. ground beef
1 onion, chopped
1 pkg. or can green beans, cooked
1 can tomato soup
1 tsp. Worcestershire sauce

Brown meat with onion. Season. Add soup and Worcestershire sauce. Place green beans in bottom of greased casserole dish; top with meat mixture. For topping use whatever is on hand: either grated cheese or cheese slices, croutons, mashed potatoes, etc. Place in oven to heat through until bubbly and browned top.

Sue Cowan

+ + + + +

BEEFBURGER PIE
(Cheese Puff)

2 tbls. shortening
2 tbls. onion, chopped
3/4 lb. ground beef
1 tsp. salt
Pepper
2 tbls. flour
2 cups tomatoes
½ tsp. Worcestershire sauce
1 cup diced carrots, cooked
1 cup green beans, cooked
1 cup sifted flour
1½ tsps. baking powder
½ tsp. dry mustard
½ tsp. salt
2 tbls. shortening
¼ cup sharp cheese, grated
½ cup milk

Brown onion and meat in shortening. Add salt, pepper and flour; mix. Add tomatoes, Worcestershire sauce; cook until slightly thickened. Add cooked vegetables and pour into greased casserole. Prepare topping: Sift together dry ingredients; cut in shortening; add cheese and milk; blend to a soft dough. Pour topping over meat mixture; spread evenly. Bake 20-25 minutes at 350°. Serves 6

Jean Moore

SLOPPY JOES

1 lb. hamburger
1 onion, chopped
1 **sm.** can tomato sauce
½-1 cup barbeque sauce (depending on flavor desired)

Brown hamburger and drain off excess fat. Add chopped onion, tomato sauce and barbeque sauce. Simmer for about 30 minutes.

Sharyn Regier

+ + + + +

SLOPPY JOES

1 lb. ground beef
2 tbls. shortening
2/3 cup chopped onion
1 tbl. prepared mustard
1 can chicken gumbo soup
¼ soup-can of water
2 tbls. ketchup
½ tsp. salt
1/8 tsp. pepper

Brown meat in hot fat until broken up, but not too dark. Add onions and cook until golden brown. Stir in rest of ingredients. Simmer over low heat for 20 minutes, stirring occasionally. Serve on warm hamburger buns.

Nancy Robinson

VARIATION: Omit mustard, ketchup and water and add ¼ cup barbeque sauce, 1 tsp. liquid smoke and 2 tbls. brown sugar. Simmer 20 minutes.

Lee Etta Lappen

+ + + + +

MRS. BELL'S SLOPPY JOES

[Very economical, goes far and is very tangy]

1 lb. ground beef
4 tbls. sugar
2 tbls. mustard
2 tbls. vinegar
6 tbls. catsup
6 tbls. chili sauce
Salt and pepper

Brown hamburger slowly. Add rest of ingredients. Simmer about 15-20 minutes. Drain off grease, serve on hamburger rolls.

Jude Mariano

198

CHASEN'S CHILI

[Tuck napkin under chin. Dig in. It's delicious!]

½ lb. pinto beans
5 cups canned tomatoes
1 lb. chopped green pepper
1½ tbls. salad oil
1½ lbs. chopped onions
2 cloves crushed garlic
½ cup chopped parsley
½ cup butter
2½ lbs. ground beef chuck
1 lb. ground lean pork
1-3 cups chili powder
2 tbls. salt
1½ tsps. pepper
1½ tsps. cumin seed
1½ tsps. MSG

Wash beans, soak overnight in water. Simmer, covered,
in same water until tender. Add tomatoes and simmer
5 minutes. Saute' green pepper in salad oil 5 minutes. Add onion, cook until tender, stirring often.
Add garlic and parsley. Melt butter and saute'
meat for 15 minutes. Add meat to onion mixture, stir
in chili powder and cook 10 minutes. Add this to
beans and add spices. Simmer, covered for one hour.
Cook uncovered 30 minutes. Skim fat from top.

Grace Frick

+ + + + +

CHILI

1 large onion, chopped
1 lb. hamburger
2 sm. cans red kidney beans
1 large can tomatoes (may use fresh)
2 tbls. brown sugar
2-4 tbls. chili powder
8-oz. can tomato sauce (opt.)

Brown hamburger with onion. Add other ingredients.
Simmer a few minutes. It's best if it stands overnight and is then reheated.

Don Van Deraa

SUSIE'S 'TATOR-TOT CASSEROLE

1 onion, chopped
1 bell pepper, chopped
1½ lbs. ground chuck
1 8-oz. pkg. cream cheese
1 can cream of chicken soup
½ soup can milk
1 sm. can green peas
1 pkg. frozen 'Tator Tots

Saute' onion and pepper. Brown meat. In small
saucepan over low heat, combine cream cheese, soup
and milk. Combine meat mixture with cheese mixture
in large casserole dish. Add peas. Place frozen
'Tator Tots on top. Bake at 425° until 'Tator Tots
are browned.

Bonnie Porter

+ + + + +

TATER TOT CASSEROLE

1 lb. ground beef, seasoned
1 onion, chopped
1 pkg. Tater Tots
1 can cream of mushroom soup
½ can milk

Brown meat and place in bottom of baking dish. Add
a layer of onion and Tater Tots. Cover with soup
mixed with milk. Bake at 350° for 1 hour.

Ruth Jones

+ + + + +

MEAT AND POTATO CASSEROLE

[Excellent for economy entertaining!]

1½ lbs. ground beef
3/4 cup oats, uncooked
¼ cup chopped onion
1½ tsps. salt
¼ tsp. pepper
1 cup tomato juice
1 egg, beaten
Mashed potatoes

Combine ingredients. Spread in a casserole dish and
bake at 350° for 1 hour. Prepare mashed potatoes for
6 and spread on top of meat (after draining off
grease). Sprinkle with grated cheese and return to
oven until cheese melts. Serves 6

Lee Etta Lappen

200

ORANGE PORK CHOPS

4 center cut loin pork chops 1" thick
Salt and pepper
Paprika
3-4 tbls. water
5 tbls. granulated sugar
1½ tsps. cornstarch
¼ tsp. salt
¼ tsp. cinnamon
10 whole cloves
2 tsps. grated orange rind
½ cup orange juice
4 halved orange slices

Generously sprinkle both sides of chops with salt,
pepper and paprika. Cook until golden brown on both
sides -- 15-20 minutes. Spoon off grease as it accum-
ulates. When well-browned, turn heat low. Add water.
Cover skillet tightly; cook chops 45 minutes to 1 hour
or until fork tender and well done, turning several
times during cooking. About 20 minutes before chops
are done, make orange glaze: in sauce pan combine
sugar, cornstarch, salt, cinnamon, cloves, orange
rind and juice, stirring and heating until thickened
and clear. Add orange slices, cover pan, remove from
heat. Serve chops with a spoonful of glaze on top,
garnish with orange slices.

Kerry Fix

+ + + + +

BAKED ORANGE PORK CHOPS

Bake pork chops with "Shake and Bake" type coating
per package directions. Ten minutes before chops are
done, make orange sauce:
5 tbls. sugar
1½ tsps. cornstarch
¼ tsps. salt
¼ tsp. cinnamon
10 whole cloves
2 tsps. grated orange rind
½ cup orange juice
Orange slices, halved

Cook in saucepan, stirring until thickened and clear.
Add orange slices; cover; remove from heat. Spoon
sauce over chops; garnish with orange slices. Nice
with corn bread, peas, and cole slaw. Enough for
4-6 chops.

Carol Barger and Linda Skulte

BAKED PORK CHOPS

Lean pork chops, seasoned
1 white onion, sliced
½ cup catsup

Place chops close together in frying pan. Slice raw
white onion and spread slices on top. Spread catsup
around top of meat and onions. Run tap water in pan
until just covering the meat. Bake at 375° for 1 hour
-- uncovering the last 15 minutes. Check water peri-
odically.
VARIATION: Sprinkle with brown sugar before adding
catsup.

                      Sandy Davis and Judy Anderson

+ + + + +

PORK CHOPS AND GRAVY

Place 12 trimmed, browned chops in baking dish.
Combine:
2 cans cream of chicken soup
1 sm. (or med.) can mushrooms
4 tbls. catsup
3 tbls. Worcestershire sauce
Salt and pepper

Thin with a little water if desired. Cover pork
chops with sauce and bake at 300° for 2 hours.
Serves 6.

                                    Jan Stevens

+ + + + +

MEAT ROLL

[Good for leftover beef]

1½ cups chopped leftover meat
1 tbl. minced onion
¼ tsp. salt
3 tbls. gravy
Mix above ingredients together.   Prepare dough:
2 cups flour
4 tbls. shortening
4 tsps. baking powder
½ tsp. salt
3/4 cup milk

Make this into a soft dough (or use Bisquick) and
roll out ¼" thick. Spread with meat mixture. Roll
up like jelly roll. Cut into 1" slices. Place cut
side up on greased baking pan. Dot with shortening.
Bake at 450° for 15 minutes.

                                    Lynn Noble

ORIENTAL DINNER

INDONESIAN PORK ROAST

1 fresh pork shoulder butt (5-6 lbs.)
1 clove garlic, minced
1 chicken bouillon cube
¼ cup sugar
1 cup water
½ cup soy sauce

Brown pork in its own fat in a Dutch oven or heavy
kettle. Combine remaining ingredients, pour over
meat and cover. Simmer, turning 2-3 times, for 2-2½
hours until tender. Place meat on heated platter;
slice and serve with plain or curried rice and applesauce or chutney. Serves 8
[Wrap any leftover meat and chill for Peking Pork.
Strain liquid and save for basting Peking Pork.]

PEKING PORK

Leftover Indonesian Pork Roast sliced thin. Arrange
on broiler rack and brush with liquid saved from
Indonesian Pork Roast. Broil about 4" from heat,
brushing often with liquid, 5 minutes on each side,
or until brown and crisp.

Arrange slices in a ring on top of Chinese Vegetable
Bowl and serve with hot buttered rice. Serves 4

CHINESE VEGETABLE BOWL

¼ cup cooking oil
1 Bermuda onion, sliced thin
2 cups thinly sliced celery
1 can (6-oz.) sliced mushrooms
1 pkg. frozen Chinese pea pods
    or 1 pkg. frozen Italian green beans
2 cups coarsely chopped Chinese cabbage
2 cups coarsely chopped escarole (or endive)
1 can (5-oz.) water chestnuts, drained and sliced
Soy sauce

Heat oil in large frying pan. Saute' onion lightly;
add celery and liquid from mushrooms. Cover, steam
5 minutes. Lay Chinese pea pods or green beans,
Chinese cabbage, escarole, water chestnuts and mushrooms in layers on top. Cover and steam 5 minutes
longer, or just until crisply cooked.

Toss together, salad bowl style. Top with Peking
Pork. Serve with rice and soy sauce.

Dorothy Brooks

+ + + + +

SWEET-SOUR PORK

[An excellent company dish. This looks complicated, but if you read it through, you will find it not so difficult. You may cut up the vegetables and meat ahead and store them in the refrigerator in tupperware.]

MEAT STEP:
3 3/4 lbs. pork shoulder, cut into 1" cubes
½ cup flour
1 tbl. ginger
½ cup salad oil

Trim excess fat from pork. Mix flour and ginger and coat pork with it. Heat oil in large skillet and brown meat. Remove meat as it browns. Place meat in uncovered pan in low oven (250-300°) for about 20-30 minutes (while you're preparing remaining ingredients).

SAUCE STEP:
2 cans (13½-oz. each) chunk pineapple (reserve syrup)
2 tbls. cornstarch
½ cup vinegar
½ cup soy sauce
1 tbl. Worcestershire sauce
3/4 tsp. pepper
1 tbl. salt
3/4 cup sugar

Add water to reserved syrup to measure 1 3/4 cups liquid; gradually stir into cornstarch. Stir pineapple syrup mixture, vinegar, soy sauce and Worcestershire sauce into fat in skillet; heat to boiling, stirring constantly. Boil and stir for one minute. Stir in sugar, salt, pepper and heat again.

VEGETABLE AND FINISHING STEPS:
2 sm. green peppers, cut in strips
1 can water chestnuts, drained and thinly sliced
4 green onions, thinly sliced
3 tbls. chili sauce or ketchup
5 cups hot cooked rice

Add meat, pineapple chunks, peppers, water chestnuts and onions to sauce and heat 10 minutes. Stir in chili sauce. Serve with rice. Garnish with sliced green onions. Serves 8-10

Carol Soderquist

SAUSAGE CASSEROLE

½ lb. sausage
2½ cups boiling water
½ stalk celery, chopped
½ can mushroom soup
1½ pkgs. dried chicken noodle soup
½ cup raw rice
½ green pepper
½ small onion

Place chicken soup in large pan. Pour hot water over. Add rice and cook 15 minutes or until thick. Add chopped celery, onion and green pepper. Fry sausage, drain, and add to mixture. Add slivered almonds if desired and stir until thick. Place in baking dish and add mushroom soup. Bake at 350° for 45 minutes.

Roselyn Shaver

+ + + + +

SAUSAGE AND RICE BAKE

1½ lbs. bulk pork sausage
4½ cups water
2 pkgs. (2 1/8-oz. each) dehydrated chicken noodle
     soup
1 cup celery, diced
1 pimiento, finely chopped (opt.)
1 med. onion, finely chopped
½ green pepper, finely chopped
1 cup uncooked rice
½ cup grated sharp cheddar cheese

Fry sausage until browned and drain. Heat water to boiling, pour into sausage and stir. Stir in chicken soup, bring to boil again and remove from heat. Add celery, pimiento, onion, peppers and rice. Put in 9 x 13" baking pan or 2-qt. casserole. Sprinkle grated cheese over top. Bake, uncovered at 300° for 1 hour or until rice has absorbed liquid and is done. If desired, serve with milk gravy. Serves 6-8

+ + + + +

SPAGHETTI PIE

1 pkg. Kraft Italian style spaghetti dinner
2 eggs, beaten
½ cup chopped green pepper
1/3 cup chopped onion
2 tbls. margarine
1 pkg. Kraft sour cream sauce mix
1 lb. pork sausage meat
Herb spice mix
1 6-oz. can tomato paste
1 cup water
Kraft low moisture part skim Mozzarella cheese cut
     in strips

Prepare spaghetti as directed on package. Add eggs
and the grated Parmesan cheese; mix lightly. Line
greased 9 or 10" pie plate with spaghetti. Cook
green pepper and onion in margarine until tender.
Stir in sour cream sauce mix and milk until blended.
Spoon over spaghetti. Brown sausage; drain, stir in
herb spice mix, tomato paste and water; simmer ten
minutes. Spoon over sauce mixture. Bake at 350°
for 25 minutes. Top with cheese strips; return to
oven until cheese melts.

Barbara Ball

+ + + + +

MACARONI CASSEROLE

Brown 1 lb. pork sausage and add
3/4 cup chopped green pepper
(If you like Mexican food, add mild chili peppers)
3½ cups canned tomatoes
2 cups sour cream
2 tbls. sugar
1 tsp. chili powder
1 tsp. salt
1 sm. pkg. macaroni

Mix; cook in electric skillet at 300° (or in deep
skillet and simmer on low) until macaroni is tender.

Roselyn Shaver

206

GOURMET CASSEROLE

3/4 to 1 lb. sausage
1 sm. onion, chopped
½ cup celery, chopped
1 can cream of mushroom soup
1 can cream of chicken soup
2 cups instant rice, uncooked
2-oz. can mushrooms
2-oz. jar pimiento, chopped
½ to 1 cup cheese, grated

Brown sausage in skillet. Add onion and celery.
Cook until limp. Pour off grease. Add rest of
ingredients. Pour into 2-qt. casserole and cover.
Bake at 325° for 45 minutes. Serves 6-8

Dorothy Gregory

+ + + + +

VEAL-PINEAPPLE SURPRISE

[A quickie dinner party meat course]

4 Veal escalopes (cutlets pounded about 1/8" thin)
4 slices cooked ham
Pineapple rings
Grated cheddar cheese
Butter

Fast fry veal escalopes in butter. Remove from frying
pan and place on pan for grilling. On each piece of
veal place cooked ham slice, a pineapple ring, and
coat with grated cheese. Grill until cheese is bubbly. Garnish with half a pineapple ring and maraschino cherry. (This meat course takes about 5-10
minutes to prepare and always receives rave compliments. Can be served with broccoli and creamed
potatoes and carrots.)

Ethelwynne Reeves

HAM ROLLS

2½ lbs. ground smoked ham
2 lbs. ground lean pork
3 cups graham cracker crumbs
1 lb. ground beef
3 eggs
2 cups milk

Mix and shape into 25 balls. Cover with the following sauce just before baking:
  2 cups tomato soup
  1 3/4 cups brown sugar
  3/4 cup vinegar
  2 tsps. dry mustard

Bake at 350° for 1 hour. (NOTE: This recipe freezes
very well. The sauce also.)
Roselyn Shaver

+ + + + +

DONNA'S HAM DELIGHTS

1½ lbs. canned ham in thin slices
12 oz. processed, sliced Swiss cheese
1 box frozen chopped broccoli, cooked (or more)
SAUCE:
4 tbls. diced onions. Cook in
4 tbls. butter until tender. Mix in
4 tbls. flour, making a paste. Add
2 cups milk and stir. (Or instead of the milk and
    flour, use 1 pkg. instant chicken gravy.) Heat
    and stir until thick and creamy. Place stacks of
ham slice, Swiss cheese slice, broccoli, Swiss cheese
slice, ham slice in a shallow pan. When all ingredients have been used, pour sauce over. Bake at 350°
for 45 minutes. Serves 6-7
Kathie Brooks

+ + + + +

DOUBLE GOOD MACARONI AND CHEESE

1 pkg. (8-oz.) elbow macaroni
1 lb. cream-style cottage cheese
3/4 cup dairy sour cream
1 egg, slightly beaten
1 tsp. salt
1/8 tsp. pepper
2 tsps. grated onion
1 pkg. (8-oz.) sharp cheddar cheese, shredded

Cook macaroni; follow label directions; drain.
Combine cottage cheese, sour cream, egg, salt,
pepper, onion and cheddar cheese in a large bowl;
mix lightly until blended. Fold in macaroni.
Spoon into a 9" baking dish. Bake at 350° for 45
minutes or until bubbly. Serves 8

Veletta Frink

+ + + + +

MACARONI AND CHEESE SQUARES

1½ cups cheese   1 tbl. minced onion
1½ cups scalded milk   ½ tsp. salt
1 cup soft bread cubes   1/8 tsp. pepper
¼ cup butter or margarine   1 cup cooked macaroni
¼ cup chopped pimiento   1 egg

Pour milk over bread cubes. Add butter, pimiento,
onion, cheese and seasonings. Mix well. Add egg
and macaroni. Pour into 8 x 12" baking dish. Bake
at 325° for 50 minutes. Serve hot with Mushroom
Sauce: Heat 1 can cream of mushroom soup with ¼ cup
milk. Stir to blend. Sprinkle with chopped parsley.

+ + + + +

MACARONI AND CHEESE WITH HOT DOGS

8 cups elbow macaroni
6 cans cheddar cheese soup
2 cups milk
3 lbs. hot dogs, cut in bite size pieces

Cook macaroni as directed. Mix cheese soup with
prepared instant powdered milk and blend with the
macaroni. Add hot dog pieces. Heat in oven until
hot. Serve with carrot sticks, apples and/or bananas
and cookies. Serves approximately 20 people. Cost
30¢ per person.

Alayne Gustafson

QUICHE LORRAINE

[Cheese pie -- good for ladies' luncheon]

1 9" unbaked pastry shell
8 slices bacon
½ lb. Swiss cheese, shredded
1 tbl. flour
½ tsp. salt
Dash nutmeg
3 eggs, beaten
1 3/4 cup milk

Bake pastry shell at 450° for only 7 minutes --
lightly browned. Remove from oven, reduce heat to
325°. Fry bacon until crisp, drain and crumble.
Reserve 2 tbls. bacon for trim. Place remaining
bacon in pie shell along with the cheese. Combine
remaining ingredients. Pour over cheese. Sprinkle
reserved bacon on top. Bake at 325° for 35-40 minutes. Let set 10-15 minutes before serving.
Serves 6-8

Joan Kendall

+ + + + +

210

CORNED BEEF CASSEROLE

[Economical and good]

1 8-oz. pkg. broad noodles -- cooked
1 12-oz. can corned beef
¼ lb. cheddar cheese (1 cup), diced
½ cup onion, chopped
1 can cream of chicken soup
1 1/3 cup milk
3/4 cup buttered bread crumbs

Flake corned beef; add cheese, onion, soup and milk
mixed together. Mix with cooked noodles and place in
buttered 2-qt. casserole. Top with bread crumbs and
bake at 350° for 45 minutes. Serves 10

Charlotte Day

+ + + + +

CORNED BEEF HOT DINNER

1 can corned beef (separate into pieces)
1 cup raw rice
1 can cream of mushroom soup
1 can cream of celery soup
2 soup cans water
½ tsp. salt
3 carrots, shredded
1 medium onion, chopped
1 bay leaf

Mix ingredients together and place in 2-qt. casserole.
Lay bay leaf on top. Bake at 350° for 1½ hours or
more.

Roselyn Shaver

+ + + + +

LIVER IN MUSHROOM SAUCE

[Delicious and nutritious!]

1 lb. liver
1 can mushroom soup
¼ cup water
2 tbls. bacon drippings

Season and coat liver in flour. Brown in skillet in
bacon drippings. Add soup and water. Simmer, covered, until liver is tender (5-10 minutes). DO NOT
OVERCOOK! Liver becomes tough when overcooked.

Lee Etta Lappen

BARBECUE SAUCE

[Delicious with a pit barbecue taste]

3/4 cup catsup
3/4 cup water
2 med. onions, chopped
2 tbls. vinegar
2 tbls. Worcestershire sauce
1½ tsps. salt
½ tsp. pepper
1 tsp. chili powder
1 tsp. paprika
1 clove garlic
1 tsp. liquid smoke
1 tbl. brown sugar

Combine all ingredients in saucepan and simmer 5 minutes. This sauce keeps indefinitely in refrigerator. For Oven Barbecued Spareribs: Cut ribs in pieces; place in baking pan and pour sauce over them. Bake at 350° for 45 minutes to 1 hour.

Lee Etta Lappen

+ + + + +

BARBECUE SAUCE

[For ribs, chicken, beef, pork or hamburger]

½ med. onion
1 tbl. oil
2 tbls. vinegar
2 tbls. lemon juice
1 tbl. brown sugar
½ cup catsup
¼ cup water
1½ tbls. Worcestershire sauce
½ tsp. prepared mustard
¼ cup celery, chopped
1 tsp. salt

Brown meat and onion. Combine ingredients and add to meat. Cover and cook slowly 1-2 hours.

Judy DeBoer

SPAGHETTI SAUCE

Brown:
1¼ lb. ground beef and 2 large onions together in
3 tbls. shortening. Add:
1 can tomato puree
2 cans tomato paste   4 cloves garlic
2 puree cans water   Salt and pepper
2 bay leaves   4 tbls. sugar
2 whole red peppers   Dash chili powder

Barbara Ball

+ + + + +

ITALIAN MEATLESS SPAGHETTI SAUCE

[Economical but good!]

½ cup butter
½ cup water
1 6-oz. can tomato paste
4 garlic cloves, minced
1 tbl. salt
2 tsps. rosemary or 1 tbl. Italian seasoning
Parmesan cheese to taste

Simmer ingredients for 1 hour. Pour over 1 lb. pkg.
of cooked spaghetti. Serves 4

Lana Jones

+ + + + +

ITALIAN SPAGHETTI SAUCE

3/4 cup chopped onion
1 clove garlic, minced
3 tbls. olive oil
2 #1 cans tomatoes
2 6-oz. cans tomato paste
1 cup water
1 tbl. sugar
1½ tsps. salt
½ tsp. pepper
2 tsps. crushed oregano
½ cup mushrooms

Cook onion and garlic in hot oil until tender, but
not brown; stir in remaining ingredients. Simmer uncovered 30 minutes; add Italian Meat Balls and cook
from 45 minutes to 2 hours longer. Serves 6

Lois Mackey and Judy Knop

(Italian Meat Ball recipe – page 193)

MEATSAUCE

1 lb. hamburger   1 sm. can tomato sauce
1 onion, chopped   Seasonings

Brown hamburger and drain off excess fat. Add rest
of ingredients and simmer about 30 minutes. Sauce
may be added to spaghetti before serving or each
person may add the sauce to his own spaghetti.

Sharyn Regier

+ + + + +

TERIYAKI SAUCE

1 12-oz. bottle soy sauce (Kikko Man)
1 cup sugar
Fresh ginger root--grate enough to taste strong

Cook soy sauce to about half the amount by boiling
in an open kettle about 20 minutes. Add sugar and
ginger root and cook 10 minutes. Strain mixture.
Keep in a jar in the refrigerator. Use to marinate
steaks (allow 2 hours). Good on pork chops - cooked
at 400° for 45 minutes.

Vonette Bright

+ + + + +

MARINATE SAUCE

½ cup oil
2 tbls. soy sauce
1 tsp. garlic salt

Blend thoroughly.   Dorothy Gregory

+ + + + +

FRUITY MEAT SAUCE

1 can cranberry jelly
1 sm. can shredded pineapple, well drained
Grated rind of 2 oranges

Mix well.   Stella Friend

+ + + + +

RELISHES TO BE SERVED WITH MEATS:

Roast Veal -
    Tomato Sauce
    Horseradish Sauce

Fried Chicken -
    Cream Gravy
    Corn Fritters

Roast Duck -
    Apple Sauce
    Currant Jelly

Pork Sausage -
    Tart Apple Sauce
    Fried Apples

Roast Beef -
    Tomato Catsup
    Grated Horseradish

Roast Mutton -
    Currant Jelly
    Stewed Gooseberries

Roast Lamb -
    Mint Sauce

Roast Pork -
    Apple Sauce

Roast Turkey -
    Cranberry or Celery
    Plum, Grape Sauce

Roast Chicken -
    Currant Jelly

Broiled Steak -
    Mushrooms
    Fried Onions

Roast Goose -
    Tart Apple Sauce

Fried Salmon -
    Egg Sauce

Broiled Mackerel -
    Stewed Gooseberries

Boiled or Baked Fish -
    White Cream Sauce
    Drawn Butter Sauce

BASIC WHITE SAUCE

<u>THIN:</u>   (like coffee cream--for creamed vegetables,
        soups, etc.)
    1 tbl. butter   1/8 tsp. pepper
    ½-1 tbl. flour   1 cup milk
    ¼ tsp. salt

<u>MEDIUM:</u>   (like thick cream--for creamed and scalloped
        dishes.)
    2 tbls. butter   1/8 tsp. pepper
    2 tbls. flour   1 cup milk
    ¼ tsp. salt

<u>THICK:</u>   (like batter--for croquettes, souffles', etc.)
    ¼ cup butter   1/8 tsp. pepper
    ¼ cup flour   1 cup milk
    ¼ tsp. salt

Melt butter over low heat in a heavy saucepan.
(Wooden spoon for stirring is a help.) Blend in
flour and seasonings. Cook over low heat, stirring
until mixture is smooth and bubbly. Remove from
heat. Stir in milk; bring to boil, stirring constantly. Boil 1 minute. Makes 1 cup.

VARIATIONS:
Cheese Sauce - to 1 cup medium white sauce add ¼ tsp.
dry mustard with the seasonings. Blend in ½ cup
nippy cheddar cheese, cut up or grated. Stir until
cheese is melted. For vegetables, rice, macaroni and
egg dishes.

Rich Cheese Sauce - to 2 cups medium white sauce add
2 cups cut-up or grated nippy cheddar cheese, 2 tsps.
dry mustard, and 1 tsp. Worcestershire sauce. Stir
until cheese is melted.

Mushroom Sauce - Add 1 cup saute'd sliced mushrooms
and 1 tsp. grated onion to the butter 5 minutes
before adding flour.

Egg Sauce - Carefully stir two diced hard-cooked
eggs into 1 cup medium white sauce. Season. Good
with salmon and other fish.

Curry Sauce - Saute' ½ tsp. curry powder with the
butter before adding flour and other seasonings to
1 cup medium white sauce. Combines perfectly with
chicken, lamb, shrimp and rice.

PIE HINTS:

It is as "easy as pie" to make a perfect pie if directions are followed correctly. Take the guesswork out--measure!

Handle dough as little as possible and work quickly.

A pastry blender is a must for more tender crusts.

Flakiness, crispness, and tenderness are the characteristics of good pastry. Glass or enamelware pie pans make a better browned crust.

Frozen fruit may be substituted for fresh fruit in a pie using only half the amount of sugar called for in the recipe.

For a more golden color, brush crust with milk and sprinkle with sugar before baking.

Sealing edges of meringue to edge of pie will prevent "weeping".

The four "too-muches" to eliminate are: too much flour, too much shortening, too much liquid, too much handling.

Try adding new flavor to your pie crusts by adding ingredients such as grated cheese, ground nuts, and cinnamon. Make 3 or 4 pies at a time. Put several unbaked ones in the freezer and bake as needed.

CRUMB CRUSTS

Variety	Butter	Crumbs	Sugar
Graham crackers	¼ cup	1 1/3 c.	¼ cup
Vanilla wafers	¼ cup	1 1/3 c.	none
Chocolate wafers	3 tbls.	1 1/3 c.	none
Gingersnaps	6 tbls.	1 1/3 c.	none
Corn, rice or wheat cereal	¼ cup	1 1/3 c.	2 tbls.

A general rule applies to all crumb crusts; let butter soften, mix with the measured crumbs and sugar and blend thoroughly with fork. Press into bottom and sides of an 8 or 9" pie pan. Bake about 8 minutes at 350°. Crust may also be chilled rather than baked.

COCONUT CRUST: Spread 2 tbls. butter on bottom and sides of 9" pie pan. Sprinkle 1½ cups coconut (4 oz.) in the pan and press evenly into the butter. Bake 15 to 20 min. at 300° or until golden brown. Cool.

NUT CRUMB CRUST: Reduce crumbs to 1 cup and add ½ cup chopped selected nuts.

BROWN PIE CRUST

20 crushed graham crackers
½ cup brown sugar
½ cup butter, melted

Mix and press into a 9 x 13" pan.   Sandy Buell

+ + + + +

NEVER-FAIL PIE CRUST

[Success for sure, even for the beginner!]

1½ cups flour   3½ tbls cold water
¼ tsp. salt   ½ tbl. vinegar
3/4 cup shortening   1 sm. egg, slightly beaten
1 tsp. sugar

Blend flour, salt, shortening. Mix water, vinegar
and egg; add to flour mixture. Mix well. Shape into
two balls; chill 15 minutes (or up to 3 days). Roll
out immediately or freeze for later use.

Bonnie Porter and Marilyn Ehle

+ + + + +

DOUBLE PIE CRUST

1½ cups flour
½ cup lard (heaping)
½ tsp. salt

Add salt to flour. Remove 4 tablespoons of flour
mixture and add 3 tablespoons water to make a paste.
Mix lard and flour until crumbly. Add paste and mix
together.
                                    Carol Barger

+ + + + +

NO ROLL PASTRY

[Yields 1 crust]

1 1/3 cups sifted flour
½ tsp. salt
1½ tsps. sugar
1/3 cup cooking oil
3 tbls. cold milk

Whip salad oil and milk together, pour over dry ingredients. Mix until completely dampened. Press dough
with fingers to line pie plate. (No rolling necessary.
Not adapted for 2 crust pies. As alternate, sprinkle
pastry crumbs over top.) Brown crust at 400° for
12-15 minutes. Cool.
                        Lana Jones and Peggy Jones

"Through wisdom is an house builded, and by under-
standing it is established; and by knowledge shall
the chambers be filled with all precious and pleasant
riches" (Proverbs 24:3,4).

+ + + + +

RASPBERRY PIE

1 graham cracker crust
1 pkg. raspberry jello
1 cup hot water
1 pt. vanilla ice cream
1 pkg. frozen raspberries, thawed and drained
Whipped cream

Dissolve jello in hot water. Add ice cream and
blend until melted. Add raspberries. When thickened, pour into crust and refrigerate. Spread
whipped cream on top before serving.

Judy DeBoer

+ + + + +

FRESH STRAWBERRY PIE

1 cup sugar
4 cups berries
3 tbls. cornstarch
1 tbl. lemon juice
1 tbl. powdered sugar
1 pie shell, baked
Whipped cream

Crush 2 cups berries and blend with sugar and cornstarch. Cook until thick. Add lemon juice and cool
thoroughly. Sprinkle powdered sugar over bottom of
pie shell. Place uncooked berries on bottom and
cover with cold, cooked mixture. Spread whipped
cream on top.

Barbara Ball

+ + + + +

TROPICANA PIE

1 (13¼-oz.) can crushed pineapple, drained
1½ cups seedless raisins
1 tbl. lemon juice
1 tbl. (1 env.) unflavored gelatin
¼ cup cold water
1 (3½-oz.) pkg. vanilla whipped dessert mix
1 cup dairy sour cream
9" baked pastry shell

Combine pineapple, raisins and lemon juice in sauce-pan. Soften gelatin in water and stir into pineapple mixture. Heat to simmer then simmer 5 minutes, stirring often. Place in refrigerator until cool. Prepare whipped dessert mix according to pkg. directions; fold in sour cream immediately. Fold sour cream mixture into raisin mixture and spoon into baked pastry shell. Chill thoroughly.

Nan Green

+ + + + +

LIME PIE

1 sm. box vanilla wafers
¼ cup margarine, melted
Crush wafers and add margarine. Press into a pie pan and chill while making filling:
¼ cup lemon juice (or lime juice)
2-3 drops green food coloring
1 can sweetened condensed milk
1 sm. can crushed pineapple, drained
Whipped cream

Add lemon juice and food coloring to milk and stir (mixture will thicken). Add pineapple and mix together. Pour into pie crust and chill 3-4 hours or overnight. Serve with whipped cream. Garnish with green sugar sparkles.

Gail Hobson

+ + + + +

FRESH RHUBARB PIE

Pastry for 2-crust pie   4 cups cut-up rhubarb
1½-2 cups sugar   1½ tbls. butter
1/3 cup flour

Mix sugar and flour and stir lightly through the
rhubarb. Pour into 9" pastry-lined pie pan. Dot
with butter. Cover with top crust which has slits
cut in it. Sprinkle with sugar. Bake at 425° for
40-50 minutes until crust is nicely browned and juice
begins to bubble through slits. Serve slightly warm.
VARIATION: Follow above recipe, except substitute
fresh strawberries or blueberries for half the rhubarb. Use less sugar.
VARIATION: Follow above recipe except substitute 1
cup drained crushed pineapple for 1 cup rhubarb.
Use less sugar.

Doris Rood

+ + + + +

RHUBARB CUSTARD PIE

Pastry for 2-crust pie   ¼ cup flour
3 eggs   3/4 tsp. nutmeg
3 tbls. milk   4 cups cut-up pink rhubarb
2 cups sugar

Beat eggs slightly. Add milk. Mix sugar, flour and
nutmeg and stir into eggs. Mix in rhubarb. Pour into
9" pastry-lined pie pan. Dot with 1 tbl. butter;
cover with a lattice top. Bake at 400° for 50-60
minutes until nicely browned. Serve slightly warm.

Doris Rood

+ + + + +

HINTS ABOUT RHUBARB:

To keep rhubarb fresh and crisp, wrap in wet towel in
refrigerator. Save time by cutting up several stalks
at once.

For mild flavor, choose early pink rhubarb. If tender
and pink, do not peel. Cut into 1" pieces (1 lb.
makes 2 cups). The amount of sugar depends on the
tartness of rhubarb. Early rhubarb requires less
sugar. Make pie shallow.

Doris Rood

PAT HEALTHFUL PIE
(A little expensive to make, but tastes good.)

Pastry:
½ cup whole wheat pastry flour
½ cup unbleached flour
½ tsp. salt
½ tsp. baking powder
½ cup vegetable oil
2-3 tbls. cold water (as needed)

Sift dry ingredients in a bowl. Add oil and mix with
a fork. Add water as needed. Work dough with hands
and shape into a ball. Put between 2 pieces of wax
paper and roll out 1/8" thick. Put into 8 or 9" pie
pan; flute edges. Prick with a fork and bake at 450°
for 10-12 minutes. Cool. Line cooled shell with
fresh or canned peach slices. Put layer of bananas
over peaches. Add another layer of peaches. Sprinkle
top with ½ cup raisins. Make a glaze of juice: 1½
cups fruit juice, 2 tbls. cornstarch, and ½-1 cup raw
sugar. Cook until thickened. Cool and pour over pie.

Pat Turanski

+ + + + +

HARVEST TABLE APPLE PIE

Pastry for 9" pie (double crust)
6 medium apples, sliced
1 tbls. cornstarch
1 tsp. cinnamon
¼ tsp. salt
3 tbls. sugar
3 tbls. margarine, melted
1/3 cup Karo syrup (blue label)

Fill bottom of pastry shell with apples. Combine rest
of ingredients and pour over apples. Cover with top
crust and bake at 425° for 45 minutes or until brown
and apples are tender. Remove from oven and spread
on topping:
Mix ¼ cup brown sugar
    2 tbls. flour
    3 tbls. Karo syrup (blue label)
    2 tbls. margarine, softened
    ½ cup chopped nuts
Spread this mixture over top of pie. Return to oven
for 10 more minutes or until bubbly. CAUTION: Pie
may drip, so be sure to place something under it in
the oven.

Janet Wagoner

+ + + + +

ROCKY ROAD PIE

1 pkg. chocolate Whip and Chill
¼ cup chopped walnuts
2/3 cup miniature marshmallows
1 graham cracker crust

Prepare Whip and Chill as directed. Add nuts and
marshmallows. Pour into graham cracker crust. Chill.

+ + + + +

FUDGE SUNDAE PIE

1 cup evaporated milk
6-oz. pkg. semi-sweet chocolate morsels
1 cup miniature marshmallows
¼ tsp. salt
1 9" graham cracker crust
1 qt. vanilla ice cream
Pecans

Mix milk, chocolate, marshmallows and salt in heavy
1-qt. saucepan. Stir over medium heat until chocolate and marshmallows melt completely and mixture
thickens. Remove from heat. Cool to room temperature. Spoon half of 1 quart ice cream over graham
cracker crust. Cover with half of chocolate mixture.
Repeat with rest of ice cream and chocolate. Top
with pecans. Freeze until firm (3-5 hours). May
be kept in the freezer for a month. Serves 8-10

+ + + + +

ICE CREAM PIE SHELL

Chocolate crust:
1 sq. chocolate
2 tbls. butter
2 tbls. hot milk
2/3 cup sifted powdered sugar
1½ cups coconut

Melt chocolate and butter together. Mix in milk,
sugar and coconut. Spread in pie pan and chill.
Fill with any flavor ice cream. Garnish with pecans
or chocolate shavings.

Lynn Noble

CHOCOLATE DREAM PIE

[Showy and delicious! The ladies love this!]

CRUST:
3 egg whites
¼ tsp. cream of tartar
1 cup sugar
16 saltine cracker squares, crushed
½ cup chopped nuts
1 tsp. vanilla

Beat egg whites until fluffy; add cream of tartar
and sugar; beat until stiff. Stir in crushed crackers
with nuts and vanilla; mix. Pour into pie plate and
press into shell. Bake at 350° for 30 minutes.   Cool
and chill.

FILLING:
½ cup margarine   1 tsp. vanilla
3/4 cup sugar   2 eggs, chilled
1 sq. unsweetened chocolate

Cream margarine and sugar; add melted chocolate,
vanilla and 1 egg. Beat 2 minutes and add second
egg; beat 2 more minutes.   Pile into chilled crust.
Top with whipped cream and serve.

Judy Anderson

+ + + + +

CHOCOLATE PIE
RICH!

3 sq. unsweetened chocolate   ¼ tsp. salt
1½ cups sugar   2 cups scalded milk
4 eggs, separated   2 tbls. butter
1/3 cup cornstarch   ½ tsp. vanilla

Mix cornstarch, sugar and salt. Gradually add milk
and put in the chocolate. Cook in top of double
boiler for at least 10 minutes until thick. Slowly
add a small amount of this hot mixture to the 4 egg
yolks. Add yolks to remaining hot mixture. Cook
5 minutes, cool. Add butter and vanilla.   Pour into pie shell and spread with meringue (using the 4
egg whites). Bake at 350° for about 8 minutes. Cool.

Sandy Buell

224

FUDGE PIE

[Quick, easy and good in an emergency]

2 sqs. unsweetened chocolate
½ cup butter
2 eggs
1 cup sugar
¼ cup flour
1/8 tsp. salt
1 tsp. vanilla

Melt chocolate in butter. Beat eggs and add sugar, flour, salt and vanilla. Add chocolate mixture and stir well. Place in greased pie plate. Bake at 350° for 25-30 minutes. Serve with ice cream.

Sandy Buell

+ + + + +

PECAN PIE

[An economical, expensive-tasting pie]

½ cup sugar
2 tbls. butter
2 tbl. flour
2 eggs, well-beaten
1 cup light Karo
¼ tsp. salt
½ tsp. vanilla
½ cup pecans, chopped
9" unbaked pie shell

Cream butter and sugar together. Add rest of ingredients in the order listed. Pour into pie shell. Bake at 350° for 40-45 minutes or until center is firm.

Gwen Martin

+ + + + +

"The only way to prepare to meet God is to live with Him so that to meet Him shall be nothing strange." (Phillips Brooks)

LEMON PIE FILLING

1 cup sugar
½ cup flour
¼ tsp. salt
Mix above in sauce pan. Gradually add:
1 to 1½ cups milk (½ to 3/4 of 1 pint of milk)
Add 3 egg yolks, mixing well. Cook over medium heat,
stirring until mixture shows signs of thickening,
then gradually add the remainder of the pint of milk.
Stir constantly. Mixture will thicken fast, so keep
on heat, stirring rapidly. When all lumps have
dissolved, set off heat and add 6 tbls. margarine
(1 spoonful at a time). Return to heat to continue
melting and smoothing out lumps. It will be very
thick. Set off to cool about 5 or 10 minutes. Add
juice of 2 or 3 lemons (approximately ½ cup lemon
juice). Stir well and cool then place in baked pie
shell. (The reason for cooling slightly before
adding lemon juice is to prevent lemon juice from
cooking.)

Lee Etta Lappen

+ + + + +

LEMON ANGEL PIE

[Out of this world - light and rich!]

4 eggs, separated
½ tsp. cream of tartar
1½ cups sugar
Juice and rind of 1 lemon
¼ cup water
1 cup (½ pint) whipping cream

Beat egg whites until frothy and add cream of tartar;
beat until stiff. Add 1 cup sugar gradually, beating
constantly until glossy. Line bottom and sides of
9" pie plate with this meringue. Bake in 275° oven
for 1 hour. Beat egg yolks until thick and light,
add remaining ½ cup sugar, lemon juice, lemon rind
and ¼ cup water. Cook over hot water (in double
boiler), stirring constantly until thick. Cool.
Cool meringue shell. Spread lemon in bottom of shell
and top with whipped cream. Store in refrigerator.

Carol Sims

MAGIC LEMON MERINGUE PIE

[A no-cook creamy lemon filling that is as easy
as a mix.]

FILLING:
1 8" crumb or baked pastry pie shell, cooled
1 1/3 cups (15-oz. can) sweetened condensed milk
½ cup lemon juice
1 tsp. grated lemon peel
2 egg yolks

In medium mixing bowl blend together condensed milk,
lemon juice, lemon peel and yolks until thickened.
Turn into pie shell.

MERINGUE:
2 egg whites (at room temperature)
¼ tsp. cream of tartar
¼ cup sugar

In small mixing bowl whip whites with cream of tartar
until they hold a soft peak. Gradually whip in
sugar; continue to whip until they hold firm peaks.
Pour onto pie filling and seal to edge of pie shell.
Bake at 325° until golden brown on top, about 15
minutes. Cool.

Peggy Jones

+ + + + +

LEMON FLUFF PIE

[Here is a good light recipe that is economical and
serves 15.]

Graham cracker crust
1 can evaporated milk, chilled
1 pkg. lemon jello
1 cup hot water
1 cup cold water
Juice from 1 lemon
Rind from 1 lemon, shredded
½ cup sugar

Blend all ingredients (except the canned milk) and
chill until syrupy. Whip chilled, canned milk until
fluffy. Blend in jello mixture and mix well. Pour
into 9 x 13" graham cracker crust and chill.

Lanita Reimer

SALAD HINTS:

"He that is of a merry heart hath a continual feast"
(Proverbs 15:15)

Chop or tear one head of lettuce. Mix in one or two
grated carrots. Add salad dressing before serving.
(Sharyn Regier)

Add cooking oil first to salad greens then add vinegar and spices; this will prevent your lettuce from
wilting. (Vonette Bright)

When preparing jello, add jello to boiling water instead of boiling water to jello. It needs less
stirring this way. (Midge Piedot)

If you make your own salad dressings, you can achieve
gourmet results at a fraction of the cost of bottled
dressings.

Think of "eye-appeal" when preparing a salad. Have
contrasts in color, texture, form and flavor.

Do not repeat a food in the salad that may be served
in another course of the meal.

Salads have two classifications: Light, as a lettuce
salad; heavy, as a meat, egg, or cheese salad.

If chopping green pepper or onion for a recipe, chop
an extra supply, then freeze the surplus for later
use.

In making salad dressing, lemon juice is more suitable to use with fruits; while vinegar is with meats
and vegetables.

Remember the Spanish proverb: "Four persons are
wanted to make a good salad: a spendthrift for oil,
a miser for vinegar, a counsellor for salt, and a
madman to stir all up."

> The kiss of the sun for pardon
> The song of the birds for mirth
> One is nearer God's heart in a garden
> Than anywhere else on earth.

"You can be too big for God to use but never too
small." (J. Hudson Taylor)

PINE-COT SALAD

1 can (13½-oz.) crushed pineapple, drained, save juice
1 can (1-lb.) apricots, peeled, drained, save juice
1 sm. pkg. orange jello
½ cup hot water
1 cup miniature marshmallows

Dissolve jello in hot water. Add ½ cup pineapple juice and ½ cup apricot juice. Cool. When jello begins to congeal, add crushed pineapple, mashed apricots and marshmallows. Let stand until firm. Spread with the following topping:
    3/4 cup pineapple and apricot juice
    ¼ cup sugar
    1 rounded tbl. flour
    1 egg, beaten
    1 tbl. butter

Cook until thick. When the mixture is cool, add ½ cup whipped cream (may use Cool Whip) and 2 tsp. Miracle Whip. Spread on jello. Cover with grated American cheese. Let stand several hours in refrigerator.

Roselyn Shaver

+ + + + +

BALLOON LAYER SALAD

2 sm. pkgs. or 1 large lemon jello
1 can crushed pineapple
2 large bananas, mashed
½ to 3/4 pkg. miniature marshmallows

Dissolve jello in 2 cups boiling water. Add 2 cups cold water. Cool until thickened or syrupy. Add drained pineapple, bananas and marshmallows. Pour into 9 x 13" pan. Chill.
DRESSING:
Pineapple juice and enough water to make 1 cup
Add: ½ cup sugar
       2 tbls. flour
       2 tbls. butter
       1 egg
Beat all together and cook until thick. Let cool; fold in 1 cup whipped cream (or Cool Whip). Spread over top of jello and sprinkle with grated cheese.

Carol Barger

GINGERALE SALAD

1 sm. pkg. orange gelatin
½ cup boiling water
1½ cups gingerale
2/3 cup Delicious apples, diced, unpeeled
¼ cup celery, diced fine
Nuts
½ cup grapes, halved and pitted
2 slices canned pineapple, cut up

Add water to gelatin and stir to dissolve. Add
gingerale and rest of the ingredients. Pour into
long cake pan. Chill. Cut in squares and place
on lettuce leaf and top with whipped cream to
serve. Serves 6-8

Elaine Karn

+ + + + +

BING CHERRY SALAD

1 sm. pkg. black cherry jello
1 can bing cherries, pitted
½ cup pecans

Add 1 cup boiling water to jello. Stir in 1 cup
cherry juice. Mix in cherries and pecans. Chill.
Serves 6

+ + + + +

RASPBERRY JELLO SALAD

1 large pkg. raspberry or cherry jello
1 8-oz. pkg. cream cheese
1 8-oz. can crushed pineapple, drained
5 cups miniature marshmallows (white or flavored)

Dissolve jello as per directions and let set until
firm. Whip cream cheese in mixer about 2 minutes.
Add the firm set jello and beat together. Stir in
pineapple and marshmallows. Pour into large jello
mold. Let set 3 hours before serving.

Toya Rennick

LIME-PINEAPPLE SALAD

[Also good as a dessert]

1 can crushed pineapple
1 sm. pkg. lime jello
6-ozs. cream cheese, softened
1 cup whipping cream
1 cup celery, chopped
Nuts (opt.)

Heat pineapple to boiling and stir in jello until
dissolved. Chill until partially set. Add cheese
to gelatin, fold in whipped cream, celery and nuts.
Chill until firm. Cut in squares and serve on lettuce
or put into individual molds.

Candace Steele

+ + + + +

LIME JELLO SALAD

Add 2 cups boiling water to 1 sm. pkg. lime jello.
Cool until lukewarm and add 1 sm. pkg. cream cheese
that has been mashed. Set in refrigerator until
partially set. Add 1 can crushed pineapple, pimiento
bits (optional), chopped pecans, and 1 sm. container
of Cool Whip. Mix together and allow to set.

Roselyn Shaver

+ + + + +

LORRAINE'S LAYERED JELLO

1 large pkg. lime jello
1 large pkg. cherry jello
1 3-oz. pkg. cream cheese
20 large marshmallows
1 8½-oz. can crushed pineapple, drained
½ pt. whipping cream

Dissolve jellos separately as per directions. Chill
the lime jello in a 9 x 12" pan. Melt cream cheese
and marshmallows in top of a double boiler. Cool.
Add sweetened whipped cream and pineapple. Mix together. Pour on top of the firm lime jello. Put
the partially set cherry jello on top of the cream
cheese layer and allow to set. Cut in squares to
serve on lettuce leaf. Serves 12
NOTE: The red and green jello is nice at Christmas;
use yellow and purple for Halloween, yellow and green
for Easter.

Toya Rennick

SUNSHINE SALAD

2 sm. (or 1 large) pkg. orange-pineapple jello
3 cups boiling water
1 large can crushed pineapple, drained
2 cans mandarin oranges, drained
1 sm. can pears, crushed
1 pint sour cream

Mix jello (dissolved in boiling water) and fruit
together. Separate into 2 parts. Put one in the
refrigerator to set. When this half is set, put
sour cream on top of it and pour the rest of the
jello on the top of it. Refrigerate.

Suzie Brenneman

+ + + + +

DREAM SALAD

1 sm. pkg. orange jello
1 8-oz. pkg. cream cheese
1 #303 can crushed pineapple
½ pt. whipping cream
1 pkg. miniature marshmallows
2 sm. pkgs. lime jello

Dissolve orange jello in 2 cups boiling water and beat
marshmallows into jello until dissolved. Let cool and
set until right consistency for beating in pineapple
and softened cream cheese. Fold in whipped cream.
Let set in large pan until firm. Mix lime jello
according to pkg. directions and cool to room temperature. Pour over orange jello mixture. Chill.

Laurie Killingsworth

+ + + + +

LEMON BLUEBERRY SALAD

1 sm. pkg. lemon jello
1 sm. pkg. black raspberry jello
1 cup boiling water
½ cup cold water
1 tsp. lemon juice (opt.)
1 21-oz. can blueberry pie filling

Dissolve jellos in hot water, add cold water, lemon
juice and pie filling. Pour into 8" pan and chill.
TOPPING: Fold ¼ cup powdered sugar into 1 cup sour
cream. Spread on chilled gelatin. Chill. Cut into
squares. Serves 8-9

Denise Kiser

ORANGE DELIGHT

1½ cups hot water
1 large pkg. orange jello
1 3/4 cups orange juice
1 sm. can pineapple chunks
1 sm. carrot, grated

Dissolve jello in hot water and orange juice. Add pineapple and carrot. Mold and chill.

Norma Galyon

+ + + + +

SUNRISE SALAD

Dissolve:
1 sm. pkg. orange jello in
1 cup boiling water and
1 pint orange sherbet ice cream.
Add 1 can mandarin orange segments. Fold in 3/4 cup whipped cream. Chill. Serves 6-8

Dixie Sylvestor

+ + + + +

ORANGE-PINEAPPLE JELLO

1 sm. pkg. orange jello
1 sm. pkg. lemon jello
1 sm. can frozen orange juice
2 3-oz. pkgs. cream cheese
1 can mandarin oranges
1 sm. can crushed pineapple

Dissolve jellos in 2 cups boiling water. Add orange juice and 1 can cold water (use frozen orange juice can). Blend in softened cream cheese and fruit. Chill in jello mold.

Barbara Herrly

+ + + + +

ORANGE BAVARIAN SALAD

Prepare one large box of orange jello. Chill until set. Add one can drained crushed pineapple and one can drained mandarin oranges or fresh orange segments. Mix in 1 cup Lucky Whip or Dream Whip. Chill.

Marcia Rieth

LIME-STRAWBERRY SURPRISE

1 sm. pkg. lime jello
1 cup crushed pineapple, drained
½ cup mayonnaise
1 8-oz. pkg. cream cheese
½ cup chopped nuts
1 sm. pkg. strawberry jello

Prepare lime flavored jello as directed on package.
Chill until slightly thickened; fold in pineapple.
Pour into 8" sq. pan. Chill until firm. Gradually
add mayonnaise to softened cream cheese, mixing
until well blended. Add nuts and spread over molded
jello layer. Chill until firm. Prepare strawberry
jello as directed on package, pour over cheese mixture. Chill until firm. Cut in squares. Serve on
lettuce; top with additional mayonnaise.

+ + + + +

STRAWBERRY-SOUR CREAM MOLD

1 large pkg. strawberry jello
2 cups boiling water
2 (10-oz.) pkgs. frozen strawberries
1 #2 can crushed pineapple
2-3 mashed bananas (or sliced)
1 cup sour cream
½ cup chopped nuts

Dissolve jello in water. Add frozen strawberries and
break apart with fork. Add pineapple with syrup and
bananas. Spoon one half of jello mixture into large
(6-8 cup) mold. Allow to set. Spread top with sour
cream and nuts. Add remaining jello mixture and
allow to set. Serves 8-10.

Lee Etta Lappen, Sharon Engel
Linda Ewing and Marcie Webb

+ + + + +

STRAWBERRY JELLO

1 sm. pkg. strawberry jello
1 cup boiling water
1 pkg. sliced, frozen, sweetened strawberries
1 cup whipping cream

Dissolve jello in boiling water. Cool. Add strawberries. When almost set, fold in whipped cream.
Mold and refrigerate.

Sharon Griffith

234

FIVE-CUP SALAD

1 cup pineapple chunks   1 cup sour cream
1 cup orange slices   1 cup coconut
1 cup marshmallow bits

Mix ingredients well. Chill 3 to 4 hours or overnight. (Serves 6 generously.)
VARIATIONS: bananas, fruit cocktail, or other fresh
fruits.

                          Doris Ryen, Sandy Davis
                       Lana Jones and Nancy Schurle

+ + + + +

WALDORF SALAD

1 cup diced apple, unpeeled   Broken nuts
½ cup diced celery   ¼ cup mayonnaise

Toss apples, celery and nuts with mayonnaise. Chill.

                                       Diane Yancy

+ + + + +

WALDORF WHIPPED SALAD

1 sm. pkg. lemon jello   ½ cup celery, chopped
1½ cups boiling water   ½ cup nuts, chopped
1 tbl. lemon juice   1 cup apples, diced
1 cup mayonnaise

Prepare jello as directed using only 1½ cups water.
Let cool to room temperature; add mayonnaise. Beat
with beater; fold in last three ingredients. Chill
until firm and serve.

+ + + + +

CINNAMON APPLE SLICES

Combine 1½ cups water
1 cup sugar
4 tbls. cinnamon candies (Red Hots)
Few drops of food coloring.
Cook until dissolved. Add apple slices and cook
just slightly (not mushy). Chill and serve as
garnish.
                                     Charlotte Day

+ + + + +

PINEAPPLE LACE FRUIT PLATE

[Direct from Honolulu!]

2 pineapples
1 cup orange segments
1 cup grapefruit segments
1 cup pineapple cubes
2 bananas, sliced
12 apricot halves
6 maraschino cherries

From one unpeeled pineapple cut very thin slices.
Arrange on plate. Cut other pineapple in half
diagonally leaving green crown on one half; scoop
out center of this half to form basket. Place on
plate and fill with fruits arranged to form an
attractive picture. Garnish with watercress and
mint. Chill; serve each portion on a pineapple
slice. Yield: 6 servings. Delicious with "Frozen
Fruit Salad Dressing" served on top of portions.

                              Eloise Knippers

+ + + + +

DATE AND APPLE SALAD

Mix:
1 cup pitted dates
2 diced apples
1 tsp. orange peel, grated
½ cup diced cheddar cheese
1 cup diced celery
Blend:
2/3 cup mayonnaise
1 tbl. orange juice
1 tsp. seasoned salt
Mix with fruit mixture.

                              Billie Thurman

+ + + + +

CHERRY PIE SALAD

[Easy for a crowd - "Yummy"]

1 can cherry pie filling
2 cans pineapple tidbits, drained
2 cans mandarin oranges, drained
3 cups marshmallow bits
3 large bananas, cut up

Mix together and chill for several hours.

                              Peggy Jones

CRANBERRY CREAM SALAD

1 6-oz. pkg. cherry jello
2 cups boiling water
1 large can whole cranberry sauce
1 cup chopped walnuts
1 cup finely chopped celery
2 cups sour cream (1 pt.)

Dissolve jello in hot water. Chill until slightly
thickened. Stir cranberry sauce, celery and nuts
into jello. Fold in sour cream. Pour into mold
and chill until firm.

Linda Morse

+ + + + +

CRANBERRY SALAD

3-4 cups cranberries
1 cup sugar
1 cup diced celery
½ cup walnuts
2 large pkgs. lemon or strawberry gelatin
3 cups hot water
2 cups cold water
1 ground orange, opt.
1 chopped apple, opt.

Dissolve gelatin in hot water, add cold water, set
aside until syrupy. Put raw cranberries (and orange)
through food chopper, using the coarse blade. Add
sugar and let stand until well mixed; add celery,
apple and nuts to prepared jello. Turn into molds
and when firm, serve on lettuce with mayonnaise
garnish.

Alice Gurtler and Linda Dillow

+ + + + +

FROZEN CRANBERRY SALAD

1 sm. can crushed pineapple, drained
1 pt. sour cream (2 cups)
1 can whole cranberry sauce
½ cup chopped nuts

Combine all ingredients. Freeze in mold. Unmold
at least ½ hour before serving or it will be too
hard to cut.

Lee Etta Lappen

FROZEN SALAD

1 8-oz. pkg. cream cheese, softened
4 tbls. mayonnaise
4 tbls. pineapple juice
1 16-oz. can fruit cocktail
1 13-oz. can pineapple tidbits
1 11-oz. can mandarin oranges
1 pkg. Dream Whip, prepared
½ lb. miniature marshmallows

Mix together cream cheese, mayonnaise and pineapple
juice. Add drained fruits (may add other fruits if
desired). Mix all together thoroughly and put in a
9 x 5" loaf pan in freezer, or in your own favorite
individual mold. Unmold from loaf pan and slice
for serving. Especially good served with Mexican
food.
                                    Edith Vander Veen

+ + + + +

ROSY FRUIT COCKTAIL SLICES

[This is an excellent salad to make ahead of time or
to have on hand for unexpected guests.]

2 3-oz. pkg cream cheese, softened
1 cup mayonnaise
1 cup heavy cream, whipped (may use Dream Whip)
1 #2½ can (3½ cups) fruit cocktail, well drained
½ cup drained maraschino cherries, quartered
1½ cups small marshmallows
Few drops of red food coloring or maraschino cherry
      juice

Blend cream cheese with mayonnaise. Fold in remaining
ingredients. Pour salad mixture into 2-qt. round ice
cream or freezer containers or empty fruit cans.
Freeze firm about 6 hours or overnight. To serve,
let stand out a few minutes, remove from containers,
slice and place on crisp lettuce. 10-12 servings

+ + + + +

BANANA SALAD

Cut bananas lengthwise, using ½ of a banana for one
salad. Cut each half again, dip in lemon juice and
roll in either crushed peanuts or pecans. Serve on
lettuce leaf, add generous amounts of mayonnaise
over the banana halves.
                                    Nellie Daniels

+ + + + +

THREE BEAN SALAD

1 can cut green beans
1 can cut yellow string beans
1 can red kidney beans
1 sm. green pepper, chopped
1 sm. onion, finely chopped

Blend: 3/4 cup sugar
        1 tsp. salt
        1½ tsp. pepper
        ½ cup vinegar
        ½ cup salad oil

Drain beans and combine with pepper and onion.
Marinate in dressing. The longer it chills, the
better it is!

                                    Thelma Stoll

VARIATION: Add 1 can Garbanzo beans and 4 strips
crisp fried bacon, crumbled. (Or 2 tbls. Baco bits)

                                    Lana Jones

+ + + + +

VEGETABLE SALAD

1 can French cut green beans
1 can peas
1 can pimientos (opt.)
1 cup celery, chopped
½ cup chopped onions

Drain above ingredients. Add the following dressing
and let stand overnight.
DRESSING: ½ cup sugar
           ½ cup vinegar
           ¼ cup salad oil
           1 tsp. salt
Drain before serving.

                                    Roselyn Shaver

+ + + + +

MEXICAN CHEF SALAD

[Tossed salad with a Mexican flare that is good
for lunch with hard rolls.]

1 onion
4 tomatoes
1 head lettuce
1 cup cheddar cheese, shredded
8-oz. Thousand Island Dressing (or French)
Hot sauce to taste
1 cup crushed Fritos
1 lb. ground beef, browned
1 can (15-oz.) drained Kidney beans
¼ tsp. salt

Toss together chopped onion, tomatoes and lettuce.
Add cheese, dressing, hot sauce and Frito chips. Add
kidney beans to browned beef and salt. Simmer 10 minutes; drain. Mix into cold salad. Decorate with
tortilla chips, avocado and tomato slices. Serve
pronto!
        Barbara Ball, Lana Jones and Lee Etta Lappen

VARIATION: Omit: salad dressing and ground beef with
kidney beans. Mix in ½ cup sliced ripe olives and
6-oz. can tuna. Add the following dressing:
    ½ large ripe avocado, mashed
    1 tbl. lemon juice
    ½ cup sour cream
    1/3 cup salad oil
    1 clove garlic, pressed
    1 tsp. sugar
    ¼ tsp. salt
    1/8 tsp. tabasco sauce

Blend together and toss with salad just before serving. Add crushed Fritos.
                              Charlotte Day

+ + + + +

TACO SALAD

Place in layers in salad bowl:
1 sm. head of lettuce
3 tomatoes, quartered
2 green onions, chopped
2 cups Mexican style chili beans, drained
1 cup grated cheese
1 cup crushed Fritos

Just before serving, top with Italian Salad Dressing.
                              Sue Myers

240

CAESAR SALAD

7 tbls. olive oil (or vegetable oil)
½ clove garlic
½ cup white bread cubes
1 head romaine lettuce, clean and crisp
1 head iceberg lettuce, clean and crisp
¼ cup grated Parmesan cheese
¼ tsp. salt
1/8 tsp. pepper
2 tbls. lemon juice
1 coddled egg
6 anchovy fillets, drained and quartered

Slowly heat 3 tablespoons oil with garlic in small
skillet. After a few minutes, remove garlic; add
bread cubes and saute' until golden on all sides.
Remove. Tear lettuce into bite size pieces into
salad bowl. Sprinkle with cheese, salt and pepper;
add remaining oil and mix. Add lemon juice and the
yolk of the egg. Toss until nicely coated. Add
bread cubes and toss lightly. Serve immediately.
Serves 4-6

Paula Carter

+ + + + +

COLE SLAW

Have ready:
1 cabbage, shredded
1 green pepper, chopped
3 grated carrots

Bring the following ingredients to a boil. Pour over
the vegetables and refrigerate:
 ¼ cup white vinegar
 ¼ cup salad oil
 1/3 cup sugar
 Salt

Garnish with tomatoes and watercress sprigs.

Lana Jones

OVERNIGHT COLE SLAW

[Very good, tart]

1 sm. cabbage, chopped fine
1 sm. onion, chopped fine
1 sm. green pepper, chopped fine
Salt, celery seed and pepper to taste
Heat: 1½ cups sugar
       3/4 cup cider vinegar
       3/4 cup oil

Combine first 3 ingredients, then layer with celery
seed, salt and pepper. Heat the last 3 ingredients
almost to boiling; pour over all and let stand at
room temperature overnight. Do not stir. In the
morning, mix and chill. Serves 8

                              Nellie Daniels

                + + + + +

OVERNIGHT CABBAGE SLAW

DRESSING:
2 scant cups sugar
1 tsp. celery seed
2 tsps. mustard seed
2 tsps. salt
½ cup vinegar

VEGETABLES:
1 large head finely chopped cabbage
1 bunch celery, chopped
1 med. onion, chopped fine
1 green pepper, chopped
2 sm. carrots, cut fine

Mix dressing with vegetables and let stand overnight
in refrigerator. Makes 3-4 quarts.

                + + + + +

ITALIAN SALAD

1 head lettuce
1 can mandarin oranges, drained
½ cup sliced almonds, toasted
French dressing

Tear lettuce, add drained oranges and sliced almonds.
Add dressing just before serving; toss and serve on
chilled salad plate.

                + + + + +

SPINACH SALAD

1 head lettuce
1 lb. fresh spinach
1 sm. can broken cashew nuts

DRESSING:
1/3 cup sugar
1/3 cup vinegar
1 tsp. celery salt
1 cup salad oil
1 tsp. salt
1 tsp. garlic salt

Mix dressing in blender until foamy. Pour over salad just before serving. Serves 8.

Louise Shukarian

+ + + + +

SPINACH APPLE TOSS

2 bags (10-oz. each) spinach
2 tart red apples, sliced
8 slices bacon, crisply fried and crumbled
2/3 cup mayonnaise
1/3 cup frozen orange juice concentrate (thawed)

Tear spinach into bite size pieces. Combine with apples and bacon. Mix salad dressing and orange juice. Pour over spinach-apple mixture and toss lightly. Serves 8.

Tarver Jo Smith

+ + + + +

SPINACH SALAD

2 lb. of fresh spinach
4 hard-cooked eggs (sliced)
3-4 tomatoes, quartered
6-8 strips bacon fried and crumbled
2-3 scallions (chopped)
1-2 tsp. Spice Right (or Lawry's seasoned salt)
Oil and vinegar salad dressing, or any good Italian
    style dressing

Clean and separate spinach, keep crisp and cool until you add the eggs, tomatoes, bacon and scallions. Pour salad dressing generously over the spinach just before serving. Add Spice Right and toss.

Judy Carpenter

+ + + + +

PARADISE CHICKEN SALAD ON PINEAPPLE BOATS

2 fresh pineapples
2½ cups cubed cooked chicken or turkey
3/4 cup diced celery
3/4 cup mayonnaise
2 tbls. chopped chutney
1 tsp. curry powder
1 medium banana, sliced
1/3 cup salted peanuts
½ cup flaked coconut
1 can (11-oz.) mandarin orange segments, chilled
    and drained

Select firm pineapple with fresh green leaves. To
prepare pineapple boats: first remove any brown
leaves from the green top with sharp knife, cut pineapple in half lengthwise through the green top. Then
cut each in half again making 4 pieces -- each with
part of the green top. Remove fruit from pineapple--
cut away eyes and fibrous shells. Cut fruit into
chunks for salad. Drain shells and fruit on paper
towels. Combine pineapple, chicken, celery in a
large bowl. In a small bowl mix mayonnaise, chutney
and curry powder. Cover and refrigerate. Before
serving, add banana and peanuts to pineapple-chicken
mixture. Toss lightly with mayonnaise mixture. Fill
pineapple boats -- sprinkle each with coconut and garnish with mandarin oranges. Serves 8.

Barbara Ball

+ + + + +

HAWAIIAN CHICKEN SALAD

1 5 lb. chicken, cooked and cooled
1 #2 can pineapple-bits
1 8 oz. pkg. shell macaroni, cooked and cooled
1 tsp. salt
3-4 stalks celery, chopped
1 cup blanched, slivered almonds
1 cup mayonnaise thinned with pineapple juice

Mix all ingredients and chill. Serve in lettuce
cups. Serves 6-8.

+ + + + +

"Live now as you shall have wished you lived when
you stand at the judgment seat of Christ."
(William Culbertson)

EXOTIC LUNCHEON SALAD

8 cups cut, cooked chicken or turkey
2 sm. cans water chestnuts, sliced thin
2 lbs. seedless grapes
2 cups diced celery
2-3 cups mayonnaise
1 tbl. curry powder
2 tbls. lemon juice
1 tbl. soy sauce
1 tsp. salt
¼ tsp. pepper

Mix mayonnaise, curry powder, lemon juice and
soy sauce. Add seasonings and other ingredients.
Serve on a lettuce leaf. Garnish with chilled
pineapple spears or chunks and litchi nuts.

Charlotte Day

+ + + + +

TUNA PROTEIN SALAD BOWL

1 med.-large head of lettuce
4 eggs, hard-cooked
4 tomatoes, cut up
4 slices cheese
4 sm. pickles, cut up
1 chopped onion
2 6-oz. cans chunk style tuna
Salad dressing

Tear lettuce into large chunks and place in salad
bowl. Quarter eggs and tomatoes, cut cheese slices
in bite-size chunks, add pickles, onion and tuna.
Salt and pepper to taste. Toss with salad dressing.
Serve chilled. Serves 4-6

+ + + + +

TUNA NOODLE SALAD

1 sm. can tuna
1 3-oz. can Chinese noodles
2 tbls. chopped onion
3 tbls. celery, chopped
3 tbls. green pepper, chopped
2 tbls. pimiento
2 hard-cooked eggs, chopped
½ cup mayonnaise
1 tbl. vinegar
1 tbl. milk

Blend mayonnaise, vinegar and milk together for
dressing. Mix with rest of ingredients just before
serving.

Thelma Stoll

CRAB AND SHRIMP MOLDED SALAD

[Elegant and lovely for ladies' luncheon]

1 large pkg. lemon jello
2 cups hot water
1 tbl. lemon juice
½ cup cream, whipped
1 tbl. grated onion
½ cup mayonnaise
3/4 cup diced celery
½ cup sliced green stuffed olives

DRESSING:
Blend
1 cup Miracle Whip
1 cup mayonnaise
¼-½ cup chili sauce
Several chopped sweet pickles
6 hard-cooked eggs, chopped
1 cup shrimp
1 cup crab

Dissolve jello in water with lemon juice. When
slightly thickened, beat until foamy. Add whipped
cream, onion, mayonnaise celery and olives. Chill.
Serve with dressing.

Judy Anderson

+ + + + +

CRAB SALAD

1 can (6-oz.) crab meat
1 can (6-oz.) shrimp pieces
2 cups cooked macaroni
1 #2 can of crushed pineapple, drained

Mix together with mayonnaise and chill before
serving.

Marilyn Heavilin

246

FROZEN FRUIT SALAD DRESSING

1 cup sugar
2/3 cup light corn syrup
½ cup water
2 egg whites
½ cup mayonnaise
1 tbl. grated orange rind
1 tsp. grated lemon rind
1/8 tsp. salt

Combine sugar, corn syrup and water; cook to thread
stage (234°). Slowly pour syrup over stiffly beaten
egg whites, beating constantly while adding syrup.
Cool. Fold in remaining ingredients. This does
not harden when frozen. Yield: 2 cups

Eloise Knippers

+ + + + +

FRUITY SALAD DRESSING

1 cup pineapple juice   ½ cup sugar
2 oranges, juiced   1 heaping tbl. flour
2 lemons, juiced

Mix sugar and flour together thoroughly. Add to
juices. Let stand about 30 minutes or more then
cook over medium heat until thickened. (Letting
it stand before cooking makes it smoother.)

Nancy Scott

+ + + + +

FRUIT SALAD DRESSING

1 cup orange juice   Dash salt
½ cup sugar   ½ pt. whipping cream
4 rounded tbls. flour   ½ tsp. vanilla

(If using frozen orange juice, dilute with 2 cans of
water instead of 3.) Mix dry ingredients in saucepan and gradually add juice, stirring and blending
well. Heat and stir until it thickens and boils.
Stir constantly to prevent scorching. Let cool.
Beat whipped cream, vanilla and orange sauce together when ready to serve.

Jean Moore

+ + + + +

FRUIT SALAD HONEY DRESSING

½ cup honey   ½ cup mayonnaise

Mix and serve over your favorite fruit salad.

+ + + + +

THOUSAND ISLAND DRESSING

Mix together:
    1 cup mayonnaise
    ¼ cup chopped mixed pickles
    ¼ cup chili sauce
    2 diced hard-cooked eggs
    3 tbls. chopped parsley

                            Mary Lou Lyon

+ + + + +

THOUSAND ISLAND DRESSING

Blend equal parts of each of the following:
Mayonnaise
Catsup
Yogurt
Pickle relish
Add chopped hard-boiled egg.

                        Dorothy Gregory

+ + + + +

GRACE'S FRENCH DRESSING

[Quick, easy and delicious!]

1 cup catsup
1 cup vinegar
1 cup cooking oil
1 cup sugar

Blend thoroughly.   Grace Frick

+ + + + +

SUPERB FRENCH DRESSING

1 cup catsup
¼ cup sugar
½ cup vinegar
1 tsp. salt
¼ tsp. paprika
½ tsp. celery seed
3/4 cup salad oil
1 sm. onion, quartered

Blend ingredients for 30 seconds.

                        Connie Burnside

+ + + + +

FRENCH DRESSING

[Delicious and easy!]

½ cup salad oil
½ cup red wine vinegar
1 cup sugar
1/3 cup catsup
1 tsp. salt
1 tsp. paprika
Garlic, if desired

Mix in blender or shake in jar. Refrigerate.

Marilyn Ehle

+ + + + +

FRENCH DRESSING

1 tsp. salt
1 garlic pod
1 tsp. strained honey
1 tsp. dry mustard
1 tsp. Worcestershire sauce
3 tbls. oil
4 tbls. vinegar

Make a paste of first 5 ingredients in salad bowl.
Mix in oil, vinegar and pepper to taste. Add herbs
to taste (such as sweet basil, tarragon, chervil,
etc.). Mix well and serve on washed and dried
salad greens. Serves 4

Stella Friend

+ + + + +

FRENCH DRESSING

Blend in this order:
1 sm. onion, sliced fine
¼ cup vinegar
½ cup salad oil
½ cup catsup
½ tsp. salt
½ cup sugar
Few drops Worcestershire sauce

Carol Barger

+ + + + +

ROQUEFORT SALAD DRESSING

1 Roka Blue Kraft Cheese jar
1 pint sour cream
½ pkg. Good Seasons Italian Dressing
¼ cup vinegar

Mix together. Add milk to thin before serving.

Suzie Brenneman

+ + + + +

ROQUEFORT DRESSING

3-oz. blue cheese, or Roquefort
1 pt. mayonnaise
3 green onions, chopped
½ tsp. dehydrated onion, fine
½ cup sour cream
1 tbl. Tarragon vinegar
Salt and garlic salt to taste
Pepper, fresh ground
1 tsp. Worcestershire sauce

Crumble cheese into bowl and gradually add mayonnaise. Add onions, sour cream, vinegar and seasonings. This may be thinned with ½ and ½ to desired consistency.

Carol Carter

+ + + + +

CABBAGE DRESSING

1 cup cooking oil
2/3 cup sugar
½ tsp. salt
1½ tsp. poppy seeds
1/3 cup white vinegar
1 tsp. dry mustard
1 sm. onion

Mix sugar, salt, mustard and vinegar. Pour oil in slowly. Add onion and poppy seeds. This can be stored in the refrigerator for a long time.

Roselyn Shaver

+ + + + +

RUSSIAN SALAD DRESSING

[This is a very large recipe and usually lasts all year. It keeps in the refrigerator.]

4 cups catsup
6 cups salad oil
8 cups sugar
2 tbls. lemon juice
¼ cup grated onion
3 cups vinegar
¼ cup salt
¼ cup paprika

Mix all ingredients together except salad oil. While beating, add oil a little at a time very slowly. Beat a half hour on medium speed. Then beat on faster speed for 5 minutes.

Roselyn Shaver

+ + + + +

GRANDPA'S SOUP

[A good hearty soup to throw together on a rainy day.]

2 tbls. bacon grease
Dash of pepper
1 large can tomato sauce (or 2 8-oz. cans)
2 cups diced celery
1 cups diced onion
2 cans water
5 diced potatoes
1 large can (#2) pork and beans

Bring mixture to a boil and cook until celery and onion are almost done. Put in potatoes. Cook until done, adding pork and beans the last 15 minutes.

Helen Lovell

+ + + + +

VEGETABLE SOUP

1 lb. ground meat, cooked and drained of grease
1 can tomatoes
1 can onion soup
1 can peas
1 can corn
1 can green beans (all cans with juice)
Spices: ½ tsp. sweet basil
         ½ tsp. oregano
         ¼ tsp. marjoram
         1/8 tsp. turmeric
         Or any spices you want

Combine all ingredients and cook about 20 minutes. May be served with clubhouse crackers to add zest. May be prepared with any canned vegetables you have on hand. Serves 10

Sally Meredith

+ + + + +

"A Bible that's falling apart usually belongs to a person who isn't." (J. Hudson Taylor)

HABITANT PEA SOUP
(Canadian)

2 cups dried yellow peas
2 qts. plus 1 cup cold water
½ lb. salt pork, blanched and minced
1 onion, minced
½ cup minced celery
2 carrots, chopped
¼ cup minced parsley
Salt and pepper
½ tsp. ground allspice

Clean peas and soak overnight or according to pkg.
directions. Boil for 10 minutes in water to cover.
Drain, discard water. Place peas in deep kettle.
Add cold water, salt pork, vegetables, salt and
pepper to taste and allspice. Simmer covered over
lowest possible heat for 2-3 hours. Makes 6-8
servings.

Diane Yancy

+ + + + +

BEAN SOUP

1 cup beans (pinto)
2 cups water
2 oz. salt pork or 3 slices bacon, chopped
¼ cup chopped onion

Wash beans thoroughly, cover with water and soak
overnight. Drain and add 2 cups water. Cook until
tender and press through a sieve if desired. Brown
salt pork or bacon and add to beans. Brown onion
in pork fat and add to soup. Thin with water to
desired consistency; season with salt/pepper and
serve very hot.

Dorothy Brooks

+ + + + +

"He who spends time on his knees has no trouble
standing on his feet." (J. Hudson Taylor)

OYSTER STEW

½ cup butter
1 onion, finely minced
½ cup celery, finely minced
2 cups milk
2 cups heavy cream
2 cups shucked oysters
¼ tsp. cayenne pepper
1 tsp. Worcestershire sauce
Salt and pepper to taste
Celery salt

Heat butter in 2-qt. saucepan. Cook onion and celery.
Add milk and cream and bring barely to a boil. Add
undrained oysters. Return to boil. When oysters
start to curl at edges, remove from heat immediately.
Add pepper, Worcestershire sauce, salt and pepper
and serve at once. Add a dash of celery salt to each
serving.

Barbara Ball

+ + + + +

CAPE ANN CHOWDER

2 cups diced potatoes
½ cup sliced celery
¼ cup chopped onions
1½ tsp. salt
2 cups boiling water
¼ tsp. pepper
¼ cup margarine
½ cup flour
2 cups milk
2½ cups shredded (10-oz.) Cracker Barrel brand sharp
    natural cheddar cheese
1 lb. haddock or cod fillets (cooked)
1 2/3 cups (7½-oz.) can crab meat (drained and flaked)

Combine potatoes, celery, onion, salt and pepper.
Add water. Cover and simmer 10 minutes. Don't
drain. Make a white sauce with margarine, flour
and milk. Add cheese and stir until melted. Add
fish that has been cut into bite-size pieces. Add
undrained vegetables. Heat but do not boil.

Barbara Ball

+ + + + +

SOUFFLE'D CHEESE SANDWICH

12 slices bread buttered
¼-½ lb. cheddar cheese
4 eggs

3 cups milk
½ tsp. salt
Dash of cayenne

Place 6 slices of buttered bread in the bottom of a greased, oblong baking dish 7 x 12". Place cheese on bread and cover with remaining slices of buttered bread. Beat eggs, add milk and seasoning and pour over bread. Let stand 1 hour. Bake at 350° for 30 minutes. Serves 6-8

Doris Rood

+ + + + +

ROLLED TORTILLA WITH SOUR CREAM

6 Tortillas (corn)
½ lb. jack cheese
2 green, peeled chilies (cut in strips)
1½ cups tomato puree
1 pt. (2 cups) sour cream
Salt and pepper

Fry tortillas in butter or margarine. Place cubes of cheese, strips of chilies and 2 or 3 tablespoons of tomato puree on each tortilla. Sprinkle with salt and pepper. Roll and place in a shallow baking dish. Pour sour cream over all and bake at 350° for 30 minutes.

Barbara Ball

+ + + + +

FIESTA ROLLS

1 dozen French rolls
2 cans tomato sauce
½ lb. Tillamook cheese
½ lb. ground meat
1 sm. can chopped olives
1/3 cup chopped onion
1/3 cup bell pepper, chopped
1 tsp. vinegar

Cook meat with onions and bell pepper. Add tomato sauce, olives and grated cheese. Add vinegar. Slice top of French rolls off and hollow out. Fill with meat mixture. Replace top of roll and wrap in foil. Heat at 350° for 1 hour.

Carol Carter

+ + + + +

HOT HAM SANDWICHES

Sliced boiled ham
American cheese
Buns (Hamburger)
Mustard
Mayonnaise
Poppy seed

Butter each half of bun, place 1 slice ham and
½ slice cheese on each bun. Spread butter and mustard
on top, then mayonnaise and sprinkle with poppy seed.
Close bun and wrap in foil. Bake 15 minutes at 350°.

Jan Vandernoord

+ + + + +

PARTY PIZZA

1 can tomato paste
½ tsp. salt
½ tsp. garlic salt
¼ tsp. thyme
½ tsp. Worcestershire sauce
½ lb. ground beef
Dash of tabasco sauce
1 pkg. English muffins
3/4 cup cheddar cheese, grated
¼ tsp. oregano

Combine tomato paste, salt, Worcestershire sauce,
garlic salt, tabasco and thyme. Cover muffin half
with thin layer of uncooked beef and then spread
tomato mixture over it. Sprinkle with cheese and
oregano. Place on cookie sheet and bake at 425° for
13 minutes.

Sandy Buell

+ + + + +

HASTY BUNS

Split hamburger buns or large dinner buns and butter
slightly. Set on baking sheet. Mix:
1 (6½-oz.) can tuna fish (flaked preferred)
2 tbls. Miracle Whip
3 tbls. chili sauce

Spread tuna mixture on each half bun. Sprinkle
grated cheese liberally over tuna and bake for 5
minutes at 400°.

Candace Steele

+ + + + +

VEGETABLE HINTS:

"God causes vegetation to grow for the cattle, and
all that the earth produces for man to cultivate,
that he may bring forth food out of the earth... and
bread to support, refresh and strengthen man's heart"
(Psalm 104:14,15 Amplified)

Cook Brussels sprouts in a small amount of milk in
place of water for a mild, delicious flavor and attractive,bright green color. (Mrs. Robert Steele)

Many of the cheapest vegetables are richest in food
value. In general, vegetables are more nutritious
than fruits.

Remember, the quicker vegetables reach the table
from the garden, the greater the flavor and nutritional value. Cook vegetables in as little water as
possible for the shortest possible time.

Vegetables will keep their color better if cooked in
hard water. When cooking red beets, if one teaspoon
vinegar or lemon juice is added, they will stay red.
If you add a little milk to water in which cauliflower
is cooking, it will remain attractively white.

When cooking cabbage, place a cup half filled with
vinegar on the stove near the cabbage, and it will
absorb the odor.

Try to buy in season; squash is a winter vegetable;
"hot-house" tomatoes, locally grown, are expensive.

Cabbage is less expensive than lettuce; is more
nutritious and keeps longer. So when you're planning
a salad, how about having cole slaw? Or try chopped
cabbage and apple moistened with (low-cal) fruit
and slaw dressing? This is even better with a few
raisins tossed in and sprinkled with paprika.

If you're lucky enough to have a freezer or a large
freezer section in your refrigerator, buy frozen vegetables in the large poly bags.

Keep your eye peeled for the "always good" fresh
vegetables such as carrots, green beans and onions.

Be fussy! Only really fresh vegetables give you the
vitamins you're looking for.

Compare the price of imported vegetables against
those which are frozen or canned. This could save
you a lot of money.

BABY FOOD:

Make your own! Much better for baby (no fillers and preservatives), economical and you really have a sense of fulfillment. You will need a blender and a friend to save you some small baby food jars.

Cook up some carrots in a small amount of water -- likewise fresh frozen green beans, squash and peas. Mash the peas through a sieve.

Chicken livers (fix as above), roast beef or pork and chicken work best for meat although you can use steak if sliced thin. Add the meat juice to the blender as well as some milk and the vegetable with its juice salted slightly.

You can fill a jar with meat only and vegetable only, or you may find that a small jar of a meat-vegetable combination (mix together in blender) is best and is adequate for baby's evening meal. Simply fill several jars with the mixture and when cool place in freezer. Rotate with other meat-vegetable combinations.

All you need to do is take a jar out of the freezer and place in refrigerator in the morning; then heat the one jar for the meal.

For lunch, feed baby yogurt or a fruit-cottage cheese dish you can also make. Bananas, peaches and pears work best. You can freeze this also and warm it up.

Breakfast can be a combination of cereal (cook your own--cream of wheat and oatmeal with raisins or dates (blend a minute) are much better than the thin bought cereals) and egg yolk; made right along with your family's breakfast. Introduce baby early (1½ years) to other vegetables such as cooked celery, cauliflower, beets, asparagus, broccoli, etc.--corn is not well digested until around three years of age.

Fill jars half full when baby is young; large baby food jars could be used for hungry boy babies.

Nan Green

"It takes time for a baby in Christ to become a man of God." (Jim Elliot)

258

ASPARAGUS AMANDINE

2 (#303) cans green asparagus spears, drained
1 can cream of mushroom soup
½ cup water, drained from asparagus
½ tsp. salt
¼ tsp. pepper
1 cup cheddar cheese
1 cup cracker or bread crumbs
4 tbls. butter
½ cup blanched almonds

Lay asparagus in oblong casserole; pour mushroom
soup mixed with water, salt and pepper over asparagus. Sprinkle with grated cheese. Melt butter,
add crumbs and sprinkle over grated cheese. Dot
with almonds. Bake at 300° for 45 minutes.
Serves 8

RiverRoad Recipe from
Sandy Schreiter

+ + + + +

CREAMED ASPARAGUS

2 large cans asparagus
Croutons (toasted bread cubes)
Cream sauce
6 hard-boiled eggs, chopped
1 sm. jar of pimientos
¼ lb. grated cheese (1 cup)

Drain asparagus and save liquid. Toast leftover
bread and cut into squares. Line bottom of casserole
with bread cubes. Add asparagus, eggs, pimiento
and cheese.
CREAM SAUCE: blend ½ cup melted butter with ½ cup
flour. (Remove from heat to blend.) Add 2 cups
milk and 1 tsp. salt. Add asparagus juice. Cook
until thickened. Pour over casserole. Top with
bread crumbs. Bake at 350° for 30 minutes.
Serves 10

Cinny Hicks

+ + + + +

CHINESE BROCCOLI BEEF

¼ tsp. salt
2 tsp. sugar
1½ tbls. soy sauce
½ lb. round steak, sliced in strips 3/4 x 1½ x ¼"
1 tbl. cornstarch
1 lb. broccoli
4 tbls. salad oil
1½ cup water

Combine salt, sugar and soy sauce. Add to steak.
Add cornstarch. Marinate 5 minutes. Wash and clean
broccoli, cut into 1¼" strips. Parboil. (Do not
overcook.) Drain. Heat oil and fry steak. Add
broccoli and water. Bring to boil and serve.
Serves 6

                                    Lana Jones

+ + + + +

CHINESE BROCCOLI

2 10-oz. pkgs. frozen broccoli
½ cup butter or margarine
½ tsp. salt
Dash pepper
1 5-oz. can water chestnuts, drained and diced
2 tbls. minced onion
3 tbls. lemon juice
1 tbl. soy sauce

Prepare broccoli according to package directions.
Drain, cut into serving pieces. Melt butter, add
remaining ingredients. Toss broccoli with butter
mixture. Heat thoroughly and serve. Serves 8-10

                                Jerri Younkman

CHINESE-STYLE BROCCOLI

2 10-oz. pkgs. frozen chopped broccoli
1 10-oz. pkg. Birdseye Japanese vegetables, frozen
½ cup butter   2 tbls. minced onion
½ tsp. salt   3 tbls. lemon juice
Pepper to taste   1 tbl. soy sauce
1 6-oz. can water chestnuts, 1 2-oz. can mushrooms
    sliced

Prepare broccoli according to pkg. instructions. Add
the frozen "Japanese vegetables" and cook 5 minutes
more.   A d d all of the remaining ingredients and
heat until butter is melted. (This may be made ahead
and reheated in a 1½-qt. casserole.) Serves 12-15

                                Diane Yancy

GREEN BEANS AND BEEF

½ lb. tender beef (round) thinly sliced in strips
2 tbls. soy sauce
1 tsp. sugar
1 tbl. cornstarch
½ tsp. salt
1 large onion, sliced
2 tbls. cooking oil
2 9-oz. pkgs. frozen French-cut green beans

Dip beef in mixture of soy sauce, sugar, cornstarch
and salt. Heat pan, add oil; saute' beef strips until
brown; push to one side. Saute' onion slices (rings)
very briefly. Prepare beans as directed on package,
but do not overcook. Add beans (with liquid) to
meat and onions. Simmer 10 minutes. Serve with hot
cooked rice and more soy sauce.

Carol Soderquist

+ + + + +

VINAIGRETTE GREEN BEANS

[This recipe was a gift to Vonette from "The Hitch-
ing Post", Austin, Texas.]

1 tsp. salt
1/8 tsp. freshly ground pepper
¼ tsp. paprika
Few grains cayenne
3 tbls. vinegar
½ cup olive oil
1 tbl. pimiento
1 tbl. cucumber pickles
3/4 tbl. green pepper
½ tbl. parsley
1/3 tbl. chives or onions
Green beans

Slowly add vinegar and oil to first 4 dry ingredients
and beat thoroughly. Finely chop all vegetables
(except beans) and add to mixture. Drain green beans
and pour dressing over them and heat slowly. This
makes about 1 cup dressing (enough for about 10
servings of beans). Dressing may be made ahead and
stored in refrigerator. (Dried pepper, onion and
parsley may be used.)

Vonette Bright

+ + + + +

REFRIED BEANS

2 (1 lb. 13 oz.) cans Mexican style beans
¼ cup bacon drippings, lard or other fat
Salt and pepper
1 cup grated jack cheese

Turn beans with liquid into a large skillet. Add bacon drippings. Cook slowly, stirring now and then and mashing some of the beans 10-15 minutes. Add salt and pepper to taste. Top with cheese.

Barbara Ball

+ + + + +

CHILI AND BEANS

2 lbs. dried pinto beans
1 cup sliced onions
2 tsps. salt
½ cup oil
2 lbs. ground beef
2 cloves garlic, minced
1 cup chopped celery
1 tbl. chili powder
1 tsp. dry mustard
½ tsp. ginger
2 tsps. A-1 sauce
1 (29-oz.) can tomatoes, drained

Cover beans with water, bring to boil. Remove from heat and soak 1 hour or overnight. Drain, add fresh water and onions. Boil and cook over low heat 3 hours or until beans are tender. (Add salt after 2 hours cooking time.) Drain. While beans cook, prepare sauce.
SAUCE: Heat oil. Brown meat and garlic, stirring constantly. Mix in celery, chili powder, mustard, ginger, A-1 sauce and tomatoes. Cover and cook over low heat for 45 minutes. Add to drained beans, taste for seasoning, and cook 30 minutes more.
Serves 6-8

Stella Friend

+ + + + +

"Blessed is the man too busy to worry in the daytime and too sleepy to worry at night." (Don Hillis)

"If you are willing and obedient, you shall eat the good of the land" (Isaiah 1:19)

+ + + + +

HAWAIIAN BAKED BEANS

[Very good to serve with hot dogs to a crowd.]

1 large can pork and beans
1 can pineapple tidbits
1 tbl. molasses
¼ cup brown sugar
½ tsp. ground cloves

Combine. Bake in casserole at 350° for 1 hour.
Serves 10-12
VARIATION: Omit molasses and cloves. Add 3 table-
spoons orange juice and 2 diced celery stalks.
Bake at 350° for 40 minutes.

Lee Etta Lappen

+ + + + +

BAKED BEANS

Use Lee Etta Lappen's recipe for Barbecue Sauce
and mix ½ cup with large (31-oz.) can Van Camps
pork and beans, drained. Bake ½ hour. Serves 4--
maybe! [Be sure to make enough of this, it goes
fast. Good to take to Pot Lucks!]

Ginger Gabriel

+ + + + +

BAKED BEANS

½ cup catsup
2 tbls. mustard
¼ cup brown sugar
2 cans pork and beans

Mix all together. Bake at 300° for 40-45 minutes.
Serve with preheated wieners.

Sharyn Regier

+ + + + +

STUFFED BAKED EGGPLANT

1 med. sized eggplant
1 med. onion, sliced thin
¼ cup shortening
1 lb. ground beef, veal, pork, lamb or leftover meat
1¼ tsp. salt
½ tsp. black pepper
¼ cup finely minced parsley
2 tbls. grated Parmesan cheese
Additional grated Parmesan for top

Cut eggplant lengthwise into 2 pieces. Pare and
cut into 1/8" slices. Saute' onion in shortening
about 5 minutes, add meat and cook 10 minutes longer or until nicely browned; season with salt, pepper,
parsley and bread crumbs. Mix well. Arrange raw
eggplant slices in flat baking dish about 10 x 11
x 3". Sprinkle lightly with salt and pepper. Cover
with meat mixture and a little sauce. Continue until
all is used reserving part of sauce for top. Sprinkle
with 3 or 4 tablespoons Parmesan cheese. Bake at
350° in covered dish 1 hour or until tender, removing
cover last 15 minutes. Serves 4-6

SAUCE:
1 can Italian style tomato paste with 2 cans water
1 sm. onion cut fine
2 tbls. shortening
1 tsp. salt
¼ tsp. pepper
1 tbl. grated cheese

Saute' onion in shortening, add combined tomato
paste and water. Cook slowly in covered saucepan
about 10 minutes then season with salt, 1 tbl.
Parmesan cheese and ¼ tsp. pepper.

                                        Nellie Daniels

                    + + + + +

264

GLAZED CARROTS

6 carrots
3 tbls. margarine
½ cup honey
½ tsp. salt

Peel carrots and cut in 1/8" disks. Cook in margarine, honey and salt on low heat until tender (about 20 minutes). Garnish with parsley.

Lana Jones

+ + + + +

CARROT AND CHEESE CASSEROLE

Cook carrots partially. Melt 2 tbls. butter; stir in 2 tbls. flour slowly. Gradually stir in 1½ cups milk. When smooth, add 1 cup or less cheese (mild or pasteurized). Add ½ tsp. salt, 1/8 tsp. paprika and ½ tsp. dry mustard. Pour over carrots in casserole dish. Top with cracker crumbs. Bake at 350° for 15-20 minutes or until carrots are cooked through. NOTE: Cheese soup may be used in place of the cheese sauce.

Karen Kuhne

+ + + + +

GOLDEN CARROTS

[A simple, company dish]

2 pkgs. carrots, peeled and sliced lengthwise.
1 lb. Velveeta cheese
4 tbls. margarine

Cook carrots in salted water until tender. Grease an oblong baking dish with margarine. Cover bottom of dish with sliced Velveeta cheese. Place cooked carrots on top of the cheese. Dot remaining butter on top. Bake at 350° for 20 minutes or until cheese melts.

Grace Frick

+ + + + +

CAULIFLOWER AND CARROTS

1 sliced head of cauliflower, fresh or frozen
1 bunch carrots
1 onion, chopped
1 cup grated cheese
White sauce

Prepare white sauce, mixing in onion and cheese. Pour over vegetables and bake at 350° for 1 hour.

Barbara Ball

CAULIFLOWER SUPREME

1 head of cauliflower
½ cup mayonnaise
1½ tbls. prepared mustard
4 slices bacon
½ cup medium or sharp cheddar cheese, grated
Salt and pepper to taste
Paprika for garnish

Cook cauliflower and place in shallow baking dish.
Combine mayonnaise and mustard, pour over top of
cauliflower. Sprinkle cooked bacon chips and shredded cheese over the top. Garnish with paprika.
Bake at 350° for 10 minutes.

                                        Pat Turanski

+ + + + +

CAULY CASSEROLE

2 pkgs. frozen Brussels sprouts
2 pkgs. frozen cauliflower
1 qt. cheese sauce
Cracker crumbs

Cook vegetables according to pkg. directions.
Butter a 2-qt. baking dish. Place cooked vegetables
in dish. Cover with cheese sauce (med. white sauce
with 1 cup grated cheddar cheese melted in).
Sprinkle with cracker crumbs. Bake at 350° for
30-45 minutes.

                                        Grace Frick

+ + + + +

CREOLE CASSEROLE

¼ cup chopped onion
¼ cup chopped green pepper
2 tbls. margarine
1 tbls. flour
¼ tsp. salt

1-lb. can tomatoes
1-lb. can green beans
1 cooked med. cauliflower
   (separate into pieces)
½ cup grated cheddar
   cheese

Saute' onions and green pepper in margarine, add
flour and salt, then tomatoes. Pour over beans and
cooked cauliflower in 8" Pyrex dish. Sprinkle with
cheese. Bake at 350° for 25 minutes.

                                        Jan Schules

+ + + + +

BAKED SPINACH

2 pkgs. frozen, chopped spinach (very well drained)
½ pkg. onion soup mix
½ cup cottage cheese
1 cup sour cream

Combine ingredients; bake at 375-400° for about
½ hour.

+ + + + +

SAUERKRAUT CASSEROLE

1/3 cup butter
3 tbls. grated onion
½ cup grated carrots
1 cup grated raw potatoes
1 #2½ can sauerkraut
1 8-oz. can tomato sauce
4 to 6 frankfurters
¼ cup grated cheese

Melt butter in skillet. Add onion, carrots, potatoes,
sauerkraut and dash of pepper. Cook 15 minutes, stirring occasionally. Remove from heat and add tomato
sauce; mix well. Pour into 2-qt. casserole. Place
frankfurter halves on top of casserole. Sprinkle
with grated cheese. Bake 15 minutes at 350°.
Serves 4-5.

Marilyn Heavilin

+ + + + +

CHEESE GRITS

[A vegetable dish or may also be used for brunch]

6 cups boiling water
1 tsp. salt
1½ cups quick grits
½ cup butter (or margarine)
1 lb. grated Velveeta cheese (or part cheddar cheese)
3 eggs, beaten
Black pepper
1 tsp. tabasco sauce
2 tsps. seasoned salt

Add salt and quick grits to boiling water. Cook 2
minutes. Add rest of ingredients. Pour into shallow
pan. Bake at 300° for 45 minutes. Serves 10-12

Carol Williams

+ + + + +

LITHUANIAN KUGELIS
(POTATO PUDDING)

½ lb. bacon, diced
½ med. onion, diced
1½ cups milk
2 eggs, well beaten
8 med. potatoes

¼ cup cream of wheat, uncooked
1¼ tsp. salt (or less)
¼ tsp. pepper

Brown bacon lightly with onion; add milk. Grate potatoes quickly into a large bowl. (Grate as fine as possible.) Pour off most of potato juice into a small bowl. Tip the small bowl a little so the starch settles. Mix salt, pepper, eggs and cream of wheat into potatoes. Heat bacon, onion and milk mixture and add to potatoes. Gradually pour off the saved juice. Scrape the remaining starch into the potato mixture. Mix well (will be mushy). Pour into heavily greased 9" square pan. Bake at 350° for 1½ hours. Serve hot with sour cream.

Bonnie Merkle

+ + + + +

SCALLOPED POTATOES AND HAMBURGER

1 lb. hamburger
2 cans cream of mushroom soup
Onion, if desired

6-7 potatoes
2 cans milk

Slice potatoes thin. Put into a 2½-qt. bowl. Add a little chopped onion if desired. Mix together. Brown hamburger. Salt and pepper as it browns. Spread the meat on top of potatoes. Heat the soup and milk together; pour over the potatoes and hamburger. Bake at 375° for 1½ hours, uncovered. Serves 5-6

Toya Rennick

+ + + + +

LEMON-CHIVE POTATOES

1 qt. new potatoes (4 cups)
½ cup butter, melted
2 tbls. lemon rind, grated
3 tbls. lemon juice
½ cup minced green onions

Cook new potatoes until done, drain very well. Pour next four items on potatoes. Serve hot.

Carol Williams

SWEET POTATO SOUFFLE

4 large sweet potatoes
6 tbls. butter
1 tbl. lemon juice
4 tbls. cinnamon
3 tbls. sugar
½ cup chopped pecans (if desired)

Bake potatoes in foil at 400° about 1 hour or until
soft when squeezed. Remove foil; cut open and scoop
potato out with spoon into mixing bowl. Add butter,
lemon juice, cinnamon and sugar. Beat thoroughly.
Add nuts, stir until blended. Turn into medium
casserole. Top with miniature marshmallows. Bake
at 325° until marshmallows are golden brown; about
15 minutes. Serves 4-5

Peggy Jones

+ + + + +

POTATO PUFF SOUFFLE'

¼ cup butter
¼ cup flour
1 cup sour cream (or sweet cream)
2 tsps. grated onion
1½ cups hot, riced potatoes, firmly packed
1½ tsp. salt
Dash of pepper
4 eggs, separated

Melt butter in heavy saucepan. Add flour and mix
until smooth. Add sour cream all at once. Cook,
stirring constantly, until just thickened. Remove
from heat. Add potatoes, onion, salt and pepper.
Beat until smooth and thoroughly blended. Add a
small amount of hot mixture to well-beaten egg yolks,
stirring constantly. Add to remaining hot mixture.
Mix well. Beat egg whites until stiff, but not dry.
Fold lightly into potato mixture. Pour into buttered
1¼-qt. shallow casserole. Bake in pan of hot water
at 325° for 50 minutes or until a knife, when inserted into center of the souffle' comes out clean.
Serves 6-8

Midge Piedot

+ + + + +

LOUISIANA CRAB STUFFED POTATOES

4 medium Idaho potatoes
1 6½-oz. can crab meat
½ cup butter
½ cup light cream
1 tsp. salt
4 tsps grated onion
1 cup sharp cheese, grated
½ tsp. paprika

Bake potatoes as usual --until fork can pierce them.
Cut potatoes length-wise and scoop out of peeling.
Whip with butter, cream, salt, pepper, onion and
cheese. With fork add crab meat and refill potato
shells. Sprinkle with paprika and reheat in hot
oven for 15 minutes. (These freeze very nicely.
Are a hit at a party with tossed salad, drink and
dessert. Relatively inexpensive - as they are a meal-
in-one.)

Libby Trest

+ + + + +

BAKED SWEET POTATO-APPLE CASSEROLE

1/3 cup brown sugar
¼ tsp. cinnamon
¼ tsp. salt
1 lb. cooked sweet potatoes

2 cups sliced apples
1/3 cup raisins
¼ cup margarine
1/3 cup almonds

Mix sugar, cinnamon and salt. Arrange layer of potatoes and cover with layer of apples and half the
raisins. Sprinkle with sugar mixture. Repeat layers. Dot with almonds and butter. Cover and bake
at 375° for 35 minutes. Remove cover and bake for
10 more minutes.

Sandy Beull

+ + + + +

SWEET POTATOES

1 #4 can sweet potatoes
¼ cup margarine
1 egg

1 tsp. vanilla
½ cup white sugar

Whip potatoes and add rest of ingredients. Place in
casserole dish and cover with topping:
Melt ¼ cup margarine
Add ½ cup brown sugar
2 tsps. vanilla
¼-½ cup pecans
Bake at 350° for 1 hour.

Sandy Schreiter

RICE PILAF

1 cup rice
2½ cups water
¼ cup butter
1 pkg. Lipton's chicken noodle soup

Heat water with the lump of chicken broth from soup package. When it boils, add rice. Meanwhile, brown noodles (from soup package) in butter. Add to rice. Stir. Simmer about 30 minutes (until rice is cooked) stirring occasionally. Let stand for a few minutes.

Dorothy Gregory

+ + + + +

RICE

Prepare 1 cup rice as directed on package, adding ½ package Lipton's dried French onion soup to the water. May be buttered or serve with gravy.

Vonette Bright

+ + + + +

DELICIOUS RICE DISH

[Always a crowd pleaser!]

Sauce:
1 pkg. frozen, chopped broccoli
1 onion
3 tbls. butter
1 can cream of chicken soup
1 med. size jar cheese sauce
½-1 cup milk
1 sm. roll of garlic cheese by Kraft

Thaw and drain broccoli. Brown onion in butter; add broccoli and cook 5 minutes. Add soup, cheese sauce, milk and garlic cheese. Cook 1½ cups rice. Add rice to broccoli mixture and place in buttered casserole. May be prepared the day before and kept in refrigerator. When ready to use, add a little milk and warm, covered in oven. Serves 8

Linda Dillow

+ + + + +

PILAF SEASONING MIXTURE

2 chicken bouillon cubes
½ tsp. rosemary

½ tsp. thyme
½ tsp. marjoram

Dorothy Gregory

CREOLE FRIED RICE

[Basic leftover. 203 calories per serving]

1 cup uncooked rice
2 eggs
¼ tsp. salt
2 tbls. cooking oil
2 tbls. bacon drippings
1 cup onion, chopped
2 tbls. green pepper, chopped
½ cup celery, chopped
1-1½ cups tuna, pork, ham, beef or chicken, chopped
2 tbls. soy sauce
Chopped green onions

Cook rice. Cool. Beat together eggs and salt. Heat
skillet to moderate temperature; add oil and cook
eggs until firm. Remove and cool. Place bacon drippings in skillet; add onions, pepper and celery.
Cook slightly. Add rice and cut-up eggs, chopped
meat and soy sauce. Serve hot or cold. Garnish with
chopped green onions. Serves 6-8

Beverly Schneider

+ + + + +

RICE AND ONION CASSEROLE

Saute': 2 tbls. butter
         ½ cup uncooked rice
         1/3 cup sliced mushrooms
Stir in: 1 pkg. dried onion soup
         1 cup water
Cook covered over low heat about 25 minutes until rice
is tender.

Lynn Noble

+ + + + +

RICE CASSEROLE

3/4 cups uncooked regular rice
1 can chicken and rice soup
1 cup water
1 tsp. Accent
1 tsp. salt
1 sm. onion, chopped
Chicken pieces

Lay pieces of chicken in baking pan. Cover with rest
of ingredients mixed together. Cover and bake at
325° for 2 hours.

Karen Kuhne

WILD RICE

1 pkg. Uncle Ben's wild rice
1 lb. hamburger meat
1 onion, very finely chopped
1 stalk celery, very finely chopped
1 tsp. dry mustard
Garlic
1 can chicken and rice soup
1 can mushrooms

Fry onion and celery until tender. Brown meat.
Drain off excess fat. Add celery and spices, onions,
mushrooms and soup (undiluted) to meat. Prepare
rice according to directions. Add rice to meat mixture, dot with butter. Bake at 350° for 1 hour.
(Also good for cornish hens).

Barbara Ball

+ + + + +

ZUCCHINI RICE CASSEROLE

½ tsp. salt
½ cup rice
1 onion, chopped
1 lb. zucchini (3-4 med.)
½ green pepper
1 8-oz. can tomato sauce
2/3 cup shredded cheese
¼ cup grated Parmesan cheese

Boil 1 cup water with ¼ tsp. salt. Add rice and
onion; reduce heat, cover and simmer until rice is
tender (about 20 minutes). Scrub zucchini and cut
into ½" slices. Boil ½ cup water with ¼ tsp. salt,
add zucchini and green pepper; cook about 5 minutes
until zucchini is tender. Remove from heat and drain.
Add tomato sauce and zucchini to cooked rice and mix
lightly. Place in 1½-qt. casserole and top with
mixed cheeses. Bake uncovered at 325° about 20 minutes. For complete meal, add ½ to 1 lb. browned
ground beef. Serves 6

Dorothy Brooks

+ + + + +

SQUASH CASSEROLE

[Delicious, even for people who don't usually like squash.)

2 (16-oz.) cans cut yellow squash,drained
3 medium-large onions, cut
1 egg
Salt and pepper to taste
8 strips of bacon
2 pieces of bread, crumbled
1 small onion, finely chopped

In a medium saucepan, place a cup of water, a slice of bacon and the large, cut onions. Cook over medium-high heat until water comes to a full boil. Reduce heat and continue cooking until onions are very soft and half of water has cooked out. About 1½ hours. Fry rest of bacon to light brown (not too done). Pour off all but 2½ tbls. of bacon drippings. Saute' chopped onions in drippings. Crumble bread into drippings to absorb the juice. Crumble bacon into fine bits, add to bread and onions. Put aside. When onions have cooked to a soft mixture and water has cooked down to half of what was originally added, remove bacon strip. Add the drained squash and mix well. Let cool. Add egg, stir thoroughly. Put in casserole. Bake at 350⁰ for 20 minutes. Remove and put bacon topping on squash. Bake 10 more minutes until topping is golden and bubbling. Serves 8

Peggy Jones

+ + + + +

ZUCCHINI OR SUMMER SQUASH

2-3 lbs. squash
1 onion, chopped
2 tbls. butter
Salt and pepper
¼ cup cream
2 eggs, slightly beaten
½ cup grated cheese
Buttered bread crumbs

Cook squash with onion in a small amount of water until dry and clear. Add butter and seasonings. Add cream and mash. Add eggs, blend; add cheese. Mix and put in a greased baking dish. Cover with bread crumbs. Bake at 350⁰ for 1 hour or until brown.

Vonette Bright

CHEESE SAUCE

[This sauce keeps forever and you can use it on practically anything, especially to pick up left-over vegetables.]

Scald 1 cup evaporated milk. Stir in:
½ lb. diced cheese
1 tsp. salt
¼ tsp. paprika
¼ tsp. celery salt
Few grains cayenne

Cook the sauce over low heat, stirring constantly until smooth. Keep in refrigerator and reheat for future use.

Helen Lovell

+ + + + +

EASY CHEESE SAUCE

[A great pick-up for vegetables!]

1 cup mayonnaise
½ cup milk
½ cup shredded cheddar cheese
½ tsp. paprika

Blend and heat, stirring. Serve over vegetables.

Midge Piedot

+ + + + +

MEAT ACCOMPANIMENTS

BERRIES N' BEANS

[This will keep your family guessing as to what is in it!]

Mix together:
    1 lb. can of cranberry sauce
    1 lb. can of pork and beans

Bake in an uncovered 8" pan for one hour at 325°. Serves 4. This is good with ham or pork chops or left-over turkey.

Dorothy Gregory

+ + + + +

BAKED PINEAPPLE

1 can crushed pineapple
1 cup sugar
3 eggs
½ cup butter, melted
4 slices bread, cubed

Mix sugar, eggs and pineapple. Mix butter and bread cubes until bread is saturated with butter. Combine both mixtures. Bake at 350° for ½ hour. (Excellent with baked ham!)

Julie Schroen

+ + + + +

BAKED APPLES AND BANANAS

Use desired number of peeled and cored apples and bananas. Put a layer of sliced apples and bananas in buttered casserole; dot with butter and brown sugar. Repeat layers, using as many as possible because the fruit will shrink. Make a crumble mixture of 2 tablespoons each of flour, sugar and butter. Spread over top. Bake at 325° for 1½-2 hours. Excellent accompaniment with meat or poultry.

Elizabeth Marks

+ + + + +

Have You Heard of the Four Spiritual Laws?

Just as there are physical laws that govern the physical universe, so are there spiritual laws which govern your relationship with God.

LAW ONE

GOD **LOVES** YOU, AND OFFERS A WONDERFUL **PLAN** FOR YOUR LIFE.

(References should be read in context from the Bible wherever possible.)

God's Love

"For God so loved the world, that He gave His only begotten Son, that whoever believes in Him should not perish, but have eternal life" (John 3:16).

God's Plan

(Christ speaking) "I came that they might have life, and might have it abundantly" (that it might be full and meaningful) (John 10:10).

Why is it that most people are not experiencing the abundant life?

Because . . .

LAW TWO

MAN IS **SINFUL** and **SEPARATED** FROM GOD. THEREFORE, HE CANNOT KNOW AND EXPERIENCE GOD'S LOVE AND PLAN FOR HIS LIFE.

Man Is Sinful

"For all have sinned and fall short of the glory of God" (Romans 3:23).

Man was created to have fellowship with God; but, because of his stubborn self-will, he chose to go his own independent way and fellowship with God was broken. This self-will, characterized by an attitude of active rebellion or passive indifference, is evidence of what the Bible calls sin.

278

Man Is Separated

"For the wages of sin is death" (spiritual separation from God) (Romans 6:23).

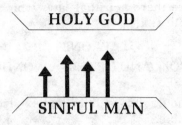

This diagram illustrates that God is holy and man is sinful. A great gulf separates the two. The arrows illustrate that man is continually trying to reach God and the abundant life through his own efforts, such as a good life, philosophy or religion.

The third law explains the only way to bridge this gulf . . .

LAW THREE

JESUS CHRIST IS GOD'S **ONLY** PROVISION FOR MAN'S SIN. THROUGH HIM YOU CAN KNOW AND EX-PERIENCE GOD'S LOVE AND PLAN FOR YOUR LIFE.

He Died in Our Place

"But God demonstrates His own love toward us, in that while we were yet sinners, Christ died for us" (Romans 5:8).

He Rose from the Dead

"Christ died for our sins . . . He was buried . . . He was raised on the third day, according to the Scriptures . . . He appeared to Peter, then to the twelve. After that He ap-peared to more than five hundred . . ." (I Corinthians 15:3-6).

He Is the Only Way to God

"Jesus said to him, 'I am the way, and the truth, and the life; no one comes to the Father, but through Me' " (John 14:6).

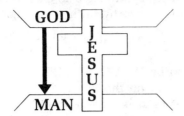

This diagram illustrates that God has bridged the gulf which separates us from God by sending His Son, Jesus Christ, to die on the cross in our place to pay the penalty for our sins.

It is not enough just to know these three laws . . .

LAW FOUR

WE MUST INDIVIDUALLY **RECEIVE** JESUS CHRIST AS SAVIOR AND LORD; THEN WE CAN KNOW AND EXPERIENCE GOD'S LOVE AND PLAN FOR OUR LIVES.

We Must Receive Christ

"But as many as received Him, to them He gave the right to become children of God, even to those who believe in His name" (John 1:12).

We Receive Christ through Faith

"For by grace you have been saved through faith; and that not of yourselves, it is the gift of God; not as a result of works, that no one should boast" (Ephesians 2:8, 9).

When We Receive Christ, We Experience a New Birth

(Read John 3:1-8).

We Receive Christ by Personal Invitation

(Christ is speaking) "Behold, I stand at the door and knock; if any one hears My voice and opens the door, I will come in to him" (Revelation 3:20).

Receiving Christ involves turning from self to God (repentance) and trusting Christ to come into our lives to forgive our sins and to make us the kind of person He wants us to be. Just to agree intellectually that Jesus Christ is the Son of God and that He died on the cross for our sins is not enough. Nor is it enough to have an emotional experience. We receive Jesus Christ by faith, as an act of the will.

These two circles represent two kinds of lives:

SELF-DIRECTED LIFE
S—Self on the throne
†—Christ is outside the life
•—Interests are directed by self, often resulting in discord and frustration

CHRIST-DIRECTED LIFE
†—Christ is in the life
S—Self is yielding to Christ
•—Interests are directed by Christ, resulting in harmony with God's plan

Which circle best represents your life?

Which circle would you like to have represent your life?

The following explains how you can receive Christ:

YOU CAN RECEIVE CHRIST RIGHT NOW BY FAITH THROUGH PRAYER

(Prayer is talking with God)

God knows your heart and is not so concerned with your words as He is with the attitude of your heart. The following is a suggested prayer:

"Lord Jesus, I need You. Thank You for dying on the cross for my sins. I open the door of my life and receive You as my Savior and Lord. Thank You for forgiving my sins and giving me eternal life. Make me the kind of person You want me to be."

Does this prayer express the desire of your heart?

If it does, pray this prayer right now, and Christ will come into your life, as He promised.

282

RECIPE INDEX

286

RECIPE INDEX

Louisiana Crab Stuffed
  Potatoes, 269
Lo-Cal Sherbet, 148
Luncheon Salad, Exotic, 244
Luncheons, 6
Luscious Apricot Bars, 101

M

Macaroni
  and Cheese Squares, 208
  and Cheese with Hot Dogs, 208
  Casserole, 205
  Double Good, and Cheese, 208
Macaroon Delite, Frozen, 122
Magic
  Lemon Meringue Pie, 226
  Marshmallow Crescent Puffs, 59
Marinade Sauce, 213
Meat
  and Potato Casserole, 199
  Armenian Sh-Kebab, 177
  Bacon-Wrapped Beef Patties, 184
  Beefburger Pie, 196
  Beef Casserole, 192
  Beef 'n Cheese Pie, 181
  Beef Pot Roast A La Province,
    175
  Beef Stroganoff, 172
  Beef-Zucchini Casserole, 182
  Chasen's Chili, 198
  Cheeseburger Turnovers, 184
  Cheese Lasagna, 185
  Chili, 198
  Chinese Beef Curry, 173
  Chinese Hot Dish, 187
  Chinese Skillet Beef, 178
  Dinner in a Skillet, 182
  Domatelli, 180
  Double Cheese Meat Roll, 179
  Earle's Specialty Roast, 174
  Easy Beef Stroganoff, 172
  Easy Tamale Pie, 189
  Enchiladas, 188
  Five-Hour Stew, 176
  Foiled Wrapped Steak
    Supper, 174
  Fondue-Teriyaki Meatballs, 187
  German Cabbage Rolls, 183
  Hamburger-Bean Casserole, 186
  Loaf, 186
  Loaf, Juicy, 186
  Loaf, Pot Roast, 186
  Pin Wheels, 179
  Roll, 201
  Sauce, Fruity, 213
Meat Accompaniments, 275
  Baked Apples and Banana
  Baked Pineapple
  Berries 'n Beans
Meatballs, 195
  Fondue-Teriyaki, 187
  Italian, 193
  Polynesian, 194
  Swedish, 193
Meatsauce (for Spaghetti), 213
Mennonite Chicken Baked in
  Sour Cream, 154
Menus See Index for Menus, Hints

Menus for Large Groups, 9
Mexican
  Chef Salad, 239
  Chicken in Orange Juice, 163
  Chile Con Queso, 38
  Pizza, 35
Mile High Fudge, 85
Milk Shake (Lo-Cal), 149
Mint Sauce for Melon Balls, 139
Miracle Cheesecake, 131
Mock Enchiladas, 190
Moist Brownies, 108
Mom Mosher's Pralines, 36
Monte Carlo, Chicken, 160
Moonshine Gingerbread, 124
Mrs. Bell's Sloppy Joes, 197
Muffins
  Oatmeal, 43
  Orange Donut, 44
  Six-Week, 44
  Spicy Apple Wheat-Germ, 43
Mushroom Soup (Lo-Cal), 146
Muzzy's Pound Cake, 71

N

Never-Fail Pie Crust, 217
New Orleans Hot Broccoli Dip, 37
New York Cheese Ball, 36
"No Cook" Marshmallow Frosting,
  82
"No Fail" Chocolate Fudge, 85
No Roll Pastry, 217
Nobby Apple Cake, 74
Norwegian Pot Roast, 174
Nuts, Spiced Mixed, 87
Nutty Banana Bread, 51

O

Oatmeal
  Cake, 80
  Cookies, 95
  Crispies, 97
  Fudge, 85
  Muffins, 43
Old-Country Chicken and Rice, 155
Old Fashioned
  Crumb Cake, 55
  Doughnuts, 59
Olive-Cheese Snacks, 34
One Bowl Jelly Roll, 80
Orange
  Angel Food Dessert, 133
  Bavarian Salad, 232
  Charlotte, 132
  Cinnamon Rolls, 57
  Delight, 232
  Donut Muffins, 44
  Kiss-Me Cake, 76
  -Pineapple Jello, 232
  Pork Chops, 200
  Pork Chops, Baked, 200

RECIPE INDEX

RECIPE INDEX

CONTRIBUTOR INDEX